THE OFFICIAL CONCEPT OF THE NATION IN THE FORMER GDR

The Official Concept of the Nation in the Former GDR

Theory, pragmatism and the search for legitimacy

JOANNA McKAY
Department of Politics and European Studies
University of Central Lancashire

LONDON AND NEW YORK

First published 1998 by Ashgate Publishing

Reissued 2018 by Routledge
2 Park Square, Milton Park, Abingdon, Oxon, OX14 4RN
711 Third Avenue, New York, NY I 0017, USA

Routledge is an imprint of the Taylor & Francis Group, an informa business

Copyright © J. McKay 1998

All rights reserved. No part of this book may be reprinted or reproduced or utilised in any form or by any electronic, mechanical, or other means, now known or hereafter invented, including photocopying and recording, or in any information storage or retrieval system, without permission in writing from the publishers.

Notice:
Product or corporate names may be trademarks or registered trademarks, and are used only for identification and explanation without intent to infringe.

Publisher's Note
The publisher has gone to great lengths to ensure the quality of this reprint but points out that some imperfections in the original copies may be apparent.

Disclaimer
The publisher has made every effort to trace copyright holders and welcomes correspondence from those they have been unable to contact.

A Library of Congress record exists under LC control number: 97078097

ISBN 13: 978-1-138-33886-9 (hbk)
ISBN 13: 978-1-138-33890-6 (pbk)
ISBN 13: 978-0-429-44142-4 (ebk)

Contents

Preface vii
Abbreviations ix

1 Introduction 1

    The East German dilemma 2
    Policy-making in the GDR 5
    The role of theorists in the GDR 6

2 The fight to preserve the unity of the German nation 13

    The divided nation 13
    The SED, the nation and the Berlin Wall 19
    Conclusion 26

3 The unity of the nation in doubt 33

    Challenges to Ulbricht's line 33
    The new socialist constitution 44
    The challenge of Brandt's *Ostpolitik* 48
    Conclusion 60

4 The 'socialist nation' in the GDR 67

    The invention of a 'socialist nation' in the GDR 67
    The consequences of the new *Nationskonzept* 80
    Conclusion 99

5 The 'socialist German nation' - from consolidation to crisis 107

Nationality: German; citizenship: GDR 108
The SED: 'heir to everything progressive in the history of 120
the German people'
The return of the nation to the political agenda 125
Conclusion 136

6 Conclusion 145

The paradoxes of official nationalism in the GDR 146
The four phases of the official line 149
The nature of East German identity 152
West German policy regarding the German nation 153
The case of the GDR and nation-building theory 155

Bibliography 161

Preface

Until the collapse of East European communism in 1989, the GDR remained a state shrouded in mystery, existing in a position of isolation surpassed perhaps only by Albania, due to its questionable *raison d'être* and obvious vulnerability. Ironically it is a state that many outsiders have become acquainted with only *after* its demise. However, it continues to be the subject of much scholarly attention and debate - not least because a better understanding of this unique and ill-fated state helps us to comprehend why the process of German reunification has proved to be so painful, particularly at a psychological level. While many questions about former communist regimes may never be answered, several writers, including the present author, have been unable to resist the opportunity to find out more about the East German state - a state born illegitimate and upheld artificially, but which nevertheless shaped the lives of millions of people who live on today, even though their former country no longer features on the map of Europe.

This study focuses on one of the most difficult tasks faced by the leadership of the GDR, namely how to explain the division of the former unitary German nation without undermining the legitimacy of the state. This was all the more pressing with various other factors gnawing away at the legitimacy of the GDR at the same time. It uses previously unavailable archive material to identify the key factors which determined the official concept of the nation throughout the existence of the GDR, and pays particular attention to the input of theorists at state-run academic institutions.

I would like to thank numerous individuals and bodies who supported and assisted me in the initial research for this study, including Prof. Gordon Smith at the LSE and Prof. Michael Burleigh, now at the University of Wales, Cardiff; in Berlin I would like to thank Prof. Siegfried Prokop, the staff of the SED archive and all my interviewees, especially Prof. Alfred Kosing and Dr Jürgen Hofmann; and I would like to acknowledge the financial support I received over the years from the Economic and Social Research Council and the German Academic Exchange Service.

Finally I would like to thank my mother for her love and for tolerating the distance academia has placed between us, and my father for his technical support and unflagging interest in my work.

Abbreviations

AdW	Academy of Sciences
AfG	Academy for Social Sciences
BArch	Federal Archives
CDU	Christian Democratic Union
CPSU	Communist Party of the Soviet Union
CSCE	Conference on Security and Cooperation in Europe
CSU	Christian Social Union
DDR	Deutsche Demokratische Republik
DKP	German Communist Party
EKD	Protestant Church of Germany
FDJ	Free German Youth
FRG	Federal Republic of Germany
GDR	German Democratic Republic
IfGA	Institute for the History of the Workers' Movement
IMF	Institute for Public Opinion Research
IPA	Internal Party Archive
KoKo	Commercial Cooperation
KPD	Communist Party of Germany
NATO	North Atlantic Treaty Organisation
NL	Estate (Nachlaß)
NPD	National Democratic Party of Germany
NVA	National People's Army
PCC	Political Consultative Committee of the Warsaw Pact
SAPMO	Foundation of the Archive of Parties and Mass Organisations of the GDR
SED	Socialist Unity Party of Germany
SPD	Social Democratic Party of Germany
UN	United Nations
ZK	Central Committee
ZPA	Central Party Archive

1 Introduction

For years social scientists have attempted to identify the essence of state and regime legitimacy and to find a means of assessing and comparing the legitimacy of individual states and regimes. It is generally accepted that legitimacy depends on voluntary acceptance of the state or regime by the majority of the population concerned, in spite of occasional opposition to specific policies or ventures, and that almost all rulers seek popular legitimacy. This may be on principle, as in democratic systems, or as a means to an end, as in authoritarian systems, for example, to enhance a claim to international recognition or to increase mass participation and productivity. Max Weber, Jürgen Habermas and Seymour Martin Lipset have all made significant contributions to the debate on the nature of state legitimacy,[1] but the appropriateness of Western models in the assessment of the legitimacy of communist regimes is questionable.[2] This is especially true in the case of the German Democratic Republic which was a truly unique state which defied categorisation and did not easily fit any theoretical models. While it could be argued that every country is unique, the GDR has rightly been described as 'more unusual than most'[3] due to the circumstances of its birth, the factors which sustained it, and the indisputable division of the German nation.

Like other ruling Marxist-Leninist parties, the *Sozialistische Einheitspartei Deutschlands* (SED) of the GDR went to great lengths to convince its citizens of the advantages of socialism and the legitimacy of the regime, and in this case, of the state itself, via a whole range of convoluted arguments and propaganda devices. This book focuses on the attempts made by the SED to fashion a *Nationskonzept*, i.e. a credible explanation of the GDR's relationship to the German nation, which had been divided into two states in 1949, that would establish the legitimacy of the socialist German state, both in the eyes of its own population and of the international community. Initially the SED portrayed the GDR as a model for a future united socialist Germany, and then later as a complete state in its own right. However, in view of the collapse of the regime in 1989 and German reunification the following year, we can tentatively conclude that the SED failed to convince its citizens of the GDR's right to exist, for given the choice in 1990, the majority of East Germans opted to become citizens of the Federal Republic.

In short, this work is not a theoretical study of the relationship between socialism and nationalism in general, but an examination of how one particular Marxist-Leninist regime handled the national question in practice. The aim is to compare the contrasting positions held by the party leadership at different points in time, and also to explain why policy changes occurred, and why they occurred when they did. Only in this way can one hope to make sense of the SED's dramatic U-turns and illogical arguments. To this end certain political factors are considered in order to assess their impact on the official line on the nation in the GDR compared with other factors such as public opinion and theoretical considerations. It will be argued that even nationhood and national consciousness were regarded by the SED as objective factors which could be manipulated and transformed to suit the needs of the party, as opposed to being permanent sources of self-identification and emotional attachment, and that policy regarding the nation was always determined by political objectives, even opportunism, and not by conventional nation-building theories or popular sentiment. In addition, particular attention will be paid to the role played by East German theorists who attempted to provide theoretical arguments to support the official party line on the nation.

The East German dilemma

From its establishment in 1949 until its demise in 1990, the GDR was regarded as temporary and artificial. It was not a result of self-determination with the popular legitimacy this brings, but a product of the failure of the victors of World War II to reach an agreement on the future of Germany. While the same could also be said of the Federal Republic of Germany, there were several reasons why the latter came to be accepted as the legitimate post-war German state, both by the outside world and by the majority of Germans on both sides of the inner-German border.

The first was the fact that the GDR was a one-party state, with power in the hands of the Marxist-Leninist SED. Although other parties did exist, the intention was merely to create a facade of democracy since they were all allied to the SED in the so-called 'National Front for a Democratic Germany' and elections were merely a sham. Thus the SED never even attempted to give the GDR genuine democratic legitimacy due to the threat this would pose to the party's position of dominance.

The second reason was that the GDR was a Soviet satellite, the jewel in the crown of the Eastern Bloc, and therefore had little opportunity for independent action. Indeed the SED had already abandoned the 'German road to socialism' in favour of the Stalinist road before the GDR was established.

The third reason was that a centrally planned, socialist economy was imposed on the East German population, with the intention of proving that it was superior to the capitalist model which in turn would enhance the GDR, since it is obvious that the legitimacy of states is always enhanced by their effectiveness in concrete terms. In fact, official emphasis on the alleged economic and material achievements of socialism was a common tactic throughout the Eastern bloc (sometimes labelled 'goulash socialism' in the West[4]). However this was a risky strategy since future economic success could not be guaranteed, as the SED was to discover. In particular the state failed miserably in the provision of quality consumer durables, cars and telephones, and East Germans were more aware of the material shortcomings of socialism than their eastern neighbours thanks to West German television and visitors.

While the same factors also undermined the legitimacy of other regimes within the Soviet bloc, they did not necessarily raise questions about other states' very right to exist because they had featured on the map of Europe in some form for years, and some, such as Poland and Hungary, were synonymous with established nations. But the GDR was a state whose population was only a small proportion of a divided nation, hence a straight forward fusion of national consciousness and state consciousness, resulting in a strong sense of identity between the people and their state, was unlikely to occur. In short, the East German regime faced an additional task which was not shared by its Eastern allies, namely the need to prove that it was more successful and more legitimate than its Western rival, the existence of which was to undermine it throughout its 40 year lifespan. Initially however the SED did not intend to compete with the Federal Republic as a separate state. Instead the intention was to prove that the GDR was the *only* legitimate German state, and the rightful political embodiment of the German nation.

The only comparable case was that of Korea, where the nation was also divided into two hostile states due to outside circumstances, and whose rivalry also symbolised the international struggle for supremacy between capitalism and communism. Even so, there were significant differences between the German and Korean cases, for example regarding the relative strength and size of the two constituent parts, the importance of nationalism, and their geo-political situations.[5] However, multinational states such as the former Soviet Union, Yugoslavia, and on a smaller scale, Czechoslovakia, also faced difficulties in gaining the allegiance of the entire population and provided further evidence of how communist regimes generally underestimated the strength of ethnic nationalism.

Unlike successive West German governments which took the continued unity of the German nation as given and then adapted their approach towards the GDR according to current circumstances and realistic possibilities, the SED took its ambitions for the GDR and for Germany as a whole as a starting point and then adapted its position regarding the state of the German nation accordingly.

Therefore the factors which determined the SED's policy regarding the German question in a political sense also determined the official line on the state of the German nation since the latter was always subordinate to the former. The first of these influencing factors were Moscow's objectives regarding the future of Germany and of Europe as a whole. According to Gerhard Wettig, the Kremlin consistently viewed the GDR 'not as a pawn or a bargaining chip but as a power position that could be used for further political advance.'[6] In other words, the GDR was the Soviet Union's prize for having won the war and the cornerstone of its security policy, hence reunification was impossible (apart from as a communist takeover of West Germany) until the East-West divide of Europe became irrelevant altogether. The second influencing factor was the West German government's *Deutschlandpolitik*. The SED was constantly on the defensive due to the Federal Republic's claim to the territory of the GDR and its emphasis on the German national bond. The party had to respond to Bonn's initiatives because it could not prevent the population of the GDR hearing about them on their radios and television sets. As a result party propaganda portrayed West German politicians as the class enemy and their advances as threatening and imperialist, although the reception given by ordinary East Germans to Willy Brandt and Helmut Kohl suggests their claims fell on deaf ears. However, while public opinion regarding the national question was monitored closely this was purely in order to bring it into line with party policy and not because the SED was willing to be influenced by popular sentiment.

An additional factor was the obligation to produce policies which could be reconciled with the basic teaching of Marxism-Leninism. While this is not the place for a detailed account of classical Marxist thought regarding questions of nationality and nationalism[7] since the focus of this work is the practical policies employed by a particular Marxist-Leninist regime, it is important to note that nationalism has always posed a theoretical problem for Marxists because it clearly contradicts and rivals socialism as the basis for the organisation of societies.[8] But even Marx himself did not condemn nationalist movements where there was a strategic advantage to be gained.[9] Subsequent attempts to reconcile socialism and nationalism have produced conflicting results. The Austrian Marxist, Otto Bauer, for example, developed a 'socialist principle of nationality' which recognised the value of national communities and cultures which he believed would continue to flourish under socialism without becoming antagonistic towards each other.[10] In contrast, Stalin devised a rigid definition of what constituted a nation which aimed not to encourage nationalism and self-determination but to limit separatist claims and to encourage multinational class solidarity.[11] In 'Marxism and the National Question', dating back to 1913, Stalin stated, 'A nation is a stable community that has arisen historically on the basis of a common language, territory, economic system and psychological character, which is manifested in a common culture.'[12] This remained the official definition in the Soviet Union and the GDR until after Stalin's death. For Lenin, the advancement of the revolution was paramount, therefore he advocated a pragmatic approach to the national question, which could be adapted to suit specific circumstances.[13] This strategy was to appeal to the leadership of the SED, a party which always put the immediate interests of the state and socialism before abstract theories.

Overall, with so many different factors to take into account it is perhaps hardly surprising that the SED's policies regarding the state of the German nation and the GDR's relationship to it often sounded artificial, contrived and self-contradictory.

Policy-making in the GDR

Since the collapse of the GDR it has become apparent that power was concentrated in the hands of a very small elite, in particular, the First Secretary of the SED (officially called General Secretary from 1976), and his close circle,[14] and even the politburo had long ceased to be a forum for debate.[15] This situation was exacerbated by the fact that individuals remained in office for decades, with most top party positions being held by only one or two people throughout the 40 years of the GDR's existence. The authority of the First/General secretary of the party was absolute, so long as it pleased Moscow, and his opinions formed the official line on any subject, especially on controversial matters such as the state of the nation and policy towards the Federal Republic. Therefore if he mentioned the subject in a speech at the party congress for example, this formed the basis of official policy and had to be quoted *ad nausium* until either he changed his mind, or Moscow changed its mind about the leader of the GDR. Consequently, the official line on the nation tended to reflect the personal convictions and ambitions of Walter Ulbricht, followed by Erich Honecker, though neither contemplated the concept of the nation in great detail. This task was undertaken by other politburo members and theorists.

As head of the Department of Sciences and the politburo member responsible for ideology and culture from 1955 until 1989, Kurt Hager was heavily involved in the formulation and elaboration of official policy regarding the national question and the production of arguments for use in propaganda material. His department controlled all academic activity in the GDR, primarily through 'central research plans' which defined which subjects should receive academic attention at state-run institutions, and allocated the necessary resources. Once formulated, it was the task of the Agitation and Propaganda departments to disseminate the party line. In charge was the State Secretary for Agitation and Propaganda (until 1978, Werner Lamberz, followed by Joachim Herrmann). These departments analysed data collected by the Institute for Public Opinion Research until its abolition in 1978 and reports from informers in order to assess the impact of official propaganda and to identify areas where it needed to be increased or improved. The fact that sciences and propaganda were the responsibility of one department until 1956 is an indication of the close relationship between the two in the GDR.

The only politburo members to address the national question out of personal interest were Hermann Axen and Albert Norden (interestingly both Jewish), both of whom attempted to prove the existence of a separate nation in the GDR. Axen was State Secretary for International Affairs from 1966 until 1989 and appears to have wanted to carve out a niche for himself once Honecker more or less took over International Affairs. Norden was a journalist, history professor and a member of the politburo from 1958-81. The rest of the politburo appear to have been more interested in the practicalities of the socialist economic and social system in the GDR and paid little attention either to theories about nationhood in general, or to the state of the German nation in particular.

The role of theorists in the GDR

The provision of theoretical justifications for changes in policy was primarily the task of theorists at state-run academic institutions.[16] This often occurred retrospectively, following a declaration by the party leadership, and involved the development of both complex academic theories and more straightforward arguments which would be comprehensible and palatable to the masses, and therefore more effective as propaganda in the SED's struggle to prove the legitimacy of the state. In fact, policy regarding the nation provides a good example of the complex relationship between the party and scholarship in the GDR. While this was in a sense a two-way relationship, it was by no means an equal one, for while the party relied on scholars to provide scholarly backing for dubious policies, the latter required official approval to fund their projects and guarantee their positions.

In common with the ruling communist party of the Soviet Union and other countries in the Soviet bloc, the SED went to great lengths to ensure that the academic community supported the regime.[17] This not only applied to scholars whose knowledge could strengthen the GDR economically and militarily, but also to theorists who could help the party win the ideological war against the Federal Republic, including philosophers, social scientists and historians. All scholars were obliged to demonstrate party loyalty *(Parteilichkeit)* in their work and individuals soon learned that it was not their place to make suggestions which would be interpreted as criticism of the leadership. Their role was merely to provide scholarly backing for party policies, in particular, to reconcile the latest declarations by leading functionaries with the principles of Marxism-Leninism. This is somewhat reminiscent of the Third Reich during which the Nazi party also employed scholars to provide academic arguments for its highly dubious policies in order to give them credibility.[18]

Various control mechanisms ensured that East German scholarship remained overtly partisan, including privileges for those who conformed, such as opportunities to travel, and discrimination against those who did not, for example, unsuccessful visa applications and poor career prospects for their children. Not surprisingly, academic appointments were not determined by academic ability alone but also according to an applicant's record of services to the party.[19] In short, theorists were by no means critical intellectuals, and even if they had hoped to change things, self-censorship was inevitable for a successful career and a quiet life.

The leading theorists on the concept of the nation in the GDR were members of the prestigious Academy of Sciences (AdW) or the Academy for Social Sciences (AfG). Such institutions were modelled on their Soviet equivalents, in particular, the Academy of Sciences of the USSR, the 'basic social function' of which was 'to safeguard the unity of science and ideology'.[20] The AdW was the largest research institution in the GDR.[21] One of its major sections was the Institute for History, which was one of several historical institutes in the GDR, suggesting that the SED recognised the significance of history as an ideological weapon and its function not only to interpret the world but also to change it.[22] The task of historians was to develop a Marxist version of German history that was 'national' in the sense that the working class was accorded its due place in history, as opposed to the traditional approach which concentrated on the actions of a tiny elite such as wars and diplomacy.[23] The smaller Academy for Social Sciences also existed to serve the needs of the party rather than to make an objective contribution to human knowledge.[24]

Those who addressed the concept of the nation in the GDR were small in number, partly because the priorities of the party leadership determined the research agenda, and the SED's schizophrenic attitude towards the subject meant that approval and funding for research and publications could not be guaranteed from one year to the next. The leading authority on the concept of the nation in the GDR was a philosopher, Professor Alfred Kosing, who eventually became director of the Institute for Marxist-Leninist Philosophy at the AfG. Other authorities who published on the subject were Professor Walter Schmidt, who became director of the Institute for Historical Research at the AdW, and Professor Helmut Meier and Dr Jürgen Hofmann, both prominent social historians at the AfG.

All publications in the GDR were strictly controlled by the party and self-censorship was the only way to ensure publication. Theoretical articles addressing the state of the nation appeared in the SED's leading theoretical journal *Einheit* (1946-89), in the *Deutsche Zeitschrift für Philosophie* (1953-89), in in-house journals of the state-run academies, and occasionally in popular form in the party newspaper, *Neues Deutschland*. A number of books on the subject also appeared and it featured in other publications such as dictionaries of political and philosophical terms and encyclopedias. The total absence of a free press or independent publishing houses made it impossible for theorists to express radical ideas in writing. Although some may now claim that there was a radical message in their work if one were to read between the lines, it was usually too subtle to be noticed among the obligatory quotations by the First Secretary of the SED and damning indictments of West German policies.

In order to achieve its objectives, in addition to published party documents, this work makes extensive use of unpublished material from the SED archive in Berlin[25] which has become accessible only since the demise of the GDR. Material from the records of Central Committee and politburo, and from the departments involved with the production and dissemination of party propaganda is particularly relevant, as are the files from offices of prominent party functionaries. In addition much evidence is provided via interviews with leading theorists engaged in the production of theoretical material on the state of the nation in the GDR and senior party functionaries. Inevitably there are limitations on how much we can know about policy and decision-making under former communist regimes, and various questions remain unanswered due to the absence of debate, or at least of records of debate. However, as other researchers have noted, many gaps can be filled if one takes into account the circumstances at the time and the position and intentions of the writer.[26]

In the chapters that follow, the SED's policy regarding the nation is examined chronologically which highlights several dramatic policy shifts over the years. Particular attention is paid to the motivation behind changes to the official concept of the nation and to the attempts made to justify these changes theoretically. Chapter two examines the period from the foundation of the GDR in 1949 until 1966 - a relatively straightforward period during which the leadership of the SED adhered to the belief that the unitary German nation continued to exist, in spite of the political division of German territory, and attempted to equate socialism with the national interest. Chapter Three covers the period from 1967 until the autumn of 1970 - a transition period during which differences of opinion regarding the state of the nation emerged within the party leadership. Chapter four examines the period from December 1970 until 1975 during which the SED adhered to the view that the unitary German nation no longer existed and that a separate, socialist nation was developing in the GDR. Chapter five deals with the second half of the 1970s and the 1980s until the collapse of the GDR which saw a return to the idea of a socialist German nation in the GDR with renewed emphasis on its German heritage. In the sixth and final chapter, we will consider the paradoxes of official nationalism in the GDR and what the collapse of the state in 1989 can tell us about its impact on the national consciousness of the East German people.

To summarise, the German national question was one of the most difficult and potentially damaging problems the SED had to face. Handled badly it would completely undermine the GDR, but handled skilfully the SED believed it could be advantageous. What was required was a convincing new *Nationskonzept*, around which a national consciousness would develop, and a new definition of the national interest, politically embodied by the GDR. Therefore for the SED, the German nation was not a fixed concept (as was the case in the Federal

Republic), but a flexible weapon in the party's ideological battle with the Federal Republic, which could be adapted to suit the needs of the moment. Each new adaptation then required a 'scientific' explanation, as was habitual among authoritarian socialist regimes. Therefore, while the theory behind the concept of the nation in the GDR was subordinate to its political usefulness, theorists did play a vital role by providing an explanation for policy changes, and it is now evident that they provided modifications which made the concept of the nation more credible, though not sufficiently so to overcome the other delegitimising factors which undermined the GDR throughout its lifetime. In fact, the search for a *Nationskonzept* that would enhance the legitimacy of the GDR continued throughout the existence of the state in spite of the ideological incompatibility between nationalism and socialism and of the fact that according to Marxist-Leninist doctrine, class is the only relevant collective identity. Together with the brutal coercion methods employed to ensure popular allegiance to the state, this was in effect a major admission that authoritarian socialism alone could not legitimise the state.

Notes

1. For a brief discussion see Peter C. Ludz, 'Legitimacy in a Divided Nation', in Bogdan Denitch (ed.), *Legitimation of Regimes. International Frameworks for Analysis* (London and Beverly Hills, 1979), pp.162-64.
2. A point made by Ludz, 'Legitimacy', pp.164, 173.
3. Mark R. Thompson, 'No Exit: "Nation-stateness" and Democratisation in the GDR', *Political Studies* 44 (1996): p.285.
4. Joseph Rothschild, 'Political Legitimacy in Contemporary Europe', in Denitch (ed.), *Legitimation,* pp.38-9.
5. For comparisons of the German and Korean situations see Jürgen Habermas, 'National Unification and Popular Sovereignty', *New Left Review* 219 (1996): pp.3-13; Paik Nak-Chung, 'Habermas on National Unification in Germany and Korea', *New Left Review* 219 (1996): pp.14-21; Chung-Won Choue, *The Integration of Korea* (Seoul, 1985), pp.155-78; Myoung-Kyu Kang and Helmut Wagner, *Korea and Germany: Lessons in Division* (Seoul, 1990).
6. Gerhard Wettig, 'The Soviet View', in Edwina Moreton (ed.), *Germany between East and West* (Cambridge, 1987), p.36.
7. The seminal work on this subject in English is Walker Connor, *The National Question in Marxist-Leninist Theory and Strategy* (Princeton, 1984).
8. See Connor, *The National Question,* p.4.
9. A.W.Wright, 'Socialism and Nationalism', in Leonard Tivey (ed.), *The Nation-State. The Formation of Modern Politics* (Oxford, 1981), p.152.

10 Wright, 'Socialism', pp.153-4.
11 Wright, 'Socialism', p.156.
12 Josef Stalin, *Der Marxismus und der nationale und koloniale Frage*, 2nd ed. (East Berlin, 1952), p.327, cited in Reiner Koenen, *Nation und Nationalbewußtsein in der Sicht der SED* (Bochum, 1975), p.12.
13 Wright, 'Socialism', p.157. See also Ian Bremmer, 'Reassessing Soviet Nationalities' Theory', in Bremmer and Ray Taras (eds.), *Nations and Politics in the Soviet Successor States* (Cambridge, 1993), pp.9-11.
14 Manfred Uschner, *Die Zweite Etage. Funktionsweise eines Machtapparates* (Berlin, 1993), p.73.
15 For an inside view see Egon Krenz, *Wenn Mauer Fallen* (Vienna, 1991); Günther Schabowski, *Das Politbüro. Ende eines Mythos. Eine Befragung* (Hamburg, 1990); Detlef Herrmann, 'The Bitter Pills of the Politburo', in Arthur W. McCardle and A. Bruce Boenau (eds.), *East Germany: a New German Nation under Socialism?* (Lanham and London, 1984), pp.128-36.
16 Throughout this book the term 'theorist' is used to describe those who were occupationally engaged in the provision of detailed theoretical justifications for official policy. In this case, it includes historians, philosophers and social scientists. The term is also by Max Weinrich for 'those who supplied the academic formulae and scholarly backing' in *Hitler's Professors. The Part played by Scholarship in Germany's Crimes against the Jewish people* (New York, 1946), pp.239-40. Naturally theorists also belong to the broader categories 'scholars' and 'academics'. Alexander Vucinich uses the rarer term 'academicians' in *The Soviet Academy* (Stanford, 1956), as does L.G. Churchward in *The Soviet Intellegensia* (London and Boston, 1973). The term 'intellectuals' is not used because it often refers to dissident intellectuals which is not appropriate here, and because the precise definition of 'intellectual' and 'intellegentsia' in the Soviet and East European context has been disputed throughout the post-war period.
17 For an examination of the situation in other Eastern bloc states see Alexander Vucinich, *Empire of Knowledge. The Academy of Sciences of the USSR, 1917-1970* (Berkeley and London, 1974) and *The Soviet Academy;* Richard B. Remnek, *Soviet Scholars and Soviet Foreign Policy, A Case Study of Soviet Foreign Policy towards India* (Durham, North Carolina, 1975); Peter Hruby, *Fools and Heroes. The Changing role of Communist Intellectuals in Czechoslovakia* (Oxford, 1980), pp.232-33.
18 On this subject see Weinreich, *Hitler's Professors;* Michael Burleigh, *Germany turns Eastwards. A Study of Ostforschung in the Third Reich* (Cambridge, 1988); Wilhelm Röpke, 'National Socialism and

Intellectuals', in G.B. De Huszar, (ed.), *The Intellectuals* (Illonois, 1960), pp.346-363.

19 See Hannelore Belitz-Demiriz and Dieter Voigt, *Der Sozialstruktur der Promovierten Intelligenz in der DDR und der BRD 1950-1982* (Bochum, 1990), pp.466-473.

20 Vucinich, *Empire of Knowledge*, p.1. Here Vucinich provides a detailed account of the role of the Academy. See also Vucinich, *The Soviet Academy*.

21 It had 24,000 members, 18,000 actively involved in research. Birgit Gebhardt, 'Reform, Evaluation, *Abwicklung*. GDR Science in the Process of Reunification: the Example of the Academy of Sciences', in Margy Gerber and Roger Woods (eds.), *Studies in GDR Culture and Society* 11/12 (Lanham and London, 1993), p.212. See also Hartmut Zimmermann (ed.), *DDR Handbuch*, 2 vols, 3rd ed, (Cologne, 1985), vol.1, pp.32-33.

22 According to Ernst Engelberg, cited in Andreas Dorpalen, *German History in a Marxist Perspective* (Detroit, 1985), p.54.

23 Dorpalen, p.52.

24 See Zimmermann (ed.), *DDR-Handbuch*, vol.1, pp.34-36.

25 In 1993 the Central Party Archive (ZPA), previously located within the Institut for the History of the Workers' Movement (IfGA), became part of the Stiftung Archiv der Parteien und Massenorganisationen der DDR (SAPMO) which was incorporated into the Bundesarchiv. In this work, files from the SED archive are prefixed by SAPMO-BArch. Files from the *Altregistratur* which had not been reclassified are prefixed by IfGA, ZPA or IPA.

26 Stefan Wolle, 'Im Labyrinth der Akten. Die archivalische Hinterlassenschaft des SED-Staats', in Werner Weidenfeld (ed.), *Deutschland - eine Nation - Doppelte Geschichte* (Cologne, 1993), p.262. According to Wolle, the more important a decision and the higher the decision-making body involved, the briefer the records. Also, in spite of kilometers of files recording trivia, many important questions remain unanswered. (pp.259-260).

2 The fight to preserve the unity of the German nation

The divided nation

When the SED was formed in a forced merger of the German Communist Party (KPD) and the Social Democratic Party (SPD) in the Soviet Zone of Occupation in 1946, its leaders proclaimed it to be 'the true national party of the German people'[1] and stressed that their long-term objective was a united socialist Germany.[2] Indeed, the defeat of Nazism and the subsequent need for a new kind of German state seemed to provide the ideal opportunity for German communists to realise their dream. The first president of the GDR, Wilhelm Pieck, declared, 'We will not rest until the portion of Germany which was illegally torn off and subjected to occupation law is united with the core of Germany, the GDR',[3] and maintained that the GDR would never recognise the division of Germany.[4] The first constitution of the GDR referred to Germany as 'an indivisible democratic republic, the foundations of which are the German *Länder*'.[5] However, a mere three years later the East German *Länder* were abolished and replaced by *Bezirke*, which facilitated a more centralised form of government, indicating the SED's lack of respect for the constitution which was ostensibly democratic, but which soon bore little resemblance to the reality of authoritarian rule in the socialist German state.

Originally the SED was not conceived as a Stalinist or Soviet-style party, but a German Marxist party with a programme 'corresponding to the interests of the German people and the peculiarities of the German economy, politics and culture',[6] and the intention was not to impose a replica of the Soviet system on Germany. Indeed, the idea of a 'specific German road to socialism', originally advocated by Anton Ackermann in 1946,[7] was supported by a large proportion of party members. However, due to Tito's attempts to achieve greater autonomy for Yugoslavia, from 1948, Moscow made it clear that there was only one road to socialism, namely the Soviet road, and Ackermann was later compelled to retract his earlier position.[8]

During the late 1940s and 1950s, no important speech by a prominent party functionary failed to stress the unity of the German nation and the SED's intention to preserve that unity.[9] For extra effect, the adjective 'national' frequently featured in the names of state institutions, for example, 'National People's Army', 'National Defence Committee', and 'National Front for a Democratic Germany' (the bloc of parties allied to the SED to give the impression of a pluralist party system). Furthermore, the party portrayed itself as the defender of national assets, such as culture,[10] and attempted to associate both it and the GDR with historical German figures such as Goethe,[11] Beethoven[12] and Schiller[13] via lavish commemorations of their achievements. It also claimed to be fighting to preserve the German language, which was apparently under threat from 'Anglo-American imperialists' who were accused of attempting to create a linguistic divide between the two German states.[14] In short, the SED portrayed itself as a truly national party, which represented the national interest in the sense of the interests of the majority of the population, i.e. the working class - not only in the GDR, but also in the Federal Republic, who it claimed to support in their 'liberation struggle' against the allied occupation forces.[15] In contrast, West German politicians were portrayed as mere agents of foreign powers, who served the interests of the latter, which was ironic, coming from a party which was clearly under the thumb of a foreign power itself. Of West German politicians, President Wilhelm Pieck commented, 'These people who call themselves Germans, but in reality no longer are, are agents of enemy imperialist forces.'[16] They were committing 'the worst form of betrayal of the national interests of the German people by their support for the policies of the Western powers'.[17] The date of the establishment of the Federal Republic was described as 'a day of national shame' which would 'go down in the history of the German people as a day of humiliating betrayal for the German nation.'[18] It was the foundation of this 'imperialist West German state' which had apparently made it necessary to found a 'peaceful German state'[19] with a 'truly German government'.[20]

For a Marxist-Leninist party, the SED's extensive use of the vocabulary of nationalism is perhaps surprising, especially since nationalism had acquired such a negative image due to the actions the Nazis on behalf of the German nation. At first the SED claimed 'We need not worry about parading our national policies because we then find ourselves in harmony with the masters of scientific socialism, with Marx and Engels, Lenin and Stalin.'[21] In fact, the SED had various political reasons for taking advantage of an ideology they claimed to despise. Firstly, by equating socialism with the national interest and portraying itself as the defender of the unity of the German nation, the SED hoped to make socialism more appealing to all Germans - not just the working class, and not only those in the former Soviet zone - and therefore to arouse support for its own vision for the future of Germany, i.e. as a socialist state. Until 1952 the SED played down the pursuit of socialism, instead emphasising the need for an 'anti-fascist democratic order'. Although the commitment of most members of the the SED to anti-fascism was genuine, both the early actions of its leaders, and soon their words too, suggested that the 'anti-fascist democratic order' was just a means to an end, namely to pave the way to socialism.[22]

The second reason why the SED stressed the unity of the nation and the national interest, was that it suited Moscow's *Deutschlandpolitik* at the time, which inevitably determined the SED's position.[23] Stalin's ultimate objective had been a united socialist Germany allied to the Soviet Union. This would provide the latter with security, both from the West and from Germany itself, would increase the Soviet sphere of influence in Europe relative to its American counterpart, and would provide a starting point for the spread of communism throughout Western Europe.[24] Stalin believed that the German desire for reunification was sufficiently strong that they would be willing to accept communism if it facilitated reunification. However, Moscow's use of this tactic was played down following the popular uprising of 1953 in East Berlin which indicated the strength of German resistance to communism.[25] Furthermore, it appears that Stalin's successors did not share his belief in the merits of a pro-unification policy, believing instead that the continued existence of two German states guaranteed Moscow's control over at least one part of Germany and prevented German power ever threatening the Soviet Union again.

During the late 1940s and the 1950s, the SED's (and Moscow's) *Deutschlandpolitik* was dealt three major blows. The first had been the establishment of the Federal Republic in 1949. In retaliation, the Soviet Zone was transformed into the German Democratic Republic, marking the beginning of the SED's struggle to prove that the GDR was a legitimate sovereign state - indeed the only legitimate German state - a struggle they continued to fight throughout the state's 40 year life-span, and one which they would eventually lose.

The second blow to the SED's all-German ambitions was Adenauer's willingness to join the European Defence Community in 1952, which was a clear indication that the Federal Republic was firmly anchored in the Western alliance, and that the division of Europe, and by implication, of Germany, was deepening. In response, the SED declared 'building socialism' to be its primary concern, although the long-term goal remained German state-unity,[26] suggesting that the leadership thought it wiser to build socialism in at least part of Germany, even if it delayed reunification, than to put the socialist system in the GDR at risk by trying to achieve too much too fast. However, Ulbricht still maintained that:

> We want German unity because the Germans in the western part of our homeland are our brothers, because we love our fatherland, because we know that the restoration of German unity is an unavoidable aspect of the logic of history and cannot be overturned.[27]

The declaration of the primacy of 'building socialism' concurred with the new Soviet twin-track strategy regarding Germany, introduced in response to Adenauer's rejection of the famous 'Stalin Note' in 1952, which was Moscow's final offer of a united, neutral Germany, although western commentators doubt the sincerity of the offer.[28] From this point, the immediate goal of the Kremlin was to strengthen the GDR, thereby increasing its own influence in one part of Germany in the hope of gaining a foothold in the struggle for the country as a whole.[29] Thus the apparently contradictory aims of recognition of the GDR on the one hand, and reunification on the other, were merely the short-term and long-term manifestations of Moscow's overall policy, to which the SED had to adhere.

The third blow to the SED's hope of a united socialist Germany was the entry of the Federal Republic into NATO in May 1955. Shortly afterwards, the Warsaw Pact was founded, including among its members the GDR, and it was clear that the situation on German soil was rapidly developing into a microcosm of the Cold War. A treaty was signed with the Soviet Union in September 1955, in which Moscow recognised the sovereignty of the GDR. Thus Moscow was simultaneously granting the GDR sovereignty, while also ensuring it would remain in the Soviet sphere of influence, thereby placing severe limitations on that sovereignty. While the treaty included a reference to the ultimate objective of German reunification, this was probably merely rhetoric since 1955 appears to mark the introduction of Khrushchev's 'two state thesis'. The key objectives behind the new line were to strengthen and stabilise the GDR, to further integrate it into the Eastern bloc, and to acquire western (particularly West German) recognition of the status quo in Europe.[30] Consequently Khrushchev himself began to speak in terms of confederation as opposed to reunification, and of the need to preserve the political and economic achievements of the GDR.[31] Superficially at least the 'two state thesis' was adopted by the SED leadership who began to refer to 'the two German states' as opposed to 'the two parts of Germany,'[32] though the assumption remained that if socialism was firmly established in the GDR, in the event of a confederation, the SED would be in a strong position to exert influence westwards until power was in the hands of communists across Germany. They even stated that reunification would only take place via step-by-step rapprochement between the two German states[33] - a whole decade before Willy Brandt advocated a similar idea to preserve the German national bond. In fact, towards the end of the 1950s, the SED proposed several confederation plans,[34] all of which were immediately dismissed by Bonn. Just how genuine these proposals were is hard to judge. By adhering to the ultimate goal of a unified state, while simultaneously strengthening the GDR, the SED was keeping its options open.

A final reason for the party's emphasis on the unity of the nation and verbal adherence to the goal of reunification during the 1950s was what could be termed the 'Ulbricht factor'. Walter Ulbricht, a veteran German communist, born in 1893, quickly acquired such a firm grip on power that his opinion was inevitably the last word on any subject. He saw the solution of the national question in the socialist reorganisation of the entire nation,[35] which had failed during the 1930s due to divisions within the workers' movement, allowing the Nazis to gain power.[36] However, 1945 provided a fresh start and it was vital that this time the workers' movement remained united. To lead a united socialist Germany was Ulbricht's dream, and it seems that he really did believe that a united socialist Germany could be created, based on his somewhat naive belief that the working class in the Federal Republic could be won over to the SED's socialist cause,[37] and that the proletariat in both East and West Germany were tied by a national bond that could not be broken. Just nine months before the construction of the Berlin Wall, Ulbricht stated prophetically that in spite of its temporary division, the re-establishment of the unity of the nation was 'historically inevitable', and described the view that two separate German nations could emerge as a 'false perspective'.[38]

However, in spite of his convictions regarding the national question, Ulbricht was by nature a pragmatist, resulting in contradictions between his words and deeds. Furthermore, he slavishly served Soviet interests, especially under Stalin, seeing himself as Moscow's right-hand man in Germany. One could almost say that he personally embodied the fundamental dilemma facing the SED, namely how to convince the population that it could serve the national interest and Soviet interests simultaneously.

In spite of all the nationalist rhetoric, in practice, the party leadership made little effort to prevent the division of Germany deepening, or to negotiate with the West, although the onset of the Cold War inevitably limited the possibility of a settlement between the leaders of the two German states. Furthermore, with the benefit of hindsight, we know that when a choice had to be made between either a unitary German state with a multi-party system or securing socialism on at least one part of German soil, the SED chose the latter.

Overall it can be seen that the SED had numerous reasons not to resist temptation to give its brand of Marxism-Leninism a national slant. However, right from the start a clear distinction was made between patriotism and nationalism. The latter was denounced as chauvinist, aggressive, and a tool used by the bourgeoisie to gain the support of the masses for their own selfish interests and to prepare them for war. This was apparently what the Nazis had done, taking advantage of Germans' typical Prussian submissiveness and deference to authority,[39] and submerging the class-consciousness of the workers under fascism.[40] In contrast, patriotism (of the socialist variety) was defined as active participation in the reconstruction of Germany and solidarity with one's fellow workers, and as having only peaceful intentions.[41] According to this argument, true upholders of the unity of the nation were patriots as opposed to nationalists, and members of the working class were the best patriots of all because they furthered the interests of the nation as a whole, unlike capitalist owners and bosses who were driven by self-interest.[42] In addition, it was argued that socialist patriotism did not pose a threat to other nations (unlike chauvinism or nationalism), because it was complemented by proletarian internationalism, the basis of which was solidarity with workers in other states as opposed to loyalty to an ethnic or cultural group, in particular solidarity with the proletariat in the Soviet Union and Eastern Bloc states and with progressive liberation movements all over the world. Proletarian internationalism was also the principle at the heart of relationships between socialist states, a relationship based on friendship, mutual assistance, co-operation and friendly competition, which was totally unlike the nationalism and 'imperialist warmongering' which characterised relationships between capitalist states.[43] It apparently had nothing in common with cosmopolitanism, which, it was claimed, 'denies the love of one's home and fatherland. It is the ideological weapon of the current American world conquerors, through which they undermine the national consciousness of peoples.'[44] Together, proletarian internationalism and socialist patriotism formed the basis of the new socialist consciousness the SED hoped to instil in the population as an alternative to the bourgeois German national consciousness of the recent past, in order to win support for the party's vision for the future of Germany.

In the end, however, the increasing emphasis the SED placed on proletarian internationalism and their subservience to Moscow, illustrated by the fact that the popular uprising of 1953 was brutally crushed by Soviet tanks,[45] severely weakened the party's claim to have the interests of the German nation at heart. In addition, the party's failure to make patriotism and internationalism seem compatible reflected the fact that they were trying to achieve two fundamentally incompatible aims at this stage, namely to reunite and to revolutionise Germany.

Meanwhile, from the late 1950s, socialism began to penetrate not just the economic and political spheres, but also people's private lives, and the seeds of a socialist consciousness were being sown which would later be advocated as an alternative to German national consciousness. An ideological campaign was waged to encourage socialist consciousness among the population, culminating in Ulbricht's 'Ten Commandments of Socialist Ethics and Morals', according to which, correct behaviour was that which furthered socialism, and incorrect behaviour was that which hindered it. In addition, writers and artists were called upon to contribute towards 'building socialism' by using 'art as a weapon' and adhering to the principles of socialist realism.[46]

While there was no shortage of political speeches and scholarly articles regarding the politics of the national question and the need to reunite Germany under socialism during the 1950s, the 'national question' remained a political question, that is to say, a question of what form a new post-war German state would take, or rather, what type of social and economic system it would have. Stalin's definition of what constituted a nation (cited in the previous chapter), was still used to support the claim that the unitary German nation continued to exist until the late 1960s, although it ceased to be attributed to him once the policy of destalinisation was implemented.[47] In short, the continued existence of the German nation was taken for granted at this stage and the SED sought to portray itself as the defender of the national interest and the guardian of the unity of the nation while accusing 'Western imperialists' of trying to destroy it.[48]

Looking back at the 1950s, it is clear that although the SED verbally adhered to the goal of reunification, the party regarded the consolidation of the GDR and its system as a prerequisite (though not yet a substitute), for reunification. While the leadership claimed legitimacy through the anti-fascist credentials of the GDR and its 'democracy' in a Marxist-Leninist sense, right from the start, Ulbricht's only concern was that it should 'look democratic'.[49] In reality, the multi-party 'National Front' hardly concealed the SED's hegemony, hence the claim of legitimacy through democracy was hardly credible. Furthermore, the SED's early economic policies failed to provide the legitimacy through prosperity which soon underpinned the Federal Republic, as the population of the GDR knew only to well. Finally, in spite of the SED's attempts to enhance the GDR's image by conducting diplomacy on behalf of the German nation, for example, by signing a treaty with Poland, recognising the Oder-Neisse Line as the official German-Polish border,[50] the international community remained unconvinced. The only remaining device which could potentially legitimise the GDR and its regime was by appealing to the German national interest. The equation of 'socialist' with 'national' or 'German' was viewed by the leadership as the solution to the problem of how make the goals of building socialism and German reunification compatible. As we have seen, this was not just a tactic - the leadership really did hope to introduce socialism nationwide. Consequently, they stressed the continued existence of the German nation and the importance of patriotism. However, the SED's relationship with the Soviet Union undermined its claims to be an independent sovereign state and to be the true representative of the German nation. Thus, by 1960, popular legitimacy was clearly lacking and ordinary East Germans were voting with their feet, regarding the Federal Republic as the real, or at least, the best German state. The increasing permanence of the GDR by the late 1950s was merely a result of the deepening division within Europe, and its right to exist depended on the continuation of the Cold War, a fact proved by its subsequent fate once the thaw began.

The SED, the nation and the Berlin Wall

In August 1961 the SED took drastic action to prevent the daily exodus of thousands of East German citizens[51] by sealing the inner-German border and dividing East and West Berlin by an impermeable wall that became the ultimate object of Cold War symbolism. But in spite of this development, official party documents continued to refer to the unity of the German nation. Furthermore, the GDR was still described as the true political representative of the entire nation because power was in the hands of the majority, i.e. the working class, hence the GDR apparently still represented the national interest. However, a change in the precise meaning of words such as 'nation' and 'national' can be perceived from the beginning of the decade, with 'national' tending to be used to mean 'GDR-wide' as opposed to all-German, although official usage was not always consistent.

The main reason for this continued belief in the unitary German nation was because the long-term objectives of the party's *Deutschlandpolitik* remained essentially the same, in spite of the construction of the Berlin Wall. They were outlined in the 'National Document', published in 1962, which stated that 'the essential interests of the nation' could only be realised 'in a united German nation-state', and described the GDR as the model for a future united Germany.[52] The two prerequisites for reunification were the victory of socialism in the GDR and the defeat of West German militarism and imperialism by the working class and other democratic forces.[53] However, the construction of the Wall did suggest that a decade without progress towards a united socialist Germany had affected official perceptions of what could realistically be achieved, and signified a reordering of priorities, with increased emphasis on the immediate objectives of international recognition and the further construction of socialism, which in practice diminished the party's chances of achieving its long-term objective of reunification. In short, the SED was still trying to use the concept of the nation to support its mutually exclusive objectives, namely to cement socialism and gain international recognition of the GDR on the one hand, and to achieve German reunification (on its own terms) on the other.

This line was confirmed in the new Party Programme of 1963 which concentrated on inner consolidation and completing the construction of socialism, which, it was argued, would strengthen the SED's position in the event of a German confederation. Although hopes for a 'democratic transformation' of the Federal Republic were fading, the party's long-term objective remained the advancement of 'the socialist revolution and reconstruction' in the GDR so that 'socialism might be victorious in one part of the country, thus establishing the basis for the future inevitable victory of socialism throughout the country.'[54] The Berlin Wall was supposed to have 'positive all-German implications' by protecting the foundations of a future united Germany (i.e. the GDR) from attacks by the 'enemies of the nation' (i.e. the West).[55] As the Party Programme stated, 'A new era in the history of the German people has begun - the era of socialism... The future belongs to socialism - not only in the GDR but throughout Germany.'[56] However, patience was clearly required and the SED regarded a relationship of peaceful co-existence based on the recognition of the equal status of the two German states as a temporary solution to the German question.[57] While Ulbricht himself still hoped to achieve German unity under socialism,[58] even he admitted: 'If we insist on a policy of all or nothing right now, we will certainly end up with nothing.'[59]

What the construction of the Wall certainly did prove was that the regime was aware of the state's lack of legitimacy, although such action was hardly likely to remedy the situation, either domestically or internationally. Reports of the views of scholars and students which were collected by the Department of Sciences revealed that scholars believed the so-called 'measures of 13 August 1961' had in fact deepened the division of Germany, and the party secretly acknowledged that most people did not accept the official explanation of why the Berlin Wall had been necessary and misunderstood 'the nature of the national question', failing to recognise that it was a class conflict.[60] Consequently, a legitimacy campaign was launched, directed towards both the population of the GDR and the international community, not least the West German government, who still referred to their eastern neighbour as 'the so-called GDR' or 'the Soviet Zone', or at best, the 'GDR' in inverted commas.

The basis of the SED's claim that the GDR was the legitimate German state was that:

> The socialist developments in the GDR correspond with all the needs of the German nation. They correspond with all the essential interests of the German people... In all areas of politics and communal life, the GDR is the national and social alternative to the imperialism that rules West Germany.[61]

However, several factors continued to discredit these claims, including the GDR's obvious lack of democracy, overt Sovietisation, and the relatively weak economy compared with the Federal Republic's *Wirtschaftswunder*. Unwilling to tackle the first two factors, and unable to deal with the third, the regime sought other ways to increase people's allegiance to the GDR. Although it could be argued that this was hardly necessary once people could no longer leave, the SED no doubt recognised that a sense of state-pride would encourage social and political participation and hard work, and that it would enhance the claim to international recognition. Consequently, during the 1960s, the regime actively sought to make socialism seem more appealing and more traditionally German, earning the GDR the nick-name 'Red Prussia' in the West by the mid-1960s.[62] The 'imperialist' Federal Republic was denounced by the party as 'a false pretender to German nationality', in contrast with the GDR, 'the true heir to the throne'.[63] Highly americanised, the FRG was apparently incapable of representing the interests of the German nation. Its leaders were portrayed as mere puppets of the Western allies, and the SED took advantage of any evidence of right-wing activity and revanchism, such as the rise of the neo-fascist National Democratic Party (NPD), and the dubious war-time records of politicians, in particular, of Chancellor Kiesinger who had been a member of the Nazi lawyers' association.

Socialist national consciousness

An integral part of the party's legitimacy campaign was a more active attempt to nurture a form of 'GDR-consciousness', officially termed 'socialist national consciousness'. Far from being a 'spontaneous national consciousness' which was considered inadequate,[64] 'socialist national consciousness' was designed according to the specifications and needs of the party. It did not reflect the actual feelings of the population but instead concentrated on what ought to bind them together, namely 'a love for the GDR and pride in the achievements of socialism'.[65] This so-called 'socialist national consciousness' was portrayed as the first truly German consciousness in the history of the German people which had not been imposed or distorted by the ruling classes.[66] It had nothing in common with the bourgeois consciousness or *Junker* bourgeois chauvinism' apparently thriving in the Federal Republic which was the consciousness of a small proportion of the population, namely the bourgeoisie, and therefore 'anti-national'.[67] The latter was also equated with German nationalism of the past, hence the SED claimed that 'any German wishing to demonstrate a fundamental change in German national consciousness would never choose to be a citizen of the FRG'[68] - not that East Germans had the choice from 1961.

The fact that 'socialist national consciousness' included subjective, cultural and ethnic elements suggests the leadership realised that the highly objective notions of socialist patriotism and proletarian internationalism alone would not create the sense of total allegiance to the state that the SED sought.[69] It is also noticeable that in the early 1960s considerably more effort was made to encourage socialist patriotism rather than proletarian internationalism, especially pride in the concrete achievements of the GDR, not only compared with the Federal Republic, which experienced its first serious slump in the middle of the decade, but also compared with the modest achievements of other members of the Eastern bloc, including the Soviet Union. This was particularly noticeable following the introduction of the New Economic System in 1963 which increased productivity and enabled the SED to portray the GDR as a model of socialist economic success for her allies to follow.[70]

The initial cause of this East German boastfulness was tension between the SED and Moscow caused by Khrushchev's desire to improve relations with Bonn after the Berlin and Cuban crises, as a result of which Ulbricht feared the GDR would be excluded from negotiations over the future of Germany, in spite of the fact that the 1964 Treaty of Friendship, Mutual Aid and Cooperation between the Soviet Union and the GDR appeared to reaffirm Moscow's commitment to the preservation of the GDR.[71] The SED also took advantage of the Sino-Soviet conflict in an attempt to assert East German interests within the Eastern bloc,[72] and another brief period of assertiveness followed the replacement of Khrushchev in the Autumn of 1964 by Brezhnev and other functionaries with less experience than Ulbricht and his veteran team. Around this time, Ulbricht boasted that the

GDR had not adopted a single Soviet idea in the field of agriculture (which was blatantly untrue), and that the Soviet Union could learn from the GDR. In addition, it was alleged that the latter had completed the transformation from the dictatorship of the proletariat to socialist democracy in 15 years whereas it had taken the Soviet Union 40 years.[73] However, this assertiveness was not to last, and the trade agreement signed between the GDR and Soviet Union in 1965 reinforced the subservience of the former to the latter.[74]

Back at home, in order to enhance 'socialist national consciousness' a 'national image of history' *(nationales Geschichtsbild)*, was devised with the help of historians. The intention was to prove that the true roots of the German nation were socialist, and that its destiny had finally been realised in the establishment of the GDR, thus supporting the party's claim that the GDR was the only legitimate German state.[75] Discussion of an appropriate view of history for the GDR began in June 1962 with the publication of an important document entitled *Grundriß der Geschichte der deutschen Arbeiterbewegung* (Outline of the History of the German Workers' Movement).[76] It had been drafted by a commission chaired by Ulbricht himself, and was debated for ten months before being accepted by the Central Committee. Reports of discussion of this document at academic institutions revealed much confusion concerning the national question. A report from the Institute for Marxism-Leninism conceded that 'many comrades have serious difficulties grasping the interrelationship between the national question and the class question in Germany since 1945',[77] which was perhaps hardly surprising.

The campaign to create a new 'national view of history' culminated in the publication of the officially sanctioned, eight volume 'History of the German Workers' Movement' which was a chronicle of the development of the movement from its origins in the 19th century to the Sixth Party Congress of the SED in 1963.[78] Its overt aim was to demonstrate 'a continuity in the development of the German workers' movement from its birth to the SED'[79] and to describe how the party had become 'the leading force of the German nation'.[80] This renewed interest in German history also led to commemorations of various historical German figures, including Goethe, Hegel and Feuerbach. In party propaganda, Stalin was replaced by German role models with whom the young could identify, such as Rosa Luxemburg and Karl Liebknecht,[81] and the centre of East Berlin received a major face-lift to make it appear more traditionally German, which indeed it did compared to the flashy materialism of the *Kurfürstendamm* in West Berlin[82] which was relatively deficient in historic architecture, unlike the eastern part of the city.

All in all, 'socialist national consciousness' was a fairly obvious attempt to combine elements of class consciousness and national consciousness, and inevitably the result was unsatisfactory due to the fundamental incompatibility of the two. This was merely a reflection of the party's mutually exclusive political objectives, namely to revolutionise and reunite Germany. However, this did not automatically mean that there was no such thing as 'GDR-consciousness'. On the contrary, once people had no choice but to make the best of things in the GDR, it appears that a distinctive East German identity did begin to take shape, although it did not necessarily correspond to the official 'socialist national consciousness' devised by the ruling party.[83]

Meanwhile the factors which had reduced the GDR's popular legitimacy continued to have an adverse effect on the state's international standing. The construction of the Berlin Wall hardly gave the outside world the impression that it was stable and consolidated, and it was clear that the state remained under Moscow's thumb.[84] Furthermore, all the efforts of the regime were further undermined by the fact that the Federal Republic was recognised as the only legitimate German state by the outside world beyond the Soviet Bloc. Consequently, the party stepped up its campaign to gain recognition of the GDR's equal status with the Federal Republic, suggesting a realisation of the fact that a united socialist Germany was likely to remain an unfulfilled dream. This was demonstrated by symbolic assertions of the GDR's sovereignty, for example, in 1964, new personal identity cards were issued, for the first time bearing the words 'citizen of the GDR', and in 1965, a separate East German team was accepted by the International Olympic Committee to compete in the 1968 games. Furthermore, from 1966, measures were introduced to limit contact between East and West Germans. For example, the East German regime imposed stricter rules governing visits by West Berliners to the GDR, banned participation by East German ministers in activities organised by the pan-German protestant church, the EKD, and terminated the regular dialogue between the SED and the West German SPD. This was the first indication that a change in the SED's *Deutschlandpolitik* was on the cards, which in turn would raise questions regarding the official line on the state of the German nation.

The theoretical dimension of the national question

From 1962, the concept of the nation began to receive attention from theorists, resulting in a marked increase in publications on the subject. There appear to have been several reasons for this. Firstly, after 12 years, the political and psychological divide between the two German states seemed to be widening, not narrowing, and there was concern about the effect of this situation on the German nation as a cohesive entity. Secondly, a rethink was necessary in order to reconcile the party's adherence to the unity of the nation, recently reaffirmed in the 'National Document', with the construction of the Berlin Wall. Thirdly, the regime now seemed to be focusing on gaining the allegiance of the population of the GDR as opposed to the entire nation. Finally, prompted by Moscow, a general policy of destalinisation was under way, which encouraged a rethink of what was meant by the word 'nation'. The resulting publications demonstrate just how difficult it was to reconcile and justify the different strands of the SED's *Deutschlandpolitik* theoretically.

Most significant was a new, more class-based definition of a nation developed by Alfred Kosing, then a philosopher at the Academy for Social Sciences. He soon became the leading East German authority on the state of the German nation and his ideas later influenced other scholars,[85] and were used in party propaganda. Initially he set out to prove that one German nation still existed, although, as we shall see, he later reversed his position and in an public act of *Selbstkritik* (self-criticism), admitted that he had been wrong in the early 1960s and that there were indeed two separate nations of German soil.[86]

The spark which ignited the smouldering theoretical debate on the state of the nation was a book by the West German theorist, Karl Jaspers, published in 1960, in which he claimed that two separate German nations were developing, in the same way as the German and Austrian nations had developed.[87] Alfred Kosing totally rejected Jaspers' view and claimed, 'The current division of the nation into two states cannot lead to the formation of two nations. Instead it will eventually be overcome via the establishment of a united socialist nation.'[88] Kosing argued that a nation was defined first and foremost by class structures, and that it was neither a condition, nor a rigid structure, but developed and changed as part of a historical process. He challenged Stalin's basic definition of a nation because it implied that nations were 'class-neutral' *(Klassenindifferent),* but believed it could still be valid if expanded upon to include more class-based elements.[89] Turning to the German case, Kosing argued that the national bond was maintained by the working class in both German states, who together constituted the German nation, which was, according to this argument, a socialist nation. Thus the 'fate of the German nation' was 'inextricably bound to the struggle of the German working class for peace, democracy and socialism',[90] and he predicted that the German working class would one day be reunited within a unitary socialist German state.[91]

If the working class formed the core of the German nation, it followed that the GDR, as a state of the working class, embodied 'the future of the German nation,'[92] hence it represented the national interest in a Marxist sense. In contrast, the Federal Republic was described as riddled with class conflict, like the former unitary German state prior to 1945, and according to Marxist-Leninist theory, its population could not possibly constitute a united nation. It failed to represent the true national interest because power was in the hands of a minority, i.e. capitalists. Therefore, the West German working class formed a nation with the population of the GDR, and the latter state was their true fatherland.[93] In short, there were now apparently two German states, two German populations in the sense of *Staatsvölker*, but one German nation, albeit at two different levels of development.

To the non-Marxist observer, and with the benefit of hindsight, there appear to be many flaws in Kosing's explanation of the state of the German nation. In particular, it is hard to ignore the fact that like the SED, theorists including

Kosing mixed socialist ideas with nationalist arguments, and took advantage of the fact that something more than proletarian solidarity bound together the working class in both German states, i.e. ethnicity, tradition and culture. The position of the West German population also remained inadequately explained. On the one hand the 'bourgeois nation' in the Federal Republic was frequently referred to as class-divided, implying that it comprised both the proletariat and the bourgeoisie. On the other hand, it was claimed that the former were in fact members of the socialist nation, which was politically represented by the GDR. It may have been more logical to refer to the West German *state* as class-divided, compared to the GDR, where everyone allegedly lived together in harmony. In the end, the SED's loyal theorists were trying to justify the unjustifiable, namely the SED's verbal adherence to the nation on the one hand, and the implementation of measures which in reality deepened the division on the other. The results of their efforts indicated that a choice would soon have to be made between a socialist German state and a reunified German state.

Conclusion

Was the SED's adherence to the unity of the German nation from the 1950s until the mid-1960s genuine? Did the professed aim of reunification demonstrate a lack of realism, or was it just plain hypocrisy to conceal separatist intentions? It seems that the leadership's adherence to the unity of the nation based on the unity of the German working class was genuine, after all, they did hope that a united socialist German state would be established one day, hence it was claimed that there was no contradiction between the goals of reunification and the construction of socialism. However, by the 1960s, the only way to achieve these aims was perceived to be via the establishment of the permanence and sovereignty of the GDR - not (yet) as a separate entity, but as a model for a future united German state.[94] But in practice of course, this worked against reunification, and the SED would eventually have to accept socialism in only part of Germany, or not at all.

In spite of the SED's claim to be the defender of the unity of the German nation, socialism in the GDR seemed neither German nor national, but Soviet, hence the state was not seen as the true representative of the German nation either by its population, or by the western world. While the party leadership seemed to be more realistic about what could be achieved in the 1960s, and recognised the significance of national consciousness, it was unrealistic to assume that the masses would automatically be sympathetic to their socialist agenda for Germany, especially since Moscow was clearly setting that agenda. And in the end, the idea of using nationalism and aspects of traditional Germanness to make socialism seem 'national' was seriously flawed, because it contradicted the basic Marxist-Leninist principle that class determines the relationship between communities.

Although accurate data on public opinion in the GDR was no longer available to western journalists and academics, several individuals recognised that the construction of the Berlin Wall had marked a turning point in the population's relationship to their state, since it suggested that the SED had given up the objective of reunification and that the division of Germany had become permanent.[95] They believed that as a consequence of this development, a state consciousness unique to the GDR was starting to evolve, although it bore little resemblance to the 'socialist national consciousness' designed by the party to support its political objectives. Socialist internationalism in particular had failed to take root.[96] Instead, really existing GDR-consciousness was essentially a 'Teutonic consciousness',[97] coloured by the collective experience of life in a socialist state, sealed off from their former countrymen and women, and often from their own families. Therefore this embryonic GDR-state consciousness had not replaced citizens' self-perception as Germans, and the regime was naive to believe that it could. Furthermore, it seems likely that the population did still believe in the existence of one German nation, and that this conviction was based not on the bond of the German working class, as the SED claimed, but on more conventional aspects of nationhood, such as shared traditions, culture, language and history. In short, the SED's actions and words regarding the national question were contradictory, hence by the late 1960s, a rethink was necessary.

Notes

1   'Manifest an das deutsche Volk,' 21 April 1946, *Dokumente der SED*, vol. 1, (East Berlin, 1951), pp.27-28.
2   See *Protokoll des Vereinigungsparteitages der SPD und KPD*, (East Berlin, 1946).
3   Wilhelm Pieck, quoted in Dieter Blumenwitz, *What is Germany? Exploring Germany's Status after World War Two* (Bonn, 1989), p.36
4   Wilhelm Pieck, quoted in Zimmermann, ed., *DDR Handbuch*, 2nd ed., p.265.
5   Constitution of the GDR, 7 October 1949, cited in Blumenwitz, *What is Germany?* p.125.
6   *Protokoll des Vereinigungsparteitages,* p.12.
7   Anton Ackermann, 'Gibt es einen besonderen deutschen Weg zum Sozialismus?' *Einheit* 1 (1946): pp.22-32. On the original nature of the SED, see Wolfgang Leonhard, *Child of the Revolution* (London and Glasgow, 1957), pp.350-357, and Harold Hurwitz, *Die Stalinisierung der SED 1946-49* (Berlin, 1997). The latter argues that the Stalinist majority on the KPD executive intended to make the SED a Stalinist party right from the start.
8   See *Neues Deutschland,* 24 September 1948.

9   For example, Walter Ulbricht, 'Die Gegenwärtige Lage und die neuen Aufgaben der SED', *Einheit* 7 (1952): p.756; ZK der SED, 'Die Gründung der SED - ein historischer Sieg des Marxismus-Leninismus', *Einheit* 16 (1961): p.351.

10   See 'Manifest an das deutsche Volk,' pp.27-28; and Franziska Rubens, 'Die deutsche Nation ist nicht zu zerstören!' *Einheit* 6 (1951): pp. 125-127.

11   See 'Unsere Aufgaben in Goethe-Jahr', *Dokumente der SED*, vol. 2, (East Berlin, 1951), pp.230-231.

12   See *Dokumente der SED*, vol. 3, pp.751, 757.

13   See *Dokumente der SED*, vol. 5, p.224.

14   I have expanded on this in 'The SED's Interpretation of Marxist-Leninist Theory regarding the Nation; the Problem of Language', in *Contemporary Political Studies 1994*, eds. Patrick Dunleavy and Jeffery Stanyer (Belfast, 1994), pp.973-984.

15   Ulbricht, 'Die gegenwärtige Lage', p.736.

16   Wilhelm Pieck, Protokoll der 22. Tagung des Parteivorstandes der SED, 4. Oktober 1949. SAPMO-BArch IV 2/1/72.

17   Wilhelm Pieck, Protokoll der 10. Tagung des Parteivorstandes der SED, 12-13. Mai 1948. SAPMO-BArch IV 2/1/46.

18   *Dokumente der SED*, vol. 2, p.338.

19   Gerhard Kegel, 'Zur Deutschlandpolitik der beiden Deutschlands', *Einheit* 23 (1968): p.737.

20   Bericht der Kommission zur Ausarbeitung der Entschließung über die Nationale Front, 4 October 1949, SAPMO-BArch IV 2/1/72.

21   Pieck, Protokoll der 10. Tagung des Parteivorstandes der SED. SAPMO-BArch IV 2/1/46.

22   See the records of the Second Party Congress, September 1947, *Dokumente der SED*, vol. 1, (East Berlin, 1951), p.230.

23   The manifesto of the 'National Front,' contained all the main aspects of the regime's early *Deutschlandpolitik:* the objective of a united, 'democratic' Germany; adherence to the unity of the nation; the portrayal of the GDR as the turning point for the whole of Germany; and the western allies' responsibility for its temporary division. 'Programm der nationalen Front des Demokratischen Deutschland', 15 February 1950, cited in Gebhard Diemer, (ed.), *Kurze Chronik der deutschen Frage* (Munich, 1990), pp.179-180.

24   On Stalin's attutude towards German reunification see Gerhard Wettig, 'The Soviet View', in Edwina Moreton (ed.), *Germany between East and West* (Cambridge, 1987), p.35; Gottfried Zieger, *Die Haltung von SED und DDR zur Einheit Deutschlands 1949-1987* (Cologne, 1988), pp.9, 13.

25   Wettig, 'The Soviet View', p.35.

26   Ulbricht, 'Die gegenwärtige Lage,' p.750. See also 'The Grand Ideas of Socialism are becoming Reality in the GDR', in Walter Ulbricht, *On Questions of Socialist Construction in the GDR* (Dresden, 1968). pp.202-234; Stefan Dörnberg, *Kurze Geschichte der DDR*, 4th ed., (East Berlin, 1969), p.210-227; Dietrich Staritz, *Geschichte der DDR 1945-1985* (Frankfurt, 1985), pp.73-77.

27   Ulbricht, 4th Party Congress, March 1954, quoted in Zimmermann, ed., *DDR Handbuch*, 3rd ed., p.924

28   For details, see Carola Stern, *Ulbricht: a Political Biography* (London, 1965), pp.182-184; Zieger, *Die Haltung*, pp.47-50; Klaus Motschmann, *Sozialismus und Nation. Wie Deutsch ist die DDR?* (Munich, 1979), pp.226-234. For a bibliography see F. Stephen Larrabee, 'The View from Moscow', in Larrabee, (ed.), *The Two German States and European Security* (London and Basingstoke, 1989), p.184, note 3.

29   Zieger, *Die Haltung*, p.9.

30   Larrabee, 'The View,' p.186.

31   Khrushchev in East Berlin, June 1955. Source: Diemer, *Kurze Chronik*, p.56. For an analysis, see Jens Hacker, 'Der Rechtsstatus Deutschlands aus der Sicht der DDR', *Ostrecht* 13 (1974): pp.133.

32   Otto Grotewohl, 26 September 1955, quoted in Ulrich Scheuner, 'The Problem of the Nation and the GDR's relationship with the FRG', in E. Schulz, H-A. Jacobsen, G. Leptin, U. Scheuner (eds.), *GDR Foreign Policy*, (New York and London, 1982), p.50.

33   Committee for German Unity, *GDR: 300 Questions, 300 Answers* (East Berlin, 1959), p.5.

34   See for example SAPMO-BArch IV/ 2/1/220; Committee for German Unity, *GDR: 300 Questions*, pp.45-48.

35   This idea dated back to the KPD's 'Programmatic Statement on the National and Social Liberation of the German People' of 1930. Source: politburo member, Alfred Neumann, Berlin 7 April 1993 and 4 May 1993.

36   See Walter Schmidt, 'The Nation in German History', in Mikuláš Teich and Roy Porter (eds.), *The National Question in Europe in Historical Context* (Cambridge, 1993), pp.165-166.

37   SAPMO-BArch IV 2/1/122 (ZK, 17-19 September 1953).

38   Ulbricht to the Central Committee, December 1960, cited in Zimmermann, (ed.), *DDR Handbuch*, 3rd ed. vol. 2, p.924.

39   Walter Ulbricht, *Whither Germany?* (East Berlin, 1962), p.117.

40   Stefan Dörnberg, *Kurze Geschichte der DDR*, 1st ed. (East Berlin, 1964), p.39.

41   Anton Ackermann, 'Der Kampf gegen den Nationalismus', *Einheit* 5 (1950): p.492.

42   Rudi Wetzel, 'Was ist Patriotismus?' *Einheit* 8 (1953): p.314.

43	Committee for German Unity, *GDR: 300 Questions*, p.55.
44	Wetzel, 'Was ist Patriotismus?' p.313.
45	For an analysis, see Arnulf Baring, *Der 17. Juni 1953* (Stuttgart, 1983); Sigrid Meuschel, *Legitimation und Parteiherrschaft in der DDR* (Frankfurt, 1992), pp.116-122; Staritz, *Geschichte der DDR*, pp.78-95. For an official East German account see Dörnberg, *Kurze Geschichte*, 4th ed., pp.227-241.
46	For details see Hermann Weber, *Kleine Geschichte der DDR* (Cologne, 1980), p.93.
47	For an examination of the use of Stalin's definition in the GDR see Koenen, *Nation und Nationalbewußtsein*, pp.12-19.
48	See Rubens, 'Die deutsche Nation', pp.124-28.
49	Stern, *Ulbricht*, p.100.
50	For the official justification for this, see the declaration of the Party executive, 19 July 1950, *Dokumente der SED*, vol. 3, (East Berlin, 1952), p.72.
51	In July 1961 30,415 East German refugees arrived in West Berlin, followed by a further 21,828 during the first 12 days of August. Source: Anthony Read and David Fisher, *Berlin. The Biography of a City* (London, 1994), p.277.
52	See Dörnberg, *Kurze Geschichte*, 4th ed, p.476, and Diemer, *Kurze Chronik*, p.73.
53	Dörnberg, *Kurze Geschichte*, 1st ed., p.451. In the 4th edition, published 5 years later in 1969, Dörnberg alleged that the first of these had been achieved.
54	Hermann Axen, 14th session of the Central Committee, December 1961, quoted in Melvin Croan, 'East Germany: a Lesson in Survival', *Problems of Communism* 11 (1962): p.10.
55	Motschmann, *Sozialismus und Nation*, pp.244-245.
56	Programm der SED, *Dokumente der SED*, vol. 9, (East Berlin, 1965), pp.171, 174.
57	Programm der SED, p.204.
58	Ulbricht in a letter to Karl Jaspers, 1 June 1966, SAPMO-BArch NL182/1306.
59	*Neues Deutschland*, 1 August 1963, cited in A. James McAdams, *East Germany and Détente. Building Authority after the Wall* (Cambridge, 1985), p.59.
60	SAPMO-BArch IV 2/2.024/1
61	Programm der SED, *Dokumente der SED*, vol. 9, p.208-209.
62	Welles Hangen, 'New Perspectives behind the Wall', *Foreign Affairs* 45 (1966): p.138.
63	*Neues Deutschland*, 19 May 1962, quoted in McAdams, *East Germany*, p.35.

64 Wolfgang Heise, 'Um die Zukunft der Nation', *Deutsche Zeitschrift für Philosophie* 9 (1961): p.1036; Jörg Vorholzer, *Willfähriger Untertan oder Bewüßter Staatsbürger* (East Berlin, 1962), p.263.
65 Programm der SED, p.247.
66 Heinrich Homann, 'Der 8. Mai 1945 und die Entwicklung des Nationalbewußtseins in Deutschland', *Einheit* 19 (1965): p.41.
67 Heise, 'Um die Zukunft,' p.1036.
68 Homann, 'Der 8. Mai,' pp.32, 39.
69 Noted by F. Kopp in 1962, in *Die Wendung zur 'nationalen' Geschichtsbetrachtung in der sowjetischen Zone* (Munich, 1962), pp.5-6, reviewed in Dietmar Kreusel, *Nation und Vaterland in der Militärpresse der DDR* (Stuttgart-Degerloch, 1971), p.278.
70 McAdams, *East Germany*, p.58.
71 See McAdams, pp.53-55.
72 McAdams, p.56.
73 Hangen, 'New Perspectives', pp.143-44; see also Ilse Spittmann, 'Soviet Union and DDR', *Survey* 61 (1966), p.165.
74 Spittmann, 'Soviet Union and DDR', p.165.
75 On the 'national view of history' see 'Grundriß der Geschichte der deutschen Arbeiterbewegung', in *Dokumente der SED*, vol. 9, (East Berlin, 1965), pp.401-594; Dörnberg, *Kurze Geschichte*, 4th ed., pp.478-9; Stefan Dörnberg, 'Zum nationalen Geschichtsbild', *Einheit* 18 (1963): p.148; Homann, 'Der 8. Mai', p.31; Berthold, 'Unser nationales Geschichtsbild', pp.225-231; Ernst Engelberg, 'Vom Werden des nationalen Geschichtsbildes der deutschen Arbeiterklasse', *Einheit* 17 (1962): pp.110-121.
76 Reprinted in *Dokumente der SED*, vol. 9, (East Berlin, 1965), pp.401-594.
77 SAPMO-BArch IV 2/2.024/1
78 Institut für Marxismus-Leninismus beim ZK der SED, *Geschichte der deutschen Arbeiterbewegung*, 8 vols. (East Berlin, 1966). For a description of the content, see Koenen, *Nation und Nationalbewußtsein*, pp.82-105.
79 Zimmermann, ed. *DDR Handbuch*, 3rd ed., p.52.
80 Berthold, 'Unser nationales Geschichtsbild', p.226.
81 For example, in the 'Nationales Dokument' of 1962. See Weber, *Kleine Geschichte*, p.111.
82 Hangen, 'New Perspectives', p.138-9.
83 Gebhard Ludwig Schweigler, *National Consciousness in Divided Germany*, (London and Beverly Hills, 1975), p.74.
84 See Spittmann, 'Soviet Union', p.165; Peter-Christian Ludz, 'Zum Begriff der Nation in der Sicht der SED', *Deutschland Archiv* 5 (1972): pp.19-

20; Welles Hangen, *The Muted Revolution* (London, 1967), p.42; Hangen, 'New Perspectives', p.144.

85 See for example, Albert Norden, 'Arbeiterklasse und Nation', *Einheit* 21 (1966): p.461; Karl Polak, 'Über fehlerhaften Auffassungen in Fragen unseres Kampfes um Frieden und nationale Wiedergeburt', *Einheit* 17 (1962): p.121; Heise, 'Um die Zukunft', p.1030.

86 Kosing, *Nation in Geschichte und Gegenwart*, pp.101-105.

87 See Karl Jaspers, *Freiheit und Wiedervereinigung* (Munich, 1960).

88 Alfred Kosing, 'Illusion und Wirklichkeit in der nationalen Frage', *Einheit* 17, (1962): p.19-20.

89 Kosing, p.15. See also Peter-Alfons Steiniger, 'Das Selbstbestimmungsrecht im allgemeinen Völkerrecht der Gegenwart', *Einheit* 21 (1966): p.1226-7.

90 Kosing, 'Illusion,' p.21.

91 Kosing, p.19.

92 Kosing, p.14.

93 Norden, 'Arbeiterklasse', p.461.

94 Kreusel also believed that the SED did not yet have separatist intentions. Kreusel, *Nation und Vaterland*, p.298.

95 Schweigler, *National Consciousness*, pp.119-120. See also Hans Apel, *DDR 1962 1964 1966* (West Berlin, 1967), pp.373, 401; Theo Sommer, 'Kommunisten oder Deutsche?' in Marion Gräfin Dönhoff, Rudolph W. Leonhardt, Theo Sommer (eds.), *Reise in ein Fernes Land* (Hamburg, 1964), pp.129, 104; Jean Edward Smith, 'The Red Prussianism of the GDR', *Political Science Quarterly* 82 (1967): p. 380.

96 Hangen, 'New Perspectives', p.143.

97 Hangen, *The Muted Revolution*, p.184.

3 The unity of the nation in doubt

Between 1967 and 1970, certain members of the SED's ruling elite began to question party policy regarding the unity of the German nation. Deviations from the official party line were first apparent at the Seventh Party Congress which took place in 1967, although the traditional line regarding the nation prevailed in the new constitution of 1968. However, in 1970, even Ulbricht started to deny the existence of one German nation. This chapter examines the reasons for this gradual policy shift, focusing on the SED's political objectives at the time and their response to new initiatives from Bonn, and also looks at the theoretical justifications for policy changes.

Challenges to Ulbricht's line

The Seventh Party Congress

At the Seventh Party Congress, for the first time in the history of the SED, differences of opinion regarding the national question among members of the party leadership became evident. On the one hand there was the traditional view based on the goal of reunification and the continued existence of one German nation; on the other hand there was the pragmatic view based on a more 'GDR-centric' line, which prioritised the aim of recognition and played down the notion of one German nation.[1] However, the divide within the party leadership was far from clear cut, and as was always the case in the GDR, many functionaries continued to adhere to the official party line regardless of their own personal convictions in order to safeguard their positions. At this point in time, Ulbricht himself combined aspects of the traditional line with a more pragmatic approach, resulting in noticeable contradictions. Only a few, for example, the State Secretary for Agitation and Propaganda, Werner Lamberz, had totally adopted the new view, but they could not enforce it while Ulbricht remained in power. What is certain however, is that by the spring of 1967, the party leadership had changed tactics on the national question, which would soon give rise to a reassessment of goals, although the immediate result of the emergence of two apparently contradictory lines was confusion within the party and among the general public.

In order to understand why a new line on the nation began to emerge from within the ruling elite of the SED, several factors which influenced the SED's thinking at the time should be considered, most notably the new initiatives from Bonn, Moscow's foreign policy objectives, public opinion, Ulbricht's own position and finally, the reality of the situation after nearly 20 years with two states on German soil.

The key to understanding the SED's policy regarding the nation during the late 1960s was the leadership's dogged determination to acquire international recognition of the GDR, an objective fully supported by Moscow as part of its plan to guarantee the status quo in Europe. Obviously the main obstacle was the existence of another state which claimed to be the true political embodiment of the German nation, and it was the attempts by the Federal government to alter the status quo that finally forced the SED to re-examine its position and to take a more pragmatic stance on the national question. Already Bonn seemed to be calling the shots, forcing the SED to respond. During 1966, there had been an exchange of views with the opposition Social Democrats, known as the 'National Dialogue', the initiative for which, according to East German accounts, came from the SED.[2] But the SPD's line was not so very different from that of the CDU/CSU. Contrary to the SED's wishes, they also refused to renounce the Federal Republic's *'Alleinvertretungsanspruch'* or to renounce the borders of Germany as they stood in 1937, hence there was little room for negotiation and the dialogue ceased.

The first real turning point in relations between the two states was the entry of the SPD (who the SED leadership could not so easily blame for the division of Germany), into the Grand Coalition in December 1966. Previously, the SED had laid the blame for the lack of progress on the national question firmly at the door of the CDU/CSU, and until this point, the matter had been on hold, due to both sides' refusal to give any ground. But now prominent individuals, including Willy Brandt and Egon Bahr, were demonstrating an interest in compromise and co-operation, hence the SED was suddenly faced with a challenge that was potentially either a golden opportunity or a serious threat. The party leadership appears to have interpreted it as the latter, hence they began to build a barricade of conditions for progress towards reunification, and stated that there would be no further rapprochement without recognition.

However, since the SED claimed that the national question was a class question it could not ignore the party that was the most credible representative of the West German working class, but in spite of this, the SED put self-interest before pan-German class solidarity, and decided not to regard the SPD as an ally. Ulbricht criticised the SPD's entry into the Grand Coalition and condemned the new

Ostpolitik due to Bonn's continued claim to the sole right of representation of the German nation and the refusal to grant the GDR recognition.[3] According to Ulbricht:

> In view of joint policies by the SPD leadership, the CDU/CSU and West German monopoly capitalists, the process of rapprochement by the working class in both German states is becoming far more difficult and the division deeper. It can be proved that every condition for the reunification of both German states is lacking and that the FRG is neither capable of negotiation nor confederation.[4]

Consequently, for the time being, the main aim could only be the preservation of peace.

Brandt sent an open letter to the Seventh Party Congress, proposing SPD-SED negotiations, but the SED leadership declined, on the grounds that Brandt had failed to acknowledge that the national question was a class struggle, and because SPD politicians and members needed to be 'cured of their nationalism'.[5] Due to what they called the SPD's betrayal of the working class, the SED leadership committed a rather petty act of revenge by temporarily referring to the SPD as the 'SP', omitting the word *Deutschlands*. Presumably the intention was to portray the SPD as unworthy of the country's name, in contrast to the SED.

Rather more significant was the renaming of the State Secretariat for All-German Affairs, which became the State Secretariat for West German Affairs. Its tasks included the production of propaganda directed at the Federal Republic, the monitoring of political activity there, and the examination of Bonn's policies towards the GDR.[6] However, such activities, and the phrase 'all-German Affairs' itself, implied that a special link between the two states still existed and undermined the SED's claim that they were nothing to do with each other. The Secretary of State concerned, Joachim Herrmann - a hard-liner, totally opposed to any compromise with Bonn - blamed 'the new situation in West Germany' (i.e. the Grand Coalition), for the name change,[7] which was approved by Ulbricht, on the grounds that the term 'all-German' had become redundant.[8] If this was the case, then surely the unity of the German nation was in doubt and there could be no reunification? It seems that Ulbricht for one was not yet ready to abandon a policy held for 20 years, but a reordering of priorities had become unavoidable.

An important catalyst was Chancellor Kiesinger's governmental declaration of 13 December 1966, in which he adhered to the aim of reunification and refused to recognise the GDR, but also expressed a willingness to intensify human, economic and cultural ties, and proposed a renunciation of force between the two German states. The offers were repeated in April 1967 and were eventually rejected by the East German prime minister, Willi Stoph, after a further exchange of correspondence in September.

But the real bombshell dropped at the end of January 1967, when Romania and the Federal Republic established diplomatic relations, marking the end of the united front upheld by the communist regimes of Eastern Europe towards the SED's German enemy and rival.[9] It also marked the death of the Hallstein Doctrine, indicating a chance for greater flexibility towards the GDR, and challenged the so-called 'Ulbricht Doctrine', whereby the GDR attempted to stop its allies establishing diplomatic relations with Bonn, so long as the latter refused to recognise the GDR.[10] Even the leadership of the SED admitted that the development was 'a success for their [Bonn's] presumption to be the sole representative of the nation.'[11] Ulbricht personally criticised Bucharest for interfering and for claiming that this action would speed up the reunification of Germany, adding, 'No one asked them to conduct such negotiations. It is nothing to do with them.'[12] Ceausescu probably did not think the German question was anything to do with him either, but was more interested in winning friends outside the Soviet Bloc for the benefit of his country and his own image.[13] The event marked the beginning of a period during which the German question became 'an object of political bargaining',[14] having previously united the Eastern bloc countries.

In order to keep up with the FRG diplomatically, the GDR needed to gain recognition from members of the western alliance, and to achieve this it would have to prove its permanence and sovereignty, indeed its very legitimacy. Though they may have not realised or admitted it at the time, the leadership was setting off on the path that would eventually lead to an unavoidable choice between recognition and reunification. From the beginning of 1967, it became clear that the former was the leadership's most immediate goal, in spite of all the rhetoric about the unbreakable bond of the German working class. Since there was no way that Kiesinger's government would agree to recognition, and the SED would accept nothing less, little progress could be made, neither side got what they wanted, and the division of Germany appeared to be becoming permanent.

One constant factor which continued to shape policy, was of course the SED's obligation to conform to the wishes of Moscow, since the German question was not just a matter for the two German states themselves, but also a microcosm of the wider struggle between two rival political systems and military alliances. During the late 1960s, Moscow pursued two immediate objectives. Firstly, from 1966, the Kremlin started to press for the formal sanctioning of the territorial status quo in Europe, and of its hold on Eastern Europe in particular.[15] This implied that a change in the situation on German soil was out of the question. Secondly in 1967 they sought to reimpose discipline within the Eastern Bloc, particularly in the realm of foreign policy, following Romania's independent action regarding relations with Bonn.[16] However, several other bloc members wanted to keep their options open with Bonn for economic reasons. In response, Erich Honecker, an increasingly influential politburo member, tried to generate solidarity against Bonn's *Ostpolitik* and criticised those who allowed 'nationalistic tendencies' to interfere with their obligations to world socialism.[17]

At the Seventh Party Congress of the SED, the Soviet leadership linked the two objectives mentioned above, demanding recognition of the GDR by the FRG and making it clear that it expected Eastern Bloc states to demonstrate their loyalty to the bloc via support for the East German cause.[18] In return Moscow required a tougher line by Ulbricht regarding the German question, resulting in the reinforcement of the 'Ulbricht doctrine' in the hope that no other Eastern bloc states would establish relations with Bonn until the latter recognised the GDR. Furthermore, for the first time, the Soviet leadership advocated a policy of *Abgrenzung* (or 'fencing off') between the two German states in a governmental declaration in January 1967,[19] which the SED was duty-bound to implement, though it can be assumed that the pragmatists among the ruling elite had no objections to this.

Another important factor was that certain members of the East German politburo, including Lamberz and Axen, were both more realistic about what could be achieved between the two German states than Ulbricht and other traditionalists, and more willing to put the interests of the GDR before the dream of a united socialist Germany. The fact that Ulbricht may have been willing to negotiate with Bonn also caused a rift among the SED's ruling elite. Politburo member Alfred Neumann objected to negotiations with Kiesinger due to his Nazi past,[20] and Albert Norden called the Federal Chancellor 'Goebbels' propagandist' and accused the current rulers of the Federal Republic of continuing 'German imperialism's policy of conquest', which had been started by Hitler.[21] Whatever their reasons, all these dissenters recognised that the prerequisites for a united socialist Germany did not exist, and were not likely to in the near future, hence they took a more pragmatic line, concentrating on improving the GDR's status and the ultimate aim of recognition. Since they had given up thinking in all-German terms, it was logical that they would soon also question whether one could continue to speak of one German nation.

Public opinion was another significant factor. According to research conducted by the GDR's Institute for Public Opinion Research (IMF) the level of acceptance of the GDR and its political system had increased considerably during the 1960s,[22] and as has already been mentioned, several western observers believed an embryonic 'GDR-consciousness' of some sort had begun to develop by the late 1960s, although it was not necessarily the combination of socialist patriotism and proletarian internationalism advocated by the SED. Nevertheless, the potential benefits for the legitimacy of the state that could be obtained by nurturing this 'GDR consciousness' were recognised by the reformers among the ruling elite. However, the public's response to lectures organised by the Department of Agitation to publicise the ideas of the *Vaterlandsdiskussion* (which is discussed below), proved that there remained considerable confusion regarding the relationship between the two German states and the implications of this for the unity of the nation.[23]

One development in particular which had provoked further confusion was the new citizenship law which came into force shortly before the Seventh Party Congress.[24] The Interior Ministry justified the move due to 'the existence of the sovereign GDR and the development of new socialist relationships between the citizens of the GDR and their socialist state, as well as our consistent rejection of the West German government's presumption to sole representation' [of the German nation].[25] Clearly aware that this appeared to contradict the GDR's constitution, the ministry continued, somewhat unconvincingly: 'The stipulation in the constitution, "there is only one German citizenship" relates to the area in which the constitution of the GDR is operative.'[26] Overall, this action could be interpreted as a further indication that the regime was starting to assert the independence of the GDR and moving away from pan-German objectives.

All of the above mentioned factors encouraged certain leading functionaries to reconsider Ulbricht's line on the national question. This began with the so-called *Vaterlandsdiskussion* (fatherland discussion) in January 1967, a discussion among secretaries for agitation and propaganda from all over the country, which was followed by a major publicity campaign. It was initiated by politburo members, Werner Lamberz and Hermann Axen, both of the emerging Honecker faction, and has been interpreted as an attempt to break with the policy of reunification via confederation behind Ulbricht's back.[27] The campaign focused on the GDR as fatherland, as opposed to Germany as a whole, and on the 'the GDR as an independent nation-state' *(die nationalstaatliche Eigenständigkeit der DDR)*.[28] Axen boldly stated, 'In these circumstances, we cannot speak of reunification... We can no longer tolerate all-German positions. "All-German" no longer fits in with our political landscape.'[29] He also regarded the normalisation of relations between the two German states as vital for European security, hence a special relationship should be rejected. Lamberz recognised the need to create a unique GDR-consciousness based on the GDR's socialist system.[30] While he did not go so far as to claim that a separate socialist German nation existed in the GDR, a report in *Neues Deutschland* stated, 'In our sovereign socialist republic, which is a whole historical epoch ahead of the western zones, we are building up the new socialist nation.'[31]

The *Vaterlandsdiskussion* has been described as 'an essential step on the road to the national concept of the Eighth Party Congress', where Honecker publicly denied the existence of one German nation.[32] This provokes speculation as to why the concept of the nation was not directly questioned at the Seventh Party Congress. Three possible reasons spring to mind: firstly, due to the general confusion surrounding the whole issue of the future of 'Germany', which intensified with the formation of a Grand Coalition in Bonn; secondly, due to the risk of reinforcing Bonn's claim to sole representation of the nation; and finally, due to Ulbricht's own all-German aspirations, which reformers could not yet criticise openly.

Shortly before the Party Congress, Ulbricht had told the Central Committee that he did not regard the mutual recognition *(Anerkennung)* and the rapprochement *(Annäherung)* of the two German states as mutually exclusive. According to his logic, recognition was a prerequisite for peaceful coexistence, which would facilitate cooperation, which could eventually lead to unification, once the 'democratic transformation' of West Germany had taken place. By refusing to recognise the GDR, he argued, Bonn was hindering peaceful coexistence and the good relations necessary for a solution of the German question. This step-by-step approach appeared to have replaced the idea of using a German confederation as a starting point for reunification, though curiously Ulbricht still made reference to the confederation proposal in his New Year message for 1967.[33]

As usual, all the speeches at the Party Congress itself received rapturous applause. Ulbricht repeated his commitment to reunification: 'A unity of the German nation under the leadership of imperialists is impossible, but we are whole-heartedly striving... for unity under the leadership of the working class.'[34] However, for the first time, he seemed to be distinguishing between short-term and long-term goals. The former consisted of the normalisation of relations between the two states, the renunciation of violence, recognition of borders and peaceful coexistence, while the latter remained reunification. He accused those who no longer believed a united socialist Germany was attainable of playing into the hands of the very capitalists he blamed for the national divide. Pre-empting Brandt's notion of 'two states of one nation' by two years, Ulbricht explained, 'Today the nation essentially consists of the German people in two German states which are independent of each other, the socialist GDR and the militaristic, imperialist West German Federal Republic', and confidently concluded, 'What imperialism has torn apart, the working class in both German states, in close alliance, will reunite.'[35]

However, Ulbricht's traditional line was somewhat contradicted by the more GDR-orientated view articulated by a worker from East Berlin, Klaus Teschendorf, who portrayed the national question as a class question more overtly than Ulbricht. According to Teschendorf, 'We are bound in every way to our socialist GDR, but we are in no way bound to the imperialist West Germany.'[36] Contrary to appearances this was no spontaneous outburst by a representative of the masses, but the view held by several members of the leading elite, who did not dare to question the official line according to Ulbricht openly. In fact Teschendorf's speech had been written by politburo member, Paul Verner, a hard-liner regarding relations with the Federal Republic, who had personally selected him to articulate the view of a growing number of the ruling elite. It was agreed in advance that the presidium of the Party Congress would express agreement with Teschendorf's speech, after pretending to discuss it.[37] However, as was customary, they also had to accept Ulbricht's speech, in spite of the fact that it was based on 'the illusion of the victorious working class' throughout Germany.[38]

By now it should be clear that by 1967, there were numerous reasons why the SED needed to rethink its *Deutschlandpolitik*, and linked to that, its stance regarding the German nation. However, one other factor also remained constant, namely the personal influence of Ulbricht. The flaws in his arguments regarding the national question were becoming increasingly obvious, as he attempted to adapt to a new situation without surrendering convictions and hopes he had held since the foundation of the GDR. However, while attempting to explain them, one should remember that at 74, Ulbricht could recall the days of the KPD as a *Reichspartei*. He continued to speak of *Deutschland* when others no longer used the word, and apparently still dreamt of the day when the working class would reunite what 'imperialism' had divided and he would become leader of a united socialist German state. In spite of signs of diverging views on the national question at the Seventh Party Congress, the new constitution in the following year showed that he was still able to exert his authority, at least, so long as it pleased Moscow for him to do so.

Academic opinion

In view of the SED's changing priorities regarding the status of the GDR and the future of Germany as a whole during this period, references to the unity of the nation were beginning to sound increasingly anachronistic, especially to educated ears. The apparent confusion surrounding the issue at the highest level, manifested at the recent Party Congress, prompted fresh discussion of the effects of continued political division on the German nation among philosophers, historians and social scientists at academic institutions.[39] Indeed, the ambiguous messages emanating from the Party leadership facilitated the consideration of various different ideas, a freedom which abruptly came to an end once Honecker declared that the national question had been 'resolved by history' at the Eighth Party Congress in 1971.[40] A report by the academic commission of the State Secretariat for West German Affairs (which included leading members of the academic establishment such as the historian, Stefan Dörnberg, and Otto Reinhold, rector of the AfG), suggested that since the 'working class' was interpreted differently in each German state, maybe it was no longer possible to speak of a united German working class. The appropriateness of terms such as 'unitary German culture' and 'German national literature' was also questioned, but a serious dilemma was recognised, namely how to avoid conjuring up incorrect and illusory all-German concepts in the minds of the population, 'without handing over essential concepts to the enemy'.[41]

Historians in particular could hardly avoid the subject of the German nation. In 1967 a group from universities and the Academy of Sciences (AdW) were commissioned by the Department of Sciences to write an officially sanctioned

'History of the German People'. The 'political and academic objectives' of the work were clearly spelled out, namely to help secure the 'socialist national consciousness' of the people of the GDR and to fill them with pride in their achievements. The work was also aimed at the working class in West Germany and intended to explain to them that their interests and those of the entire nation were best served by the GDR. The foundation of the GDR was to be portrayed as the turning point in German history and the completion of socialism its high point so far.[42] However, the Department of Sciences, headed by Ulbricht's ally, Kurt Hager, insisted that certain points be stressed which bore the hallmark of Ulbricht's approach to the national question, for example, his prediction that socialism would one day be victorious in West Germany and that the working class would then reunite what imperialism had divided.

In spite of the relative freedom for discussion behind the closed doors of academic institutions at this time, published work on the nation was tricky due to the obligation to adhere to an official line that was becoming increasingly hard to define, hence relatively few books and articles on the subject appeared during the late 1960s. However, one significant new publication was the first edition of the *Kleines politisches Wörterbuch*, which was the official reference book of political terms in the GDR. The entry for 'nation' was composed by the theorist, Alfred Kosing. While some elements of Stalin's definition of a nation remained, namely the existence of a common economy, territory, language, culture and social psyche,[43] the basis of Kosing's argument was that the character of a nation was determined by its ruling class, hence there were two types of nation. Socialist nations were based on a socialist means of production and were characterised by the political and moral unity of the whole population, which made them more stable than bourgeois nations. The working class was the dominant force in a socialist nation, under the leadership of the Marxist-Leninist Party. In contrast, bourgeois nations were based on a capitalist means of production and their dominant power was the bourgeoisie. Consequently they were divided into antagonistic classes and plagued by class struggles and social conflicts. Only through a socialist revolution could a bourgeois nation be transformed into a 'qualitatively higher type of national community, the socialist nation'.[44]

On the subject of the German nation in particular, the writer attempted to combine sound Marxist-Leninist arguments with the official line according to Ulbricht:

> The German nation currently consists of the populations of two states... By completing the construction of a socialist society, the GDR represents the interests of the entire German nation... and smooths the way into a socialist future for the whole nation... The unification of the German nation can only be achieved via a long, not yet specific process of development.[45]

A description of the components of national consciousness in general followed, probably also penned by Kosing. Like the nation, national consciousness was also defined in Marxist-Leninist terms, hence one could distinguish between socialist and bourgeois national consciousness (which was equated with nationalism), in the same way that one could distinguish between socialist and bourgeois nations.[46] In the GDR, 'socialist national consciousness' was based on the acceptance of four claims, namely:

> a) the anti-imperialist and socialist renewal of our nation which was necessary in our time has already been successful in the GDR; the GDR embodies the realisation of the national interests of our people; b) the solution of the German question can only take place under the leadership of the working class and its Marxist-Leninist Party; c) West German imperialism is the chief enemy of the German Nation; d) the completion of socialism does not only lie in the interest of the population of the GDR but is their best contribution to the conquest of imperialism and militarism in West Germany.[47]

An entry for 'socialist national culture' in the same volume called the GDR the 'protector of both the cultural heritage and the current progressive democratic culture of the entire German people', and claimed that the GDR's socialist national culture represented the 'future path of the culture of the entire German nation'.[48]

Overall, this definition of the nation and national consciousness, which was frequently quoted elsewhere, was riddled with contradictions. On the one hand, the German nation was described in Marxist-Leninist terms as divided into a socialist nation and a bourgeois nation, but on the other hand, the ethnic German link was retained. We can only conclude that the author was trying to find a theoretical justification for the increasingly contradictory messages emanating from the party leadership.

The aftermath of the Seventh Party Congress

After the Seventh Party Congress, contact between the two German governments continued in the form of letters exchanged between Stoph and Kiesinger, but in spite of their claims to have the same goal, namely reunification, their understandings of the word, and how it should be achieved, were so totally irreconcilable that no progress could be made. Furthermore, by this stage, it was clear that the SPD was not going to lead a socialist transformation of the Federal Republic, hence from this point, the emphasis was placed on the bond with the West German proletariat themselves, as opposed to their 'right-wing Social Democrat leaders'.[49]

Overall, by accepting two contradictory approaches to the national question, the Seventh Party Congress had raised more questions regarding the future of

Germany than it had answered. Over the next few months, differences of opinion within the party leadership intensified, especially between Ulbricht and the senior functionary Professor Albert Norden. In a letter to the latter, Ulbricht confirmed his ultimate objective: 'The West German Press claims I want socialism in Germany. That has been the goal of the progressive forces of the German working class since Karl Marx, is also contained in the programme of the Social Democrats, and was clarified by Bebel.'[50] However, in December 1967 an article by Norden in *Neues Deutschland* publicly challenged Ulbricht's line for the first time and raised doubts about the unity of the nation. Norden criticised Bonn's claim that the GDR was not a foreign country and therefore could not be treated as such, and accused 'imperialist' West German politicians of breaking the German national bond for good by the incorporation of the FRG into NATO.[51] The article also highlighted the fact that the notion of a unitary nation was undermining the regime's claim to sovereignty and legitimacy, a view advocated by none other than the First Secretary of the SED himself. In retaliation, Ulbricht commissioned an academic, Wolfram Neubert, to write a response, which appeared in the paper nine days later. Neubert argued that the reality of the German situation was that two states existed on German soil, but this did not mean that the German nation had ceased to exist However, they were not merely 'two German constituent states' *(Gliedstaaten)* as Bonn claimed, but two sovereign states, and this fact was of greater importance than the existence of one nation. With classic Ulbricht-style logic, he concluded, 'If equal status and mutual recognition of sovereignty are increasingly used as sensible and progressive principles between states of different nationalities, why shouldn't they also be valid, if not more so, for inter-state contact within one nation?'[52] After the Eighth Party Congress this article became such a source of embarrassment for Neubert that he left the Academy for Social Sciences.[53]

A few symbolic changes took place after the Seventh Party Congress which aimed to reinforce the GDR's independence from the FRG, thus prioritising *Abgrenzung* before *Annäherung*. For example, what until then had been the 'German Issuing Bank', was renamed 'State Bank of the GDR' in December 1967, and the currency, previously the 'Mark of the German Issuing Bank', became the 'Mark of the GDR'.[54] Around the same time, two separate German teams entered the winter Olympics in Grenoble and the summer games in Mexico City the following year. As the Department for Sport commented, 'This visibly underlined the existence of two German states and dealt a blow to Bonn's claim to sole representation of the nation. The team has justified the trust placed in it through politically aware behaviour and good sporting achievements, and in this way contributed to raising the profile of the GDR.'[55]

However, regular reports by the Agitation Department provided further evidence that the Party Congress had failed to clarify the SED's position on the national question. Clearly the popular desire for reunification remained strong and any contact between the SED leadership and Bonn was interpreted as a move towards reunification. Furthermore, people thought the SED's claims that the West Germans were aggressive and threatening were exaggerated.[56] Other polls confirmed an unwillingness among East Germans to regard West Germans as their enemies and a general belief that living standards were higher in the Federal Republic than in the GDR.[57]

Not surprisingly, the contradictions in the SED's proposals did not go unnoticed in the West. After Ulbricht's new year message for 1968, one West German journalist wrote:

> With the formula 'normalisation of relations between the two German states', the SED is making two totally irreconcilable demands. They are demanding recognition in accordance with international law, as though they are a foreign country in order to complete their consolidation and the final division of Germany. At the same time they do not want to be a foreign country, in order to use their status as a recognised independent state more energetically in an attempt to spread their power over the whole of Germany. Thus recognition is not the final goal for the SED, but a halfway-house... The short term goal of the recognition of the GDR and the long-term goal of a united communist Germany are at present running side-by-side.[58]

A report from the State Secretariat for West German Affairs seemed to confirm this by describing 'the national mission of the GDR' as at minimum peace and peaceful coexistence, and at maximum a socialist Germany.[59]

The new socialist constitution

In 1968, the old anti-fascist constitution, dating back to 1949, was replaced by a new 'socialist' constitution, which was hailed by Ulbricht as the most democratic constitution Germany had ever had.[60] In its references to the national question, the new constitution was a triumph for the traditionalist wing of the party, and emphasised the aim of reunification and the unity of the German nation, based on the unity of the German working class. The new preamble began,

> Impelled by the responsibility of showing the *entire German nation* the path into a future of peace and socialism - in view of the historic fact that imperialism... has split Germany in order to construct West Germany as a base for imperialism and for the fight against socialism, which is contrary to the essential interests of the German nation - the people of the GDR have given themselves this socialist Constitution.[61]

Article 1 described the GDR as 'a socialist state of the German nation', replacing the outdated statement that Germany was 'an indivisible democratic republic, composed of *Länder*.' However, it still maintained that there was only one German nationality. Article 8 contained the ultimate goal of reunification:

> The establishment and cultivation of normal relations and cooperation between the two German states on the basis of equality are the national concern of the GDR. The GDR and its citizens are striving beyond that towards overcoming the division of Germany forced upon the German nation by imperialism, and towards the step-by-step rapprochement of the two German states until their unification on the basis of democracy and socialism.[62]

The referendum on the constitution held in April 1968 could hardly be called impartial, but then state-sponsored referendums rarely are. The party encouraged people to vote in favour with slogans such as 'Do you want peace? Then vote yes to the socialist constitution of the GDR!' or 'If you want your children to have a happy future, then say yes to the socialist constitution of the GDR!' The ballot paper was designed with a large circle labelled 'yes' in the centre, and a small one labelled 'no' in the bottom right-hand corner.[63] The constitution was accepted by 94.49 per cent of the electorate,[64] which the SED portrayed as an indication of the GDR's democratic legitimacy, compared with the Federal Republic where the Basic Law had never been put to the people, and which, conveniently for the SED, was experiencing serious social unrest in 1968.[65] The referendum was followed by a campaign to popularise the constitution, during which the contribution of the 'first socialist state of the German nation' to peace and security in Europe was emphasised.[66]

Unlike its predecessor dating back to 1949, and its successor of 1974, the constitution of 1968 was the only one to stress both the Germanness and the socialist character of the GDR, and as mentioned earlier, Article 8 adhered to the (increasingly unrealistic) aim of a united socialist Germany. Nevertheless, 19 years had passed since the first constitution was ratified, during which time the existence of two German states had more or less become an accepted feature of post-war Europe, therefore many of the changes were perfectly justifiable and long overdue, and as Ulbricht noted, the conditions of 1949 clearly had been overtaken.[67] In spite of the fact that the SED claimed to regret the existence of 'two independent states of the German nation with opposing political and social orders,' they claimed it was a historical fact that Bonn ought to acknowledge, as they had via the new constitution,[68] and blamed 'West German imperialists' for the need to remove the phrase 'Germany is an indivisible republic' from the preamble 'against our wishes'.[69] Consequently, the normalisation of relations in the interest of peaceful coexistence remained the most pressing goal for the time being, as Article 8 stated.

However, the party leadership soon became aware that the new constitution had again caused confusion among the public regarding the state of the German nation. As a result, Ulbricht personally addressed the issue at a meeting in East Berlin where he explained:

> If the question is raised as to whether the German nation has a future, I reply, yes indeed, the German nation has a future - in the establishment of unity in one socialist Germany... The time has come to fix in the constitution that our republic is a socialist state of the German nation, the first state in the history of the Germany that acts entirely in the interest of the nation. But at the same time, these words bear in mind that an imperialist state of the German nation exists in the form of the West German Federal Republic, which is contrary to the national interest. Thus the assumption of the constitution expresses the current reality in the struggle between socialism and imperialism on German soil.[70]

Since the new constitutional line on the nation seems like a regression to the days before the Seventh Party Congress, and out-of-step with other more pragmatic pronouncements of the period, an examination of the domestic and international factors at work at the time is required. Overall, the line on the nation enshrined in the new constitution proved that Ulbricht was still unwilling to abandon his dream of a united socialist Germany, and was still sufficiently powerful to get his own way. However, events would soon force him to change his mind and challenge his very position of power.

Two other factors appear to have helped shape the new constitution. The first was the SED's continuing struggle to win the allegiance of the population of the GDR. Superficially at least, the party tried to involve the population in the process of drafting the constitution, and it appears that they took considerable interest in the project, especially the sections on the future of Germany. In total, the Constitutional Commission received 10,237 suggestions from the public, which resulted in 118 changes.[71] However, such figures do not reveal the qualitative influence of the general public on the end result, and the suggestions may well have been initiated by party functionaries. During February and March 1968, shortly before the referendum, research was conducted into popular attitudes towards the contents of the draft constitution. Common areas of confusion included the nature of inner-German relations, the likelihood of reunification and the state of the nation.[72] In one survey, respondents were asked 'Which do you consider to be your fatherland, the GDR or all of Germany?' Initially 60 per cent replied the latter, and later on in the campaign, 42 per cent still did.[73] Therefore it could hardly be denied that many people, especially the elderly, still retained 'all-German illusions'. Questions were also being raised regarding the appropriateness of name German Democratic Republic, but according to official sources this was 'entirely appropriate for a socialist state of the German nation'.[74]

While it was difficult for the public to influence the content of the new constitution, the same was also true of theorists, including those who studied the concept of the nation. The constitutional commission did include some academics, but they were heavily outnumbered by representatives from the party, who ensured that the constitution was a totally political document. Both academics and constitutional lawyers could see that it contained both all-German concepts and references to *Abgrenzung*, but since the leadership was still keeping its options open, there was no way that these contradictions would be corrected. Alfred Kosing has claimed that up to 1968, both politically and theoretically, the view prevailed that the unity of the nation should if possible be preserved, and knew of no suggestion to delete reunification as a long-term objective.[75] However, due to the lack of progress towards that goal, theorists began to question the validity of a theory which had grown out of the Soviet Union's original plan for a neutral, demilitarised, unitary Germany. While some Party functionaries had begun to think in terms of a much longer and more gradual process, even in the late 1960s, illusions continued regarding the prospects for social change in the Federal Republic.[76]

The second factor which may have affected the content of the new constitution was the need to raise the GDR's international profile, in particular, to encourage other governments to take up diplomatic relations with the GDR, and to gain equal status with the FRG. As mentioned earlier, the positive result of the referendum was portrayed as proof of the legitimacy and sovereignty of the GDR. On the first anniversary of the referendum, the Agitation Department proclaimed 'The constitution raised the international authority of the GDR as a sovereign state which shows the whole German nation the way into the future.'[77] No doubt Moscow also wanted the international profile of its German ally raised to match that of America's German ally, the Federal Republic, and to enhance the status of the Warsaw Pact as a whole. We know that Brezhnev was sent a copy of the proposed constitution,[78] and can assume that the Soviet politburo would have debated it, and there is no evidence to suggest that it did not meet with their approval.

In October 1969, official celebrations of the 20th anniversary of the foundation of the GDR took place, and the tone was a strange mixture of the traditional and alternative views regarding the GDR's relationship to Germany as a whole. On the one hand, emphasis was placed on 'GDR-consciousness' and the GDR as 'our fatherland', suggesting that the realists were reasserting their influence, possibly through Lamberz, who was in charge of propaganda.[79] On the other hand, official slogans for the celebrations included 'The SED and its allies are resolutely committed to a unitary democratic Germany',[80] and Ulbricht proclaimed that the socialist German state was the conscience of the entire German nation.[81] However, his short-term goal remained the same, namely the normalisation of relations between the two German states as the first step towards rapprochement, a strategy approved of by Moscow, so long as it strengthened the international position of the GDR, and served the interests of the community of socialist states.[82]

In spite of the all-German rhetoric, incidents between the two German states from the middle of 1968 until autumn 1969 suggested a preference for *Abgrenzung* rather than *Annäherung*. The GDR increased restrictions on travel between the Federal Republic and West Berlin; a huge row erupted over the proposed election of the Federal President in West Berlin; and a separate union of East German protestant churches was founded, severing ties with their West German counterparts for good.[83] Furthermore, the participation of troops from the National People's Army during the invasion of Czechoslovakia in August 1968, in spite of memories of the last time German troops had entered the country in 1938, increased the rift between the two German states.[84] The Czechoslovak experiment proved that alternative forms of socialism would not be tolerated by Moscow. This soon became known as the Brezhnev doctrine, and also applied to the GDR, as Ulbricht was to about find out during his final years in power.

In short, by October 1969, the seeds of change in the SED's *Deutschlandpolitik* and the official line on the nation had been sown. However, in order to germinate, a change in the external climate was required, followed by a change of gardener, if the shoots of a new approach were to thrive. That new climate began within a month of the 20th anniversary of the GDR.

The challenge of Brandt's *Ostpolitik*

In his first governmental declaration of 28 October 1969, Willy Brandt spoke of 'two states of one nation', effectively stealing Ulbricht's argument. He declared his willingness to negotiate as equals, but ruled out full recognition because the two states existed under a kind of national umbrella and therefore could not be considered foreign to each other. Consequently, a sudden change of tactics was necessary if the SED was to achieve its primary goal of recognition. However, although all the members of the ruling elite shared this goal, Ulbricht saw it as a means to an end, believing that full recognition could lead to a relaxation of tension and rapprochement,[85] whereas other members of the ruling elite viewed recognition as an end in itself.

The SED's immediate response to Brandt's declaration was an increase in propaganda in support of recognition and the rejection of a special relationship between the two German states. The party leadership claimed that in spite of his more flexible methods, Brandt was really just adhering to the principles of West German imperialism, after all, the Federal Republic still claimed the right to sole representation of the German nation, apparently illustrated by the use of the word *Deutschland* as an abbreviation for the Federal Republic, by refusing to recognise the citizenship of the GDR or to renounce the borders of the German Reich of 1937, by the use of phrases such as 'inner-German travel' and 'inner-German affairs', in the blocking of the GDR's membership of international organisations, and even by the *Deutsche Bundesbahn's* treatment of Germany in its entirety.[86] According to *Neues Deutschland* '"Germany as a whole", in the borders of 1937 only exists in the Federal Republic's weather forecasts.'[87] An official assessment of the new administration in Bonn stated, 'Several times in his government declaration, Brandt conjured up the *totally non-existent unity of the nation* in order to arouse national feelings yet again.'[88]

Erich Honecker was the first politburo member to respond to Brandt's declaration. After welcoming the latter's acceptance of the existence of 'two German states within Germany', Honecker went on to accuse him of not really offering anything new (or rather, nothing of interest to the SED), since the Federal Republic remained an expansionist monopoly-capitalist state.[89] Although certain aspects of the declaration were worthy of consideration, Honecker felt it better to concentrate on the all-round strengthening of the GDR and the campaign for international recognition, and to take a class-based view of the national question. The SED's demands would remain unchanged, namely recognition of the GDR's sovereignty and equal status with the FRG.[90] The prime minister, Willi Stoph commented that Brandt's recognition of the existence of two German states was a mere 20 years overdue, but nevertheless, was a sign of progress. However, they would judge Brandt not on his words, but on his deeds.[91]

Just how perturbed the SED leadership was by Brandt's approach is obvious from the amount of attention devoted to the subject at the 12th plenum of the Central Committee in December 1969. In the first version of his speech to the Central Committee, Ulbricht accepted Brandt's idea of 'two states of one nation' but added, 'That means the German nation is divided.' Whether the division was permanent or only temporary, he did not make clear, although he accused Brandt of using the fact that both states were of the same nation as an excuse to interfere in the GDR's internal affairs, which implied that he personally still believed in the existence of that nation. However, while the 'one nation' aspect was of primary importance to Brandt, it was the existence of two states that was stressed by Ulbricht.[92]

The actual speech to the Central Committee was a mixture of familiar 'Ulbrichtisms' on the national question, interspersed with new elements, in response to Brandt's governmental declaration:

> As is written in our constitution, the GDR and its citizens are striving to overcome the division of Germany, which was imposed on the German nation by imperialism, and for the step-by-step rapprochement of the two German states until their reunification on the basis of democratic socialism.[93]

Though he denied that they had a special relationship, Ulbricht undermined this somewhat by saying:

> Certainly there can be special features in a normal diplomatic relationship between the GDR and the West German Federal Republic... for example, politicians can negotiate with each other in their own language, although already, the extensive penetration of Americanisms into West German usage sometimes makes it difficult for us to understand this linguistic mixture.[94]

Ulbricht also included a large portion of a speech made at a meeting of Warsaw Pact members in Moscow ten days earlier on 'the enigmatic sphere of the term "Germany".' He criticised the press of other countries for using the term 'Germany' in ways which contradicted the SED's usage, for example, to refer to the Federal Republic alone, or as though a unitary state called Germany still existed. Furthermore:

> Since they have grown far apart, it is illusory to try to construct an artificial umbrella, roughly in the sense of the Holy Roman Empire of the German nation, which arches over the first German peace state, the GDR, and the West German Federal Republic, which is ruled by militaristic and monopoly-capitalist forces.[95]

Interestingly, Ulbricht admitted that the bloc system in Europe determined the national question, not nation theories. Consequently, the 'solution to the German question' was 'a regulated, peaceful existence, side by side, on the basis of equality and mutual diplomatic recognition'. Most importantly, he concluded, 'We regard the declaration by the government of the FRG regarding the existence of two German states as a step forward. It is *de facto* recognition of the GDR.'[96] A few days later, Ulbricht sent a proposal for a treaty between the two states to normalise their relations on the basis of equality to the new federal president, Gustav Heinemann, which was immediately rejected.[97]

What motivated the SED's defensive response to Brandt's declaration? The official explanation was that in spite of a new vocabulary and more flexible methods, Brandt still had the same old goals, namely to continue the Federal Republic's claim to sole representation of the nation, to undermine the GDR, and to represent the interests of NATO,[98] but even so, it seems that his declaration in October 1969 deeply disturbed the party leadership.

After waging war against the CDU/CSU for 20 years, the SED had welcomed their exclusion from government at long last, and initially they portrayed the SPD's victory as indicative of West Germans' desire for a change of course, including regarding relations with the GDR.[99] However, due to its participation in the 1966-69 Grand Coalition, the SPD was certainly not viewed as an ally. In reality, Brandt's *Ostpolitik* put the SED on the defensive, and throughout his first year in office, relations between the two states almost functioned like a tennis match, with Brandt always serving and the SED receiving. However, his acceptance of the existence of two German states and proposals for an exchange of views on a non-discriminatory basis made it harder for the SED to decline talks, therefore they accused the SPD of using new methods to achieve the same objectives simply because the old ones had failed.[100]

In reality, however, the time for utopianism and procrastination was over, and the leadership of the SED would soon have to choose between adherence to the unitary German nation and non-recognition of the GDR on the one hand, and the denial of the existence of one German nation to support the claim of sovereignty on the other. Of course the party was bound to reject any proposals which they believed undermined the GDR, although traditionalists like Ulbricht were reluctant to do anything that would completely rule out a unified socialist German state. Unfortunately records of discussion of this matter within the politburo are not available, but drafts of speeches are, and they indicate uncertainty as to how to react to Brandt's ideas, and a sense that the leadership was being overtaken by events quicker than it could formulate responses to them. It seems that this may well have been the turning point in the SED's policy on the German nation, or at very least, it forced them to set off on the road leading to an unavoidable choice between one German nation or two.

But the leadership of the SED could not act without first consulting Moscow. At the Warsaw Pact meeting in December 1969, Brezhnev warned that Brandt was working together with other NATO states which sought to undermine the socialist community, hence his motives were not to be trusted. Bonn was apparently trying to split the socialist block via separate treaties with individual states, but Brezhnev reminded his allies that they were all in it together, and added, 'The image of the GDR is the result of our joint policies'.[101] This was a warning, in case Ulbricht was considering independent initiatives. Finally, according to the Soviet leader,

> Imperialism has divided Germany and the German people. Brandt's government is now trying to put its hope in the national sentiment of the Germans via self-righteous suggestions of a national rapprochement. But there can be no return to the past. As our German friends again declared, the reunification of Germany is only possible on the basis of democracy and socialism.[102]

Ulbricht's reluctance to give up his dream remained an obstacle, though he too must have realised that a more pragmatic approach was required if the GDR was to gain recognition. However, as mentioned earlier, by agreeing that there were two states of the German nation, Brandt had stolen Ulbricht's argument, thereby forcing the latter to look for a new one. At this stage, Ulbricht was attempting to keep his options open, hence his initial response was ambiguous, with frequent references to the divided German nation and the constitutional aim of reunification, on condition that the 'democratic transformation' of the Federal Republic took place.

A final factor was that the winter of 1969 was characterised by shortages and low morale in the GDR, which may have encouraged widespread public interest in Brandt and hopes for a better relationship between the two German states, leading to increased personal freedoms.[103] Consequently, the SED decided to take a firm line in order to 'put a damper on the détente-euphoria among the population.'[104] An official report admitted that the Party had failed to find convincing arguments to counteract the 'changed methods of the imperialists' fight against socialism as expressed by the "new *Ostpolitik*".[105] Clearly, even after 20 years, the legitimacy of the GDR had not yet been established in the minds of the population, hence drastic measures would be required to sever the tie with the other German state for good.

The first indication that the SED leadership had finally decided to change its position regarding the state of the nation was a press conference held by Ulbricht on 19 January 1970, in response to Brandt's recent 'Report on the State of the Nation'. For the first time, Ulbricht unambiguously portrayed Brandt's references to the unity of the nation as unrealistic and even hypocritical, in view of his adherence to the Paris Treaties which had apparently cemented the division, and as a device to avoid the normalisation of relations. Suddenly, he seemed to have abandoned his own argument of the national bond of the German working class. He even claimed that it was not possible to defend a unity that had not existed for 20 years,[106] although that was what he personally had done until this point! Finally he questioned the Federal Republic's legitimacy as a German state, calling it merely 'a capitalist NATO state' and 'a state with limited national sovereignty'. From this point, the GDR was officially referred to as the 'socialist German nation-state', as opposed to the 'socialist state of the German nation'.[107]

Ulbricht welcomed the fact that Brandt had recognised a great deal - the existence of two German states, the fact that their relations were bad or rather non-existent, and that it would not be possible to overcome the division for the foreseeable future, the fact that the western powers were not keen on the idea of a reunification anyway, and finally that two different social systems could not be merged. Even so, the First Secretary claimed it was regrettable that Brandt chose to 'avoid the consequences of this realisation', i.e. that it was time for mutual recognition. However, in a characteristic lapse back to his previous stance, he added, 'As our constitution says, we hope that the nation that was divided by imperialism, both German states and their citizens, will one day grow closer together on the basis of democracy and socialism, and maybe will find themselves together again.'[108]

Several conclusions can be drawn from Ulbricht's remarks at the press conference in January 1970. Clearly many of his comments were pretty radical and indicate that even he had felt obliged to reconsider his position following Brandt's declaration. He adopted a noticeably more pragmatic approach, putting the interests of the GDR first, although his tendency to refer to the possibility of rapprochement and the constitutional imperative of reunification indicated just how hard it was for him to give up hope entirely. He may also have been pressurised by Moscow to warn other Eastern Bloc states of the dangers of Brandt's more conciliatory approach.[109]

Just what other members of the politburo thought of Brandt's comments is hard to assess due to the absence of records. Those close to Moscow, such as Honecker, had lost interest in the Federal Republic several years earlier, preferring to concentrate on consolidating socialism and securing international recognition of the GDR. According to the Minister for Foreign Affairs, Otto Winzer, the question of the unity of the nation was irrelevant: 'Mutual diplomatic recognition is an elementary condition for the establishment of relations between sovereign states. Whether they are nation-states, nationality-states or states whose population includes just part of a nation is entirely insignificant.'[110] Politburo member, Hermann Axen continued to stress that the national question was a question of class, adding, 'German imperialism divided the German nation and as long as imperialism rules West Germany there cannot and will not be a unitary German nation.'[111] For Albert Norden, who had been reprimanded by Ulbricht for questioning the unity of the nation prematurely, it was the ideal opportunity to voice his long-held view. He claimed that out of pure class interest, the West German monopoly-capitalists had destroyed the unity of the nation and therefore one could not preserve what no longer existed.[112]

Erfurt and Kassel

Chancellor Willy Brandt suggested negotiations on the exchange of documents renouncing force to Willi Stoph, eventually resulting in the historic meeting in Erfurt on 19 March 1970, which aroused great interest among the local population. Ulbricht claimed that the aim of the talks was to achieve normal, peaceful, diplomatic relations and to relax tension between the two states,[113] though he may personally have hoped that this would eventually bring them closer together. The fact that the meeting took place at all was quite remarkable, indeed it was nearly cancelled due to a row concerning Brandt's plan to travel to Erfurt via West Berlin.[114]

Although many practical aspects of the relationship between the two states were also addressed in Erfurt,[115] this work will concentrate on what was said regarding the state of the German nation. In the first draft of his speech (prepared before he had heard what Brandt had to say, of course), Stoph stated, 'It would be groundless to talk about a "unity of the nation" which, through no fault of our own, has not existed for a long time.'[116] In a revised version of the speech, he did not deny that the populations of both states were both German, but argued:

It is futile to try to disguise the refusal to establish diplomatic relations with the phrase 'we are still all Germans'. The issue is not so simple. Since the beginning of the last century, there have always been Germans who stood on the side of progress, the working class and working people, and others who stood on the side of reaction and capitalism.[117]

Nevertheless, he said that the SED hoped for the victory of socialism everywhere, including in the Federal Republic, which could facilitate reunification, but this was not to be discussed at Erfurt.[118] Stoph prepared an answer to all the possible arguments Brandt might use to avoid the establishment of normal relations, most significantly, the existence of one German nation. But there were signs that his position and its consequences had not been sufficiently thought through. Though the unity of the nation was denied, there was no talk of two German nations or two entirely separate nations, merely of 'two autonomous states with opposing social orders'.[119]

After the meeting, Stoph concluded, 'There is no such state as Germany, therefore there can be no special or particular conditions in the relationship between our two states.'[120] The politburo discussed the problems arising from Erfurt in a closed session on 24 March 1970, but there is no record of exactly what was said. However, while Brandt had regarded Erfurt as proof of 'the reality of the unity of the nation', Hermann Axen maintained that it proved that there was no unitary German nation, but instead two fundamentally different states which were independent of each other and sovereign.[121]

After Erfurt, few people would have expected much to come of the meeting in Kassel two months later, not even Stoph himself, who had already prepared a closing speech assuming that Bonn had refused to recognise the GDR.[122] (In fact Brandt produced a 20 point plan for the regulation of their relations on the basis of equality.[123]) In his opening speech, Stoph declared that the destruction of the unity of the nation by imperialism could not be undone via 'conceptual constructions professing a fictitious continuation of the unity of the nation' and he accused Bonn of 'misusing national feelings for non-peaceful purposes'. He added, 'There will never be an "inner-German umbrella" through which NATO can enter the community of socialist states.'[124]

The State Secretariat for West German Affairs prepared arguments to counteract those that they expected Brandt to make in Kassel. If he said that by rejecting a special relationship, the GDR was contradicting its own constitution in which it was described as a 'socialist state of the German nation', Stoph was simply to respond that imperialism had destroyed the unity of the nation and that independent sovereign states now existed on German soil. He would point out that according to the constitution, the unity of the nation would only be possible on the basis of socialism, hence to talk about the possibility of reunification would be totally unrealistic at this time. Therefore, it would be totally wrong for

Bonn to try to use the constitution of the GDR to justify a special relationship between the two states.[125] If Brandt argued that full diplomatic recognition was impossible due to the need to safeguard the unity of the nation, Stoph would reply that it was impossible to safeguard something that did not exist, and that due to their opposing social orders, the prerequisites for unification did not exist, hence peaceful coexistence was the best situation that could be hoped for.[126] These counter-arguments were somewhat evasive, and Stoph also seemed to be using the division of Germany as a state, and the division of the unity of the nation interchangeably. Even so, the SED's arguments and objectives were at least becoming more compatible than they had been until this point.

After the meeting, the East German side blamed the inevitable lack of progress on Bonn's intransigence and used the presence of anti-communist demonstrators in Kassel to show the Federal Republic in a poor light. In an assessment of the meeting by the politburo, it was seen as ironic that those who had apparently destroyed the unity of the German nation and made West Germany a foreign country to the GDR should emphasise the unity of the nation. While the GDR was labelled 'the socialist German nation-state' which had learnt the lessons of history, implemented the Potsdam Protocol and was ruled by the working class, who had allegedly freely chosen to tread the road to socialism, the Federal Republic was branded an 'imperialist NATO-state'.[127] Brandt's use of 'the unity of the German nation' was condemned as a sign of nationalism and expansionism, which showed that Bonn was still trying to keep open the possibility of assimilating the GDR into the Federal Republic[128] (which was essentially true of course).

Kassel also dominated the 13th Plenum of the Central Committee in June 1970. The above arguments concerning the motivation behind Brandt's concept of the 'unity of the German nation' were voiced by several leading functionaries who had fewer scruples about breaking with past positions than Ulbricht. Albert Norden claimed Brandt's concept 'contradicted political and social reality', and said that anyone who claimed that it corresponded to the position expressed in the constitution of the GDR obviously could not read, since it clearly stated that a unity would only be possible on the basis of democracy and socialism.[129]

It should be remembered, however, that Ulbricht himself was still interested in negotiating with Brandt. In his speech to the Central Committee he concentrated on the undeniable existence of two German states, but made no mention of the nation. Ironically he claimed that Bonn's discrimination against the GDR and its citizens had 'constructed a barrier of hostility between the two German states, which was, so to speak, the cement with which the division was cemented'![130] He attempted to play down features common to both states, such as language and culture, saying that 'one can no longer speak of a common German language - there is a huge difference between the traditional German language of Goethe, Schiller, Lessing, Marx and Engels, which is full of humanism, and language which has been contaminated by imperialism and manipulated by capitalism.'[131]

He dismissed the significance of family ties with the argument that 'the two German states and their social orders are not related at all.' According to Ulbricht, the feelings the mattered were not those between relatives but the feeling of hatred for imperialism, militarism, neo-nazism and the forces in the Federal Republic who had divided Germany and damaged the GDR whenever they could.[132] He also refuted Bonn's demand for the right to self-determination for all Germans with the argument that the citizens of the GDR had already used that right when they voted to accept the new socialist constitution.[133]

At the end of the day, little was achieved at Erfurt and Kassel because both sides arrived with different objectives regarding the future of their relationship. The leadership of the SED admitted that the 'central question' *(Kernfrage)* was the full diplomatic recognition of the GDR by the Federal Republic,[134] and even Ulbricht publicly put the immediate goal of recognition before reunification, although his later comments suggest that reunification remained in the back of his mind. The realisation that something would have to be given up finally seemed to be sinking in, at least to some members of the ruling elite, and since Brandt based his argument for a special relationship which ruled out full diplomatic recognition on the fact that both states were of one nation, and could not consider the other foreign, it was this argument which had to be refuted. Symbolically from July 1970, all exports bore the words 'Made in the GDR', as opposed to 'Made in Germany'.

In fact, the main reason why direct negotiations were doomed from the start was because the Soviet leadership opposed them on the grounds that they contradicted the policy of *Abgrenzung*. Those close to Moscow within the SED, such as Honecker, shared this view and thought nothing could be achieved through negotiations, although they were not able to say so openly while Ulbricht remained in power.[135] Moscow had insisted that Stoph should represent the GDR - officially on the grounds that Brandt was not the head of state, but no doubt also for fear that Ulbricht would try to find out how far Brandt would go towards a confederation and would give too much ground.[136] However, Brezhnev, who wanted to emphasise the co-operation and unity of the SED and CPSU regarding the German question, regarded Erfurt as having at least achieved one thing, namely the acceptance of the existence of two German states by Brandt.[137]

Challenges to Ulbricht's authority

It is widely believed that by the late 1960s, Ulbricht was beginning to overestimate his own importance within the Warsaw Pact, even in relation to the Kremlin.[138] However, due to recent events, Moscow was no longer prepared to allow its satellites the freedom to act without prior consultation, and a confrontation occurred between Brezhnev and Ulbricht just before the Warsaw Pact meeting in August 1970, where the former made it clear to the veteran leader of the GDR that the Brezhnev Doctrine not only applied to Czechoslovakia.[139]

Having just signed the Moscow Treaty with the FRG,[140] Brezhnev's aim was to cement the status quo in Europe, thus preserving the Soviet Union's sphere of influence, and Ulbricht's dream of German reunification simply no longer fitted in with this plan. The impact of this meeting is apparent from the change of tone in Ulbricht's letters and speeches afterwards, in particular, the increased emphasis on the GDR's allegiance to the Soviet Union.

In an exchange between Brezhnev and Honecker from July 1970, the Soviet line was clear: there could be no unity between the socialist GDR and the capitalist Federal Republic. According to Brezhnev, nothing favourable came out of Erfurt and Kassel because 'Brandt has different goals to us regarding the GDR'. No doubt the Soviet leader had Ulbricht in mind when he criticised 'a certain air of superiority among you towards other socialist countries... also towards us', and he warned against unilateral action on the part of the GDR:

> Erich - I'll be frank - never forget that without us, the Soviet Union, with our power and strength, the GDR would not exist. Without us there would be no GDR. The existence of the GDR is in accordance with our interests and those of all socialist states. She is the result of our victory over Hitler's Germany. Germany does not exist anymore and it is better that way. There is the socialist GDR and the imperialist FRG. Why is there suddenly a problem?... The enemy will try to drive a wedge between us, but will not be allowed to succeed.[141]

In August delegations from the SED and CPSU met to discuss the future of relations between the two German states and the prospect of treaties with the Federal Republic. Brandt's concept of the unity of the nation was described as unrealistic: 'The destruction of the unity of the nation goes back to the military defeat of Hitler's Germany. It was finally laid down in the Federal Republic's Paris Treaties with the USA, Britain and France.'[142] The sovereignty of the GDR was of paramount importance and Ulbricht had to agree that he would not behave in a conciliatory manner towards the Federal Republic,[143] which meant abandoning his long-standing hope for rapprochement, and agreed to cooperate fully with Moscow on the issue. It is alleged that during a tête-à-tête, Brezhnev warned Ulbricht that the GDR's economic ties to the Soviet Union would have to be strengthened if he wished to remain in office. Ulbricht had to accept this, but resented the attack on the GDR's freedom to manoeuvre, saying, 'During cooperation we want to develop as a genuine German state. We are not Belorussia, we are not a province of the Soviet Union.'[144] He is alleged to have also said that although the CPSU had Lenin, the SED had Marx and Engels.[145] Comments such as this were later used against Ulbricht by his opponents to lower his standing in the eyes of Brezhnev.

After three months of negotiations, Brandt visited Moscow in August, resulting in the signing of a treaty to normalise their relationship. In a separate 'Letter regarding German unity', Bonn stressed that the treaty did not contradict the ultimate aim of German reunification.[146] In the East German press, the treaty was officially hailed as a great success for the Soviet Union, and as laying the path for the normalisation of relations between the GDR and FRG by accepting the inviolability of borders, including the one dividing the two German states.[147]

Ulbricht must have felt insulted by his exclusion from the negotiations. In a letter from October 1970, Brezhnev warned him that Brandt's rhetoric regarding the special character of relations between the two German states and the so-called unity of the nation were just an attempt to shake the social and economic foundations of the GDR, hence a consistent policy of *Abgrenzung* was the only answer to what he called 'the nationalistic and anti-communist tendencies of the policies of the FRG'.[148] Ulbricht had little choice but to agree to support the campaign to secure socialism in Europe and the GDR's permanent place in the socialist bloc, thus ending any chance of compromise with Brandt,[149] although he himself was reluctant to use the term *Abgrenzung*.[150] Even so, in November Ulbricht conceded that 'there is nothing "inner-German" left'. Furthermore:

> When Herr Brandt speaks of the German nation, he speaks of some sort of *fata morgana...* that floats somewhere in the sky. When one asks him what this nation actually consists of in his opinion, he cannot offer a single argument, because there is no common economic area, but two separate social orders, opposed in principle; there is no common state, but instead two, which are principally opposed to each other; and there is no longer a common culture, for this squalid, americanised West German culture cannot be described as German culture. That is merely what Brandt earlier called 'the blue sky over the Ruhr.' In place of 'the blue sky over the Ruhr', he now calls it 'nation'.[151]

The contrast to Ulbricht's proclamations just over a year earlier is striking. Although it is hard to believe that he had really changed his mind, it illustrates the fact that he was prepared to give up his convictions to enhance the legitimacy of the GDR as a sovereign state, and to save his own skin.

Just how much public opinion affected the party line on the nation at this point is hard to judge. On the basis of opinion poll data and the reaction of the population of Erfurt to Brandt, the SED must have known that even though reunification was looking increasingly unlikely, most people still hoped for a closer relationship with the Federal Republic, which in their eyes was not just another neighbouring state.[152] The party claimed that the majority of the people on the streets of Erfurt had been demonstrating in favour of the recognition of the GDR and supported the line of the party leadership. West German journalists were accused of organising the demonstration of support for Brandt and of encouraging a minority of 'hostile elements' to cause trouble, who were 'mainly young people who had not been sufficiently politically influenced by us'.[153]

The politburo acknowledged the contribution made by the Institute for Public Opinion Research[154] which monitored popular allegiance to the state, and must have known that popular support for the regime and its policies was good for the image of the GDR abroad and thus for the campaign for recognition around this time. Increased attention was paid to the personality traits which were supposed to form part of GDR-consciousness, based on the 'socialist morality' defined in the 1950s, combined with elements of the traditional German (or rather, Prussian) character which were regarded as positive, such as hard work and obedience to authority, which clearly served the interests of the regime. A leading functionary defined the 'spiritual and moral countenance of the new person in our republic', which was based on 'pride in the GDR' *(DDR-Stolz)*.[155] From 1969, empirical research into 'GDR-consciousness' and in particular, historic consciousness was undertaken by researchers at the AfG, which continued until 1985. According to Professor Helmut Meier, who coordinated the project, respondents were asked what they considered to be their fatherland, the GDR or Germany, and whether or not it was acceptable for Germans to shoot Germans. The results showed that people no longer saw reunification as possible in the near future, which was interpreted negatively so long as Ulbricht's theory of the 'socialist state of the German nation' prevailed, but positively by those who wanted to abandon it and to emphasise the GDR as an independent entity.[156]

Academic activity

It does not appear to be the case that the SED's reaction to Brandt's statements was the result of an in-depth theoretical examination of the state of the nation. More likely was that the leadership was caught off guard and had to cobble together a response quickly without having time for serious analysis or discussion, and there is no evidence that those best able to do this were consulted. Indeed it was only after the party had changed course that the services of theorists were required, once the party recognised the need for a theoretical justification for the dramatic change in policy.

While most leading functionaries did not bother with theoretical explorations of the national question, Albert Nordon continued to take an interest, no doubt encouraged by the fact that the official Party line was moving towards his hard-line stance. According to Nordon:

> The content of the national question is determined by which class rules the nation... National policy, in the fullest sense, consists of the liberation and leadership of the working-class, which itself forms the socialist nation. That is the path that the GDR has trod. 'National' means hitting out against social and political reaction. When we annihilated the hostile imperialism in our own state, we solved the national question... Just because Messrs Flick, Abs and Siemens spoke German, are the workers supposed to form

a nation with them?! Hitler and Himmler also spoke German and murdered hundreds of thousands of German speaking communists, Social Democrats and progressive members of the bourgeoisie.[157]

On the whole, the uncertainty as to whether the line on the nation enshrined in the constitution was still valid, following statements at the highest level which contradicted it, discouraged academics from addressing the question of the German nation for fear of saying the wrong thing. Even so, they continued to consider the problem of the nation among themselves. Indeed, as reunification on the SED's terms became increasingly unlikely, and the difference between the two halves of Germany became more apparent, many had begun to contemplate the effect of this on the unity of the nation and national consciousness, and Brandt's acceptance of the existence of two German states further encouraged such considerations. According to Alfred Kosing, some saw 'a new form of national community' emerging as a result of the increasingly obvious independence of the GDR from the FRG, which they began to view as a potential nation in a Marxist sense.[158] Around this time, at the request of the Department of Sciences, a lengthy paper was produced by historians at the Academy for Social Sciences in preparation for yet another comprehensive new account of German history. However, it was never published due to uncertainties regarding the delicate subject of the German nation. To deny the existence of the unitary German nation fitted in well with the concept of *Abgrenzung* favoured by the Honecker faction within the ruling elite, but the constitutional line was still officially the last word on the subject.[159]

Overall, it was clear that the state of the German nation required more theoretical attention. Even Brezhnev recognised this in a letter to Ulbricht in which he outlined the 'ideological tasks' ahead: 'Working out the national question from a Marxist-Leninist position is of primary importance, in particular the basic principles concerning the establishment of the socialist human community, the forging of socialist patriotism and finally the formation of the socialist nation in the GDR.'[160] But before the task could be completed, one obstacle had to be removed, namely Ulbricht himself.

Conclusion

The period 1967-70 began with adherence to the unity of the German nation as the official policy of the SED, and ended with its denial. In between was a transitional period during which the traditional line overlapped with a more pragmatic, GDR-centric approach, manifested both by differences of opinion between leading party functionaries, and inconsistent statements by individuals. This was most apparent at the Seventh Party Congress.

The key factor was the GDR's struggle for legitimacy which eventually forced the leadership to choose between a united socialist Germany (supported by the idea of a unitary German nation), on the one hand and international recognition as a sovereign socialist state on the other. Clearly no other government was going to recognise a state that appeared temporary or incomplete. Though the two German states had been growing apart for nearly two decades and the consequences of the division were already deeply ingrained, a catalyst was required to force the SED leadership to decide between German unity and recognition of the GDR.

That catalyst was Brandt's notion of 'two states of one nation'. As a result, from January 1970 (and not from the Eighth Party Congress in June 1971 as is often stated[161]), pragmatism took precedence over the theory of the national bond of the German working class. Bonn had used the continued existence of the German nation to avoid full recognition of the GDR, hence the SED leadership had to deny this in order to gain the legitimacy and security they wanted so badly. No doubt several prominent members of the politburo would have gladly set off on the pragmatic road earlier, but due to the power of the First Secretary and the desire to hang on to their own positions, they could not challenge the official line. But due to Soviet pressure, Ulbricht eventually showed that he too could be pragmatic when the future of the GDR's socialist system, indeed, his own future, was at stake. Overall the period provides considerable evidence of the fact that the leadership of the GDR was not entirely in control of its own destiny, but was caught between the ambitions of Moscow on the one hand and of Bonn on the other.

However, many of the SED's arguments still seemed half-baked, and the consequences of the demise of the unitary German nation had not yet been adequately thought through. This may have been due to the fact that the new policy on the nation did not have a theoretical basis. In short, by 1970, pragmatism, as opposed to either theoretical consideration, or even the basic principles of Marxism-Leninism, determined policy regarding the German nation. However, the last word on the subject was still to come.

Notes

1 Some writers argue that a change of position by the entire politburo took place, led by Ulbricht himself, but the evidence suggests otherwise. For example, Gerhard Naumann and Eckhard Trümpler, *Der Flop mit der DDR-Nation 1971* (Berlin, 1991), p.21. This work, written by two members of the academic establishment in the GDR, chronicles the SED's line regarding the nation between 1966 and 1971, drawing extensively from official documents, but does not explain policy changes.

2 See Jürgen Hofmann, *Ein neues Deutschland soll es sein* (East Berlin, 1989), pp.203-210.

3   For details see N. Edwina Moreton, *East Germany and the Warsaw Alliance: the Politics of Détente* (Boulder, Colerado, 1978), pp.54-55, 67-68.
4   SAPMO-BArch IV A2/9.03/2
5   SAPMO-BArch IV 2/1/356
6   See Jochen Staadt, *Die geheime Westpolitik der SED 1960-1970. Von der gesamtdeutschen Orientierung zur sozialistischen Nation* (Berlin, 1993) for a detailed account of the SED's attempts to infiltrate and destabilise the FRG during this period.
7   SAPMO-BArch IV A2/2.028/122
8   SAPMO-BArch J IV 2/2A/1202
9   See Moreton, *East Germany*, p.51.
10 Croan, 'The Development,' p.201.
11 SAPMO-BArch J IV 2/2A/1211
12 SAPMO-BArch J IV 2/2A/1211
13 On Ceausescu's motives see Mark Almond, *The Rise and Fall of Nicolae and Elena Ceausescu* (London, 1992), pp.103-104; Julian Hale, *Ceausescu's Rumania* (London, 1971), p.48; Aurel Braun, *Rumanian Foreign Policy since 1965* (New York, 1978).
14 Moreton, *East Germany*, p.5.
15 For example, from July 1966, the Kremlin wanted a pan-European security conference to ratify the status quo in Europe. McAdams, *East Germany*, p.73.
16 One such attempt was made by Moscow at a meeting of Warsaw Pact foreign ministers in February 1967. See Moreton, *East Germany*, p.59.
17 McAdams, *East Germany*, p.84.
18 McAdams, p.74.
19 *Neues Deutschland*, 30 January 1967, cited by Klaus-Uwe Koch, 'Die Vaterlandsdiskussion am Vorabend des 7. Parteitags', *Thematische Information und Dokumentation* 42 (1984): p.104.
20 Alfred Neumann, Berlin, 7 April 1993.
21 SAPMO-BArch IV A2/2.028/14
22 SAPMO-BArch IV A2/9.02/31
23 BArchP, D-2/13; SAPMO-BArch IV A2/9.02/3
24 SAPMO-BArch IV/A2/9.02/3
25 SAPMO-BArch J IV 2/2A/1205
26 SAPMO-BArch J IV 2/2A/1205
27 The view of Jürgen Hofmann, Berlin, 5 February 1993.
28 Koch, 'Die Vaterlandsdiskussion', p.99.
29 Koch, p.101.
30 Koch, p.102.
31 *Neues Deutschland*, 30 January 1967, cited in Hofmann, *Ein neues Deutschland*, p.217.

32 Koch, 'Die Vaterlandsdiskussion', p.104.
33 *Neues Deutschland,* 1 January 1967. See also Moreton, *East Germany,* pp.54-5
34 Walter Ulbricht, *Die gesellschaftliche Entwicklung der DDR bis zur Vollendung des Sozialismus* (East Berlin, 1967), pp.51-2.
35 Ulbricht, pp.51-2. For his comments about the West German government and those of Brezhnev, see Moreton, *East Germany,* pp.62-65.
36 *Protokoll der Verhandlungen des 7. Parteitags* (East Berlin, p.152.
37 SAPMO-BArch J IV 2/2A/1218
38 Jürgen Hofmann, Berlin, 5 February 1993.
39 Walter Schmidt, Berlin, 3 June 1993.
40 Jürgen Hofmann, Berlin, 5 February 1993.
41 BArchP, D-2/67
42 SAPMO-BArch NL182/1362
43 Waltraud Böhme et al (eds.), *Kleines politisches Wörterbuch,* 1st ed., (East Berlin, 1967), p.427, and also *Kleines Wörterbuch der Marxist-Leninistischen Philosophie* (East Berlin, 1966), p.192.
44 *Kleines politisches Wörterbuch,* 1st ed., pp.427-428.
45 *Kleines Politisches Wörterbuch,* 1st ed., pp.428-429.
46 *Kleines Politisches Wörterbuch,* 1st ed., p.429-30.
47 *Kleines Politisches Wörterbuch,* 1st ed., p.429-30.
48 *Kleines Politisches Wörterbuch,* 1st ed., p.603
49 SAPMO-BArch J IV 2/2A/1281
50 IfGA, IPA NL2/31
51 *Neues Deutschland,* 19 December 1967.
52 *Neues Deutschland,* 28 December 1967, p.4.
53 According to Prof. Helmut Meier, Berlin 28 March 1993.
54 For a justification see SAPMO-BArch J IV 2/2A/1265
55 SAPMO-BArch NL182/1179
56 SAPMO-BArch IV A2/9.02/44
57 SAPMO-BArch IV A2/9.03/32
58 Renate Marbach, 'SED Nation', *Stuttgarter Nachrichten,* 8 January 1968, in SAPMO-BArch NL182/1312
59 BArchP, D-2/2
60 SAPMO-BArch J IV 2/2A/1275
61 Blumenwitz, *What is Germany?* pp.125-126, my italics.
62 Blumenwitz, pp.125-126, my italics.
63 A copy of the ballot paper is located in SAPMO-BArch J IV 2/2A/1287
64 Hofmann, *Ein neues Deutschland,* p.223
65 Gerhard Kegel, 'Zur Deutschlandpolitik der beiden Deutschlands', *Einheit* 23 (1968): pp.734-43.
66 SAPMO-BArch J IV 2/2A/1296

67	SAPMO-BArch NL182/1106
68	SAPMO-BArch NL182/1106
69	SAPMO-BArch NL182/1106
70	The meeting was entitled 'Yes indeed, there is a German Nation!' SAPMO-BArch NL182/1107
71	SAPMO-BArch NL182/1107. For an extensive examination of the submissions from the public, see Jürgen Hofmann, 'Studien zur Entwicklung der sozialistischen deutschen Nation und zur Nationspolitik der SED', (Doctoral thesis, IfGA, 1983).
72	SAPMO-BArch NL182/1107
73	SAPMO-BArch IV A2/9.02/32
74	SAPMO-BArch NL182/1107
75	Alfred Kosing, Berlin, 3 March 1993.
76	Alfred Kosing, Berlin, 11 February 1993.
77	SAPMO-BArch IV 2/2.033/9
78	SAPMO-BArch J IV 2/2A/1265
79	For the advice given to newspaper editors by the Agitation Commission see SAPMO-BArch IV 2/2.106/6
80	SAPMO-BArch IV 2/2.106/6
81	SAPMO-BArch IV A2/2.01/31
82	SAPMO-BArch IV 2/2.035/61
83	For more details see Zieger, *Die Haltung*, pp.120-122.
84	On the official East German reaction, see Moreton, *East Germany*, pp.75-80; McAdams, *East Germany*, pp.83-93; 'Die Haltung der SED im Konflikt mit Prag', *Deutschland Archiv* 1 (1968): pp.620-646.
85	*Neues Deutschland*, 24 October 1969.
86	SAPMO-BArch J IV 2/2A/1399
87	*Neues Deutschland*, 9 November 1969.
88	SAPMO-BArch J IV 2/2A/1399, my italics
89	Heinz Lippmann, *Honecker and the New Politics of Europe*, trans. Helen Sebba, (London, 1973), p.208.
90	IPA NL2/32
91	Willi Stoph, Rostock, 12 November 1969. Cited in *Deutschand Archiv* 2 (1969) p.327.
92	SAPMO-BArch J IV 2/2A/1403
93	SAPMO-BArch IV 2/1/402
94	SAPMO-BArch IV 2/1/402
95	SAPMO-BArch IV 2/1/402
96	SAPMO-BArch IV 2/1/402
97	For details of the treaty, see *Europa Archiv* 5 (1970): D. 191-3, and for Heinemann's response see Zieger, *Die Haltung*, p.125.
98	SAPMO-BArch J IV 2/2A/1405
99	SAPMO-BArch J IV 2/2A/1399

100 Lippmann, *Honecker*, p.209.
101 IfGA, IPA NL2/32. This file, a unique, leather-bound volume on the circumstances of Ulbricht's removal, was specially compiled for Honecker in February 1989.
102 SAPMO-BArch IV 2/1/402
103 Lippmann, *Honecker*, pp.209, 213.
104 Siegfried Kupper, 'Political Relations with the FRG', in Schulz et al (eds.), *GDR Foreign Policy*, p.297.
105 Report on the results of the ideological training year *(Parteilehrjahr)* 1969/70, SAPMO-BArch J IV 2/2A/1440
106 *Neues Deutschland*, 20 January 1970.
107 *Neues Deutschland*, 20 January 1970.
108 *Neues Deutschland*, 20 January 1970.
109 Kupper, 'Political Relations', p.297.
110 Letter from Otto Winzer to Joachim Herrmann, 16 February 1970, BArchP, D-2/59
111 SAPMO-BArch IV 2/2.035/166
112 SAPMO-BArch IV/2/408
113 *Neues Deutschland*, 19 March 1970.
114 See Ilse Spittmann, 'Deutscher Gipfel in Erfurt', *Deutschland Archiv* 3 (1970): pp.431-439.
115 For details see Zieger, *Die Haltung*, pp.126-127.
116 SAPMO-BArch J IV 2/2A/1425
117 SAPMO-BArch J IV 2/2A/1428
118 SAPMO-BArch J IV 2/2A/1428
119 SAPMO-BArch IV 2/2.033/10
120 *Europa Archiv* 5 (1970): D.222.
121 SAPMO-BArch IV 2/2035/166
122 SAPMO-BArch J IV 2/2A/1441
123 For details see Zieger, *Die Haltung*, pp. 128-129.
124 SAPMO-BArch J IV 2/2A/1441
125 BArchP, D-2/186
126 BArchP, D-2/186
127 SAPMO-BArch J IV 2/2A/1443
128 SAPMO-BArch J IV 2/2A/1445
129 SAPMO-BArch IV 2/1/408
130 SAPMO-BArch IV 2/1/408
131 SAPMO-BArch IV 2/1/408
132 SAPMO-BArch IV 2/1/408
133 SAPMO-BArch IV 2/1/408
134 SAPMO-BArch IV 2/2.033/10
135 Alfred Kosing, Berlin, 3 March 1993.

136 Alfred Neumann, Berlin, 7 April 1993; Manfred Uschner, Berlin, 23 July 1993.
137 IfGA, IPA NL2/32
138 See Moreton, *East Germany*, p.5.
139 According to Prof. Helmut Meier, Berlin, 15 March 1993.
140 For details of the impact of this event on East German-Soviet relations see Moreton, *East Germany*, pp.149-58; McAdams, *East Germany*, pp.104-06.
141 Peter Przybylski, *Tatort Politbüro*, 2 vols. (Berlin, 1992), vol. 1: Die Akte Honecker, p.281.
142 SAPMO-BArch J IV 2/2A/1460
143 Przybylski, *Tatort*, vol. 1, p.290.
144 Przybylski, *Tatort*, vol. 1, p.110.
145 Helmut Meier, Berlin, 15 March 1993.
146 See *Dokumentation zur Ostpolitik der Bundesregierung* (Leck, 1988), pp.13-20.
147 SAPMO-BArch J IV 2/2A/1459
148 IfGA, IPA NL2/32
149 SAPMO-BArch J IV 2/2A/1478
150 Alfred Neumann, Berlin, 7 April 1993.
151 IfGA, IPA NL2/32
152 SAPMO-BArch IV A2/9.02/33
153 SAPMO-BArch IV/2/1/409
154 SAPMO-BArch J IV/2/3A/1784
155 Alexander Abusch, 'Das geistig-moralische Antlitz des neuen Menschen in unserer Republik', *Einheit* 24 (1969): pp.1085-6. See also Bernd Bittighöfer, 'Das Menschenbild unserer sozialistischer Gemeinschaft', *Einheit* 24 (1969): p.418-429.
156 Interview with Helmut Meier, Berlin, 15 March 1993.
157 SAPMO-BArch J IV 2/2A/1425
158 Kosing, Berlin, 7 July 1993.
159 Helmut Meier, Berlin, 28 May 1993.
160 IfGA, IPA NL2/32
161 For example, Hofmann, *Ein neues Deutschland*, pp.246-247.

4 The 'socialist nation' in the GDR

Within a few months of Erich Honecker's elevation to the position of First Secretary of the SED, dramatic changes in the official line on the German nation occurred. At the Eighth Party Congress in June 1971 he declared that a purely 'socialist nation' was developing in the GDR - a move which was to have serious practical consequences. Evidently the new leadership believed that by denying the existence of the unitary German nation, and by claiming that the population of the GDR constituted a nation in their own right, the legitimacy of the GDR as a sovereign state could be enhanced. However, while official acceptance of the unity of the German nation had inevitably preserved a link with the Federal Republic, thus undermining the permanence and legitimacy of the GDR, it would soon become clear that the German origin and character of the population and the state could not suddenly be changed at the behest of the First Secretary of the SED.

In order to justify such a dramatic U-turn, the Party leadership required some convoluted theoretical arguments, and it has recently emerged that the theorists who provided them were highly sceptical about the notion of a non-German, socialist nation. Nevertheless, it was their duty to make sense of the SED's radical new stance. However, the fact that this was later officially replaced by the concept of the 'socialist *German* nation' indicates that the leadership itself eventually recognised the lack of credibility of the socialist nation and its shortcomings as a means to legitimise the GDR.

The invention of a 'socialist nation' in the GDR

The beginning of the end for Ulbricht

Before the new line on the nation could be introduced, one obstacle remained, namely Walter Ulbricht, who had publicly adhered to the unity of the German nation for over 20 years. The 14th plenum of the Central Committee in December 1970 was the first of four which dealt with the preparations for the Eighth Party Congress where the official line on the nation was unambiguously altered. It has been common knowledge since before the collapse of the GDR that the 14th plenum marked the beginning of the end for Ulbricht. More recently, it has emerged that this had less to do with his economic policies, as was widely believed, and more to do with his *Deutschlandpolitik* which had become unacceptable to Moscow. Although Ulbricht was still involved in preparations for the congress, his rival, Honecker, was chairman of the commission responsible for the highly significant report from the Central Committee. In fact the national question was rapidly becoming a pawn in the power struggle within the SED, and as a result, Ulbricht had to sacrifice the idea of one German nation in order to buy time, although by this stage it was already too late.

Peter Przybylski has interpreted the fact that no guests were invited to the 14th plenum as a sign that the discussion was to be more frank than usual.[1] There, Ulbricht delivered a report on the meeting of the Political Consultative Committee of the Warsaw Pact states (PCC), which had taken place nine days earlier. However, the Central Committee heard a revised version of his speech to the PCC, and even the latter did not hear the original version presented to the politburo for approval a few days before. On that occasion Ulbricht had boasted about the SED's tireless struggle to re-establish a unitary German state during the first 12 years of the GDR's existence, and claimed it was grotesque that those who had destroyed the former unitary nation and who had written it off via the Paris Treaties were trying to avoid the recognition of current realities. He had also rejected the notion of 'inner German relations' and a 'common German umbrella'.[2] In contrast, the PCC merely heard him stress the sovereignty of the 'socialist German national state' and its desire to join the UN, socialist solidarity with the CPSU and other communist parties, and his approval of the treaties Moscow and Warsaw had recently signed with Bonn. Large chunks referring to the 'former unitary German nation' had been removed from the speech. A concluding declaration gave assurance that the SED would continue policies in the interest of international security and détente, that they would further strengthen the 'German state of workers and farmers' politically, economically, culturally and militarily, and that they would secure their membership of the community of socialist states, and totally fence themselves off from the imperialist FRG. Surprisingly, only Brezhnev referred to Bonn's attempt to create a 'national community of all Germans'.[3] In his report of the PCC meeting to the Central Committee, Ulbricht again stressed these goals, especially socialist solidarity, but made no reference to the German nation, and only this uncontroversial version was published.[4]

Exactly why these references to the nation were removed, when on the surface they seemed to concur with the new line, is open to speculation. Maybe it was thought that even to mention the 'former unitary nation' would undermine the emerging theory of two irreconcilable nations on German soil, one socialist and the other bourgeois, and would arouse fears among Warsaw Pact member-states that its re-establishment was still desirable. It has been suggested that Ulbricht clashed with Brezhnev at the PCC meeting as a result of differences between the two men, particularly regarding a settlement of the Berlin question,[5] and it is possible that the former came under pressure to stress the GDR's loyalty to the community of socialist states. In addition, other leading functionaries may have wished to distance Ulbricht from the German question all together, in view of his past (and they suspected, continuing) convictions. What was certain was that the current First Secretary's authority was no longer accepted in Moscow or in East Berlin.

During the 14th plenum, Honecker reinforced the message that Bonn's adherence to phrases such as 'the so-called unity of the nation' and 'special inner-German relations' were merely ploys which aimed to upset the social and economic foundations of the GDR. He stressed that a process of *Abgrenzung*, as opposed to *Annäherung* was taking place, and added that peaceful coexistence between states with opposing social orders and the uncompromising fight against bourgeois ideology were not incompatible, but two sides of the same coin.[6] Here he was overtly demonstrating his allegiance to the Soviet line, since the concept of *Abgrenzung* had originally been dreamt up in Moscow, as mentioned earlier.[7] However, in spite of tangible differences between the two German states by this stage, Honecker's claim that they were no closer than any other two states with different political systems was hardly credible, and he himself would later exploit the fact that a special bond between them did exist, particularly during the 1980s.

The report of the politburo to the Central Committee reiterated the line taken by Honecker. It emphasised the character of the social order of a state as the decisive factor which determined her relationship with other states, and stated, with an air of finality, 'The unity of the nation was destroyed as a result of the Second World War and above all by the division enforced afterwards by American and West German imperialists', though the GDR was still described as the 'socialist German national state'. The politburo pledged support for the West German communist party, the DKP, and expressed confidence that one day, the road to socialism would be opened in the Federal Republic.[8] Interestingly, this comment was omitted from the version of the speech published in *Neues Deutschland*,[9] presumably because it raised questions about what might follow if this occurred, and whether the SED had closer ties with the DKP than with communist parties in other countries.

In the discussion which followed it was clear that the Honecker faction was gaining the upper hand, and most speakers now expressed his 'GDR-centric' line and support for *Abgrenzung*, which complimented the campaign for recognition and the need to refute Bonn's claim that the GDR was less than an independent sovereign state. However, many members of the Central Committee evidently found the new line hard to grasp. Hans-Joachim Hertwig for example, committed a *faux pas* when he unwittingly described the GDR as the 'country of birth' *(Geburtsland)* of Marx and Engels, which was changed to 'homeland' *(Heimatland)* in the published record of the proceedings, and another speaker,

Alois Bräutigam, recognised that many ordinary citizens still believed that the two German states were growing closer together.[10]

The most significant aspect of the 14th plenum was the reaction of the rest of the politburo to Ulbricht's closing remarks. Suddenly it was not only Ulbricht's long-held convictions that were being overturned - he was now also fighting for his political life. On the subject of the German question, his remarks coincided with those of the other main speakers and even he claimed that the Brandt/Stoph talks had led to a dead-end due to Brandt's attempts to undermine the GDR via the concept of 'inner-German relations'.[11] However, the inclusion of a reference to the GDR's past efforts to achieve a confederation and the absence of the word *Abgrenzung* no doubt failed to satisfy his opponents within the ruling elite.

But it was the section concerning the economy which gave politburo members an excuse to write to Ulbricht individually, urging him not to publish the version of the speech he had read to the Central Committee, on the grounds that it contradicted the report of the politburo and recent utterances by the prime minister, Willi Stoph. This was an unprecedented occurrence and indicated that they all knew Ulbricht's days were numbered.[12] In particular, Honecker attacked Ulbricht for saying that economic co-operation with the Soviet Union was necessary because the GDR lacked raw materials, instead of saying it was an obligation of socialist internationalism.[13] There can be little doubt that Honecker and his supporters were intentionally using Ulbricht's comments to further undermine the reputation of the latter in Moscow by questioning his commitment to the socialist community, and hinting that he might unilaterally attempt to negotiate with Bonn. It seems that for these reasons, rather than for his economic policies themselves, Brezhnev approved Ulbricht's removal, which was engineered by Honecker and his faction which included Stoph and Verner. There is no evidence to suggest that Ulbricht tried to resist pressure to withdraw his remarks on the economy, with the result that only an edited version of his speech, without the controversial section, appeared in the published record and in *Neues Deutschland*. Interestingly, Jürgen Hofmann's officially acceptable account of the evolution of the nation in the GDR, written in the late 1980s, only refers to Honecker's speech at the 14th plenum of the Central Committee, and makes no mention of Ulbricht at all,[14] a sign that according to official history, Ulbricht had already been written off.

Less than a week later, at a meeting of the commission for the preparation of the 25th anniversary of the foundation of the SED, Ulbricht suddenly altered his position and for the first time talked about *Abgrenzung* and criticised Bonn's advances towards the GDR on the basis of 'fictitious national common ground' *(fiktive nationale Gemeinsamkeit)*. At last he seemed to recognise that if the unity of the nation no longer existed, there must now be two separate nations, and spoke of 'the process of evolution of a socialist nation' in the GDR and 'the old bourgeois German nation' in the Federal Republic,[15] although his use of the adjective 'German' remained somewhat inconsistent.

Commentators have wondered what occurred that week to make Ulbricht suddenly speak in such finite terms, but the answer remains unclear.[16] Politburo member Alfred Neumann, a supporter of Ulbricht, has rejected the suggestion that Ulbricht changed his mind regarding the nation, on the grounds that he, Ulbricht, had always maintained that there could be no unification of socialism and capitalism. In Neumann's opinion, the first secretary was a pragmatist, and had merely switched tactics to suit the changed circumstances, which now dictated that the GDR needed to gain equal status with the Federal Republic, in order to compete economically and politically. Therefore by the end of the decade, recognition inevitably took precedence over reunification. So how else can Ulbricht's new position be explained? The idea that if the unitary German nation no longer existed, there must be something else in its place, presumably two nations, seems logical, if far-fetched, and one wonders why Ulbricht had not come to this conclusion earlier. Presumably this was because he did not want to admit that the division of Germany was irreversible, and that his dream to head a united socialist German state would never be realised. Certainly it would have been more characteristic for him to be motivated by pragmatic considerations than by a genuine change of heart regarding the German nation, and his subsequent return to his previous stance after his removal from office supports this.[17] Some commentators see the change as more to do with personal rivalry, that is to say, Ulbricht wanted to knock the wind out of Honecker's sails and not be seen as an old has-been, merely expressing ideas that had been overtaken. But none of these reasons explain why he amended his stance *when* he did. The most likely explanation is that realising how fragile his position had become, Ulbricht had to toe the Soviet line in view of the controversy over his recent speech before the Central Committee.

At the end of December 1970, Ulbricht had sent a draft publication on the national question to the Soviet politburo for approval. The latter responded: 'As we in Moscow understand it, the main aim of the proposed publication is a complete, theoretically justified orientation of party activities regarding the development of the GDR as a sovereign socialist state and the people of the GDR as a *socialist nation.*'[18] Unfortunately, the actual material is not available, but this comment indicates the line desired by Moscow, which inevitably became the official line of the SED. It is worth noting that the importance of 'theoretical justification' was recognised from the start. Once again, the national question had become subordinate to other political objectives, to the extent that an individual's position regarding the nation had become an indicator of their loyalty (or lack of it) to the Soviet Union and the socialist bloc. Furthermore, since the issue had been determined by political considerations, it had nothing to do with popular feeling in the GDR.

Ulbricht fights back

At the 15th plenum of the Central Committee on 28 January 1971, Ulbricht concentrated on domestic policy, in particular, on his plans for a 'developed social system of socialism' and a 'socialist human society',[19] and advocated 'national solutions' to the GDR's problems.[20] The occasion is widely seen as an attempt by Ulbricht to regain some lost ground and he certainly seemed more confident.[21] He had begun 1971 with a New Year message in which he stated that 'in the GDR, we are experiencing the birth of the socialist German nation'. The latter was firmly rooted in 'humanist and democratic German traditions', unlike the Federal Republic, which had distanced itself from them and had been created to serve the purposes of American imperialism. He went on to list many figures who had 'shaped our socialist German national state and its socialist national culture', including Bach, Beethoven, Fichte, Kant, Marx, Engels, Rosa Luxemburg, Ernst Thälmann, Heinrich and Thomas Mann, and Bertolt Brecht.[22]

Ulbricht's speech to the Central Committee focused on 'the development of the GDR into a socialist German national state, inextricably and forever bound to the Soviet Union and the community of socialist states', and *Abgrenzung* from 'the imperialist NATO-state, the FRG', which was said to have reached the point of no return.[23] His apparent 'conversion' away from the idea of one nation existing in two states that would one day be reunited was apparent, but knowing the factors at work at the time, it can be assumed that he was acting in the interest of recognition, although it must have been painful for him, in view of his previous grand designs for Germany as a whole. However, Ulbricht still used nationalistic language, in contrast to the class-based arguments put foreword by Honecker, who re-emphasised the need to sever links with the Federal Republic and to strengthen them with the Soviet Union and other socialist states.[24]

On 28 January 1971, Brandt issued his next 'Report on the State of the Nation', in which he pointed out that in spite of its rejection of a special relationship, the GDR was more involved with the Federal Republic than with any other state.[25] The fact that the East German population and media were preoccupied with the Federal Republic, and that the SED still had special bodies such as the State Secretariat for West German Affairs confirmed that the relationship was still far from ordinary. Quite justifiably, Brandt accused the party leadership of wanting it both ways, distinguishing between the 'socialist nation' and the 'bourgeois nation', but also using the phrases such as 'the remainder of the old bourgeois *German* nation' and the 'socialist *German* nation-state'. He added that the shared national basis was causing the leadership in East Berlin not to relax its view of the East-West conflict but to over-exaggerate it, and concluded, 'The nation is a question of consciousness and will. East Berlin's polemics against the nation are evidence of the existence of a consciousness and will that have been preserved over there too.'[26] Clearly there was plenty of truth in Brandt's comments, and some leading functionaries must have realised that words such as 'nation,' 'national' and 'German' still had resonance.

An assessment of the last two sessions of the Central Committee by the Department of Sciences acknowledged that the problem of the nation had not yet been resolved. It condemned what were described as West German manifestations of nationalism such as the celebrations of the foundation of Bismarck's Reich in 1871 and Brandt's recent report on the state of the nation, and argued that the existence of two autonomous states with opposing social orders could not be denied or concealed by 'nationalist phraseology'. Indeed, it was claimed that nothing particularly 'national' characterised the relationship between the GDR and the FRG because according to Lenin, the crucial factor in any national question was the nature of the social system(s) concerned.[27] The report repeatedly stressed the need to get this message across to the population in order to counteract West German attempts to convince them of the 'unity of the nation' and of 'national similarities' *(nationale Gemeinsamkeiten).* For once the need to provide an alternative was recognised: 'we must make our citizens proud to live in the GDR and to take part in its formation. As Walter Ulbricht stated at the 15th plenum, it is a matter of filling our people with socialist national consciousness and socialist patriotism for the socialist German nation-state.'[28] However, the question of the relationship between the East and West German proletariats remained unresolved. Paraphrasing the famous phrase from the Seventh Party Congress, the report concluded, 'As with the workers of other countries, we are bound to the working class of the FRG by the relationship of proletarian internationalism. However, this is no class-indifferent national relationship, but a relationship based on class.'[29]

The Department of Sciences was clearly aware that the population was still unsure about the state of the nation. By monitoring discussion at universities it was discovered that many students and academics were not sure what a nation actually was, what the difference was between the phrase 'socialist state of the German nation' and 'socialist German national state' which superseded it, and whether the German nation could simply cease to exist after a mere 25 years of division.[30] Reports from local party secretaries provided further evidence that many people, including party members, did not understand the change in official policy regarding the nation or why the GDR had to sever its ties with the Federal Republic.[31] However, this was hardly surprising in view of the brevity of official statements, and the issue clearly required far more detailed attention to make the change in policy comprehensible and acceptable.

Meanwhile, Ulbricht continued to prepare for the Eighth Party Congress on the assumption that he would still be First Secretary, and planned to emphasise the GDR's national achievements, as opposed to those of the Eastern Bloc as a whole.[32] A resolution drawn up by a commission chaired by Ulbricht claimed that the official line on the nation had to be altered due to 'changes in the world situation which have arisen from the clashes between the socialist and imperialist world systems since the Seventh Party Congress'.[33] The question of national culture was also addressed: 'With the formation of its socialist German national culture, the social system of our GDR also sharply fences itself off from the Americanised philistinism *(Unkultur)* dominant in the imperialist social system of the FRG.[34]

At the same time, a separate commission chaired by Honecker was preparing the Central Committee's report for the Party Congress. The report emphasised the successful strengthening of the GDR since the previous congress and the bond of socialist internationalism. The issue of the nation was not addressed in early drafts, but reference was made to 'the new socialist constitution - an expression of socialist reality and prospects', in spite of the fact that the constitution still contained the aim of reunification. Meanwhile, at a consultation meeting with the West German DKP and KPD, Honecker repeated his usual arguments against a 'common German umbrella' and unitary nation, and stated that the parties needed a clear 'class position' on the national question. He welcomed their statement that 'the national question in the FRG consists of conquering imperialism', and hoped that the door to socialism would be opened for the Federal Republic, and offered 'international fraternal assistance' in spite of the SED's policy of *Abgrenzung*. Hinting at events to come, he promised that, 'At the Eighth Party Congress, everything will be precisely formulated and justified from scratch, and we will provide answers to the new questions that life poses.'[35]

Material now available proves that Ulbricht's revised vocabulary concerning the German question was insufficient to save him, and that his past words and deeds had not been forgotten by his enemies and rivals. A week before the 15th plenum of the Central Committee, most politburo members were plotting against him. His independence of thought regarding relations between the two German states was used as the main reason why he should be removed before the Eighth Party Congress:

> Not only in domestic policy, but also in policy towards the FRG, Walter Ulbricht pursues his own personal line, to which he rigidly adheres. This constantly interferes with the reliable course of action that was co-ordinated by the CPSU and the SED, and the agreements struck regarding the FRG... In addition he transfers his exaggerated estimation of himself onto the GDR, which he increasingly tries to manoeuvre into a role of model and example: 'After all, we, the GDR, are no Belorussian Soviet Republic.'[36]

Two further reasons why he had to go were given a month later: 'a) Comrade Ulbricht has again and again raised questions and made assessments which do not conform to the reality of the situation or our tasks and decisions; b) unfortunately his health and his physical state has become visibly worse.'[37] While there can be no doubt that Ulbricht was not in good health, indeed this had been the case since 1968, especially due to arteriosclerosis, which caused him to take frequent holidays,[38] it seems that his rivals took advantage of this to exclude him, and in particular, to disassociate him from the German question.[39] Clearly by this stage, power was in the hands of those who put the interests of the GDR (and of the Soviet Union) before reunification.

Unfortunately we do not know the precise course of events which led to Ulbricht's 'resignation' announced at the 16th plenum of the Central Committee. His fall had certainly occurred very rapidly and came as a complete surprise to GDR-watchers in the Federal Republic and the United States.[40] The most likely explanation is that opposition to his economic policies and *Deutschlandpolitik* had been growing within the Party's ruling elite for several months, but a change at the top would only occur when Moscow thought it necessary. However, during this period, Ulbricht's growing obsession with his own importance, his tendency to act autonomously with regard to relations with the Federal Republic, and his failure to acknowledge 'the major role the USSR had played as midwife to the GDR and guarantor of its security',[41] were causing the rapid erosion of support for him in the Kremlin. Ulbricht's defence of the interests of 'his' GDR was particularly unwelcome at a time when Brezhnev wanted to regain the Soviet Union's hegemony within the Eastern Bloc.[42] Furthermore, there is no evidence that any leading members of the SED violently objected to his removal, since it was clear that his time was up, and that Honecker was now the favourite in Moscow.

It is widely accepted that the final straw was Ulbricht's assertion of the GDR's sovereignty, which continued to threaten the rapid resolution of the Berlin question desired by Brezhnev in order to advance détente in Europe.[43] The fact that his removal could not even wait until the Eighth Party Congress in June 1971 is a sign of the urgency of a change at the top. Ultimately Moscow made the decision to replace Ulbricht, although his enemies closer to home may have decided the actual date of his departure.[44] In short, 'His definition of the GDR's sovereignty on the one hand, and Soviet international interests on the other, clashed over the very issue that had given him the opportunity to begin moulding the GDR's identity: Berlin. And it was his definition of the GDR's needs that fell victim to the forces of change around him.'[45] Although Ulbricht's language had changed, he had failed to back up his words with deeds, and even though he had recently assured the CPSU, 'We have rejected a so-called "special German road to socialism",'[46] his rhetoric was unlikely to convince Moscow that its satellite was safe in his hands.

Once Ulbricht had gone, the Soviet leadership could 'embark on the next phase of its German and European policy with a new man at the helm in the GDR - a partner more agreeable than Walter Ulbricht.'[47] For Moscow, the German question was a matter of strengthening the GDR with the aim of attaining equal status with the Federal Republic and of continued *Abgrenzung*. It was no coincidence that a new agenda for the Eighth Party Congress had already been drawn up, on the assumption that Honecker would be First Secretary, and with a new orientation in domestic policy based on the Soviet model.[48]

'History' settles the national question

On 18 May 1971, Honecker addressed the CPSU and sought to reassure them that his position on the German question coincided with their own, after all, as Brezhnev had pointed out, the GDR was the child of their joint parentage. Honecker attacked Brandt's claim that 'we are still all Germans and still belong to one German nation', and his attempts to persuade other states to delay recognising the GDR on the grounds that it might disturb the 'inner-German dialogue'. Bonn's motive was clear, he said: 'They want us to move closer towards the FRG as a sign of alleged "national common ground". They want to embrace the GDR in order to crush her. After all, Brandt has visited Nixon five times since his election as Chancellor and agreed his *Ostpolitik* there.' For Honecker, the most important goal was the GDR's entry into the UN, but he admitted that there was work to be done at home: 'We will carry out active explanatory work among our population and will educate them in the spirit of class-based *Abgrenzung* from the FRG, whereby signs of negative tendencies regarding the national question and all-German illusions will not be tolerated.'[49]

Throughout May and June, a commission was working on Honecker's report for the forthcoming Party Congress. Politburo member Hermann Axen, a firm believer in a class-based definition of the nation, was responsible for the section on the national question, according to his personal adviser, Manfred Uschner. Uschner has claimed that Axen urged Honecker to pay more attention to the national question in order to ward off the advances of 'the enemy', i.e. Bonn,[50] but there can be no doubt that the basic concept of this section of the speech was agreed between them. However, early versions differ from the final draft. Honecker deleted the description of the national question as 'an extremely complicated problem', preferring to say it had 'already been resolved by history'. In addition, he rejected Kurt Hager's suggestion to emphasise the 'bond with forces in the FRG who oppose the anti-national policies of the monopoly-capitalists'.[51]

On 1 June 1971 a draft of the full speech was presented to the politburo, which included the following extract:

> Two fundamentally different German nations exist on German soil, the developing socialist nation in the GDR, and the bourgeois nation in the FRG. They will no doubt exist beside each other for a long historical period. The world-wide historical process of transformation from capitalism to socialism will certainly not make a detour around the FRG in the long run. If sometime in the future the power of the monopoly-capitalists in the FRG is overthrown and the way to socialism is pursued, then a socialist nation under the leadership of the working class will also develop in West Germany. This would result in totally new historical conditions for the solution of the national question on German soil.[52]

But by the 17th plenum of the Central Committee on 10 June, this section had been removed from the speech and Honecker's only reference to the national question was that it should be examined according to its class content. His primary objectives for the immediate future were the consolidation of the 'developed socialist society in the GDR', *Abgrenzung* towards the Federal Republic, and entry into the UN.[53] Presumably he felt that to even mention the possibility of change in the status quo would prejudice these aims. For the same reason, the adjective 'German' was used increasingly rarely.

The Eighth Party Congress was a marked contrast to the previous one. With power securely in the hands of Honecker and his immediate circle, there was now only one acceptable point of view regarding the national question. By design, Honecker's style raised expectations that it was the beginning of a new era, with the emphasis placed on social policy and solidarity with the Soviet Union, though hopes of reform and liberalisation were soon to be dashed. The new First Secretary's speech provoked much interest in the West German media and among Western scholars,[54] and, as mentioned earlier, is often incorrectly portrayed in secondary literature as the SED's first official rejection of the unity of the nation. Honecker stated, 'All this talk in the West about the so-called unity of the German nation and the apparent special nature of relations between the German Democratic Republic and the FRG is obviously to encourage those whose policies still aim to undermine the social and economic foundations of our republic.' He rejected such claims on the grounds that the national question had 'already been settled by history'. Furthermore:

> In contrast to the FRG, where the bourgeois nation continues to exist, and where the national question is determined by the irreconcilable class contradictions between the bourgeoisie and the working masses... a *socialist nation* is developing here in the German Democratic Republic, the socialist German state.[55]

The language used was significant, especially since the First Secretary's speech at the Party Congress was regarded by many as the definitive line in all policy areas. However, many inconsistencies remained. While the intentional use of 'German Democratic Republic' in full, compared with the abbreviation 'FRG,' implied that the GDR was the legitimate German state, from this point on, the term 'socialist nation' became the norm, as opposed to 'socialist German nation'. In fact, only Brezhnev referred to 'Germany' and 'the German people',[56] and it was generally the socialist aspect of the GDR that was stressed, its 'socialist national culture' and permanent place in the community of socialist states, giving the impression that the division of Germany had reached an irreversible stage.

So how can Honecker's drastic and decisive statement on the nation be explained? Four important influences can be identified. Firstly, as James McAdams has pointed out, Honecker had to do something drastic because the Federal Republic was getting dangerously close as a result of détente and Brandt's

Ostpolitik.⁵⁷ Until this point, official statements had been a confusing and often contradictory mixture of old tenets and new responses to Brandt, which needed clarification. It was blatantly obvious that the GDR had gained nothing, and maybe even undermined itself, by maintaining the idea of the unity of the German nation and the aim of reunification via the socialist transformation of the Federal Republic. Consequently, it was logical to believe that more might be gained by giving up this long-standing, but ultimately unobtainable goal, and now that the existence of two sovereign states had more or less been accepted, it made sense to reconsider the notion of a 'national umbrella' arching over them. Thus it was not necessarily the case that the leadership had given up the aim of reunification and a unitary nation because they no longer desired it, but because it had become unrealistic and incompatible with the more pressing objectives of enhancing the legitimacy and securing the permanence of the GDR.

Secondly, strengthening the GDR's international position with the ultimate aim of UN membership had become the SED's immediate objective. Although there is no evidence that the SED ever used the claim that a separate nation existed in the GDR to support its application for UN membership (using instead the indisputable existence of two independent states), failure to deny the unity of the German nation could have prejudiced their case. In a letter to the UN General Secretary, the Foreign Minister, Otto Winzer, stressed the GDR's commitment to the UN's aims regarding the preservation of peace: 'As one of the successor states of the former German Reich, the GDR sees preventing another war from ever breaking out on German soil as its great historical task.'⁵⁸

Thirdly, Honecker wanted to demonstrate his allegiance to the Soviet Union, particularly compared to his predecessor, who had become far too autonomous for Moscow's liking. As a result, he asserted the sovereignty of the GDR on the one hand, while at the same time subordinating it to Moscow on the other. In February 1971 a paper written by historians entitled 'The Development of the National Question in German History' was discussed with the CPSU, and afterwards the director of the Department of Sciences, Hörnig, reported that the paper generally conformed to the view of both parties:

> Our Soviet comrades are in agreement with the formulation that the socialist German nation is developing in the GDR. They recommend that this development should be even more strongly embedded in the international struggle, and that we should show that together with the all-round development of the socialist nation, the GDR is taking on and further developing all the progressive achievements and experiences of the German nation, so that the devaluation of national feeling or a slide into national nihilism can be avoided.⁵⁹

However, the latter advice was soon ignored by Honecker, as was 'the task of presenting the joint interests of the workers of the GDR and the working class in West Germany in the struggle against West German imperialism.'⁶⁰ The CPSU also recommended a more extensive and theoretically accurate portrayal of the 'development of the socialist German national state'. While some of these comments seemed to be a few years behind current statements of the leadership, notably in the continued use of the adjective 'German', they indicate the SED's obligation to consult Moscow regarding the concept of the nation, and also show that Moscow saw the national question in Germany as just part of the larger international conflict between socialism and capitalism.[61]

Overall, the Soviet leadership was undoubtedly more interested in the practical aspects of the German question than complex theories and national concepts, and in particular, in cementing the status quo in Europe, thereby preserving its sphere of influence. But they did like to check that East Berlin was not becoming too German, therefore the concept of the socialist nation in the GDR, permanently allied to the Soviet Union, should not have been unwelcome in Moscow.

Fourthly, Honecker needed to promote himself as the man who would bring new policies and new success to the GDR. This must have been the reason why subsequent official accounts of the development of the nation in the GDR gave the impression that this was the turning point.[62] However, it should be born in mind that the state of the German nation was not of primary importance to him, indeed he personally believed that *Abgrenzung* alone was sufficient, and publicly expressed his intention to concentrate on new social policies.

Whether or not a fifth factor, namely public opinion, influenced the new leadership's stance, is questionable. As we have seen, they were aware of popular confusion caused by different messages emanating from the politburo, and of wide-spread enthusiasm for Brandt's new approach. But the leadership could hardly expect the population to turn their backs on their western neighbour unless they were offered a credible alternative with which to identify, hence a replacement for the former unitary German nation was artificially created and called simply the 'socialist nation in the GDR'. This concept was very much imposed from on high, more as an ideal desired by the regime, as opposed to being a reflection of the subjective feelings of the population. Nevertheless, it was hoped that the people would accept it, since one of Honecker's primary goals was to secure internal stability by making the GDR more appealing.

Meanwhile, Ulbricht, now very much yesterday's man, was originally supposed to open the Party Congress. His prepared speech contained strong words which echoed the tone of the new line (although he still used the term 'socialist German national state'): 'The objective process of their [the two German states'] *Abgrenzung* from each other has reached the point of no return... That the ruling classes of imperialism in the FRG carry the mark of Cain, of national treason, on their foreheads, while the working class of the GDR have taken the solution of the national question into their own hands, is a genuine historical fact.'[63] However, the politburo rejected this version, and not only did the actual speech not refer to the German question at all, it was read by Hermann Axen, since Ulbricht was not even present. It seems that his successor wanted to exclude both him and all reminders of his policies on the nation. One analyst claims that Ulbricht refused to appear at the congress due to the way he was treated after his resignation,[64] while another commentator has more recently suggested that Honecker conspired with Ulbricht's doctors to prevent him attending the Party Congress.[65]

In summary, the Eighth Party Congress was an attempt to break with the past and to indicate a fresh start for the GDR in the post-Ulbricht period. This was true of all policy areas, not least the German question. Honecker had applied a political solution to the emotive problem of the German nation with no regard for the consequences. He tried to deal with the nation as swiftly as possible so as to avoid controversy. However, while the vacuum left by the abandonment of the unitary German nation had officially been filled, it was hardly sufficient just to declare that the national question had been resolved by history, and that a socialist nation (no longer the socialist *German* nation), was developing in the GDR. Former politburo member Alfred Neumann, privately condemned Honecker for having given up the fight regarding the national question, and secretly accused him of misusing the concept of the socialist nation as it appears in the Communist Manifesto.[66] A leading West German commentator noted that the new leadership ignored factors which played a leading role in discussion of the nation in the Federal Republic, in particular the relationship between *Volk* and nation, and the geographical borders of the nation. He concluded that they were more or less using whatever meaning of words such as '*Volk*' and 'nation' they liked, in order to suit current policy objectives.[67]

Not surprisingly, this drastic attempt to settle the national question for good confused the population, and reminded theorists of the fact that in the GDR, academic research was determined, even hindered, by the needs of the party. However, within a few years, the leadership evidently realised that the creation of a credible concept of the nation would require considerably more work, and called upon the services of East German philosophers, social scientists and historians to devise a theoretical framework and a 'national' consciousness and history for the socialist nation in the GDR.

The consequences of the new *Nationskonzept*

Honecker wanted to be rid of the national question once and for all in order to mark the beginning of a new era in the history of the GDR and to achieve internal stability. However, because the concept of the socialist nation in the GDR was merely an objective or ideal desired by the leadership and not an expression of popular sentiment, it was necessary for the party to impose identification with the new *Nationskonzept* from above.

Official justifications for the new line

After the Eighth Party congress Honecker's references to the German nation were usually brief, lacking in detail and heavily cloaked in the language of class struggle. The policy of strict *Abgrenzung* from the Federal Republic seemed to have paid off, since only two years into his leadership, he could boast that 82 states had established diplomatic relations with the 'socialist state of workers and farmers', i.e. the GDR. Only at the end of 1974 did Honecker recognise that his virtual silence on the complex subject of the German nation had not erased it from people's minds, but instead had nurtured confusion.

The rare occasions when Honecker mentioned the topic attracted much coverage by the West German media, for example, his speech during an inspection of troops in Rügen in January 1972. There he stated:

> There is no unity between the socialist GDR and the imperialist FRG and there can never be a unity... Constant talk about the 'unity of the nation' does not change this. Moreover, it is an attempt to interfere in the internal affairs of the GDR... The FRG... is a foreign country, and furthermore, an imperialist foreign country.[68]

A year later at a consultation meeting with local functionaries and members of the Central Committee in January 1973, Honecker addressed the national question quite extensively, in response to Brandt's most recent governmental declaration. Once again Brandt had put Honecker on the defensive by stating that it was not normal for a border to divide members of the same people *(Volk)*. But according to Honecker, Brandt was 'intentionally overlooking the fact that it was not a case of a border dividing members of the same people, but one between sovereign states that were independent of each other and which had different social systems'. Furthermore:

> At the centre of this policy of rapprochment during the past few years, stands the notion of the German nation, which apparently exists unchanged. In fact there are two German nations, the socialist one, or as they occasionally say in the West German press, the 'GDR-nation', and the capitalist nation in the FRG.[69]

Apparently Honecker did not object to the term 'GDR-nation', but one problem remained, namely the need for an alternative to the adjective 'German' in the GDR. 'East German', which was commonplace in the West, was never used by the SED, but one could hardly describe something as *DDRsch.* Then there was the problem of how to describe everything associated with the German nation which predated the division of Germany, such as culture, if the unitary German nation no longer existed. Finally, even Honecker was sometimes inconsistent in his use of the word

'German' and on this occasion, still spoke of 'both German states' and 'two German nations'.

Honecker's next reference to the nation occurred during the ninth plenum of the Central Committee in May 1973. The very fact that he returned to the subject suggests that contrary to his claims and wishes, it was still an issue. Yet again he seemed to be responding to Brandt's government, which had justifiably accused the SED of trying to run away from their shared culture, history and language. Evidently, he had not formulated his arguments himself, but instead adopted those of other politburo members such as Axen and Norden.

Norden had been critical of Ulbricht's line on the nation for several years. He adopted Marx and Engels' idea that by taking over the leadership of a nation, the proletariat would become the national class and therefore would itself constitute the nation. Since power was said to be in the hands of the working class in the GDR, they and their allies had created a socialist nation-state and themselves constituted the nation.[70] He claimed that economic and social factors defined a nation, not the factors previously identified by Stalin, and in any case, the absence of a common German territory and common economy, the differences in the psychological and moral characteristics of the populations of the two states, in their lifestyle and way of thinking, and the lack of common contemporary culture disproved the claim that the unitary German nation still existed. Even a shared history apparently no longer united them, due to their conflicting interpretations of it.[71] In addition, Norden dismissed the notion that a common language was an indicator of nationhood, since the members of several different countries spoke German.[72] After all, no-one would suggest that all English or Spanish native speakers around the world should form one nation, so why should this be the case for all German native speakers? According to Norden:

> With reference to this argument of the common German language - it is well known that the Austrians also speak German, and the people in large parts of Switzerland, Luxembourg and Eastern France too. With this argument of a common language, one comes dangerously close to the greater German concept of Hitler, who justified his first annexations with the need for all German speaking people to belong together in one state. But the Russian speaking workers of Moscow, the English speaking miners of Scotland, the French speaking work force at Renault, and Italian farm labourers are a thousand times closer to us than the German speaking Messrs Siemens, Abs and Krupp.[73]

At the ninth plenum Honecker borrowed Norden's argument, saying that just because citizens of Switzerland, Austria, the GDR and Federal Republic all spoke German, it did not necessarily follow that they all belonged to the same nation. He stressed that it was not language and culture that had drawn a border between the GDR and Federal Republic, but their different, or rather conflicting social and political structures, adding that 'the common language cannot magically change this reality. Apart from that, such things in common have not been equated with a joint state or a joint nation for a long time.' However, he did acknowledge the fact that East Germans had the option of tuning in to West German television and radio if they wished, hence more home-grown counter-propaganda was required, together with an improvement in programme quality.[74]

But even Honecker seemed to have difficulties with the common heritage shared by both states on German soil. Somewhat defensively, he counteracted Bonn's accusations that the SED was trying to run away from their shared history, culture and language with the argument, 'German history was... always a history of class struggles'. Furthermore, 'Today, the GDR is the state that embodies the best traditions of German history, the peasants' uprising of the Middle ages, the struggle of the revolutionary democrats in 1848, the German workers' movement founded by Marx and Engels, Bebel and Liebknecht, and the heroic acts of the anti-fascist resistance fighters.'[75] Presumably Honecker could now afford to refer to the past without undermining the GDR because by this stage, the Basic Treaty (signed by both German governments), had made the position of the East German state more secure. Finally, he criticised the Chinese leadership for believing in the idea of a unitary German nation and the possibility of reunification, and accused them of collusion with Bonn.[76] However, somewhat disingenuously he added, 'In which form the peoples of Europe arrange their co-existence once Western Europe, including the FRG, has travelled down the road to socialism, only time will tell.'[77]

Much to the annoyance of theorists concerned with the nation, other members of the ruling elite followed Honecker's lead and avoided the subject following the Eighth Party Congress. Those closest to the First Secretary, such as Günter Mittag and Joachim Herrmann, tended to adopt a purely pragmatic approach to such issues, rather than trouble themselves with theories and justifications. However, there were exceptions, for example, Kurt Hager, Hermann Axen and Albert Norden, who put some flesh onto the bare bones of the new official position, though their arguments often sounded highly polemical. The sudden increase in their attention to the subject was undoubtedly caused by renewed hopes among the masses that the two German states would grow closer together as a result of the Basic Treaty. However, even top functionaries had to adhere to the basic line expressed at the most recent party congress in order to safeguard their positions and future careers.

This was particularly true of the head of the Department of Sciences, Kurt Hager, who had previously supported Ulbricht's line on the nation. As mentioned earlier, Hager played a significant role due to his overall control of academic institutions, and via the Department of Sciences' Central Research Plan and consultations with those responsible for elaborating upon and propagating the official line. However, Hager had apparently rather carelessly commented that Honecker was an intellectual lightweight, which was conveyed to the First Secretary by a third party. After this indiscretion, Hager did not dare to challenge Honecker, even though he must have been aware that the idea of a purely socialist nation was being taken to ridiculous lengths. Certain academics found such cowardice unforgivable for a man of Hager's intelligence.[78] However, his opinion of Honecker was not totally unfounded, hence the latter needed experienced, educated people like Hager to work out detailed policies. Due to the power structure within the Department, Hager's deputies rigidly enforced the line to which he himself was obliged to adhere, which placed great constraints on scholarship and resulted in the reproduction of the views and mistakes of the leadership.

In a speech on the tasks of social scientists following the party congress, Hager was the first leading functionary to elaborate on the concept of the socialist nation. He claimed that far from being eternal and unchanging, nations were products of social developments and the class struggle. After all, as Marx, Engels and Lenin had stated, the socialist revolution would lead to the renewal of all forms of existence in human society. The implications for scholarship were clear:

> The Eighth Party Congress of the SED orientates the theoretical and ideological work of social scientists towards a convincing debate with bourgeois nationalism. Next to anti-communism, nationalism is the other main strand of the struggle by West German imperialism against socialism in the GDR.[79]

A draft of a speech by Hager to functionaries in Brandenburg in September 1971 stated, 'It must not be forgotten that for Marxist-Leninists, the socialist nation is not the ultimate goal. The flourishing of socialist nations is logically accompanied by their growing closer together and in the long term will lead to their merging together.'[80] This was removed from the final version, suggesting that Hager realised it would be going too far.

The most common arguments used in support of the notion of a socialist nation in the GDR can be summed up as follows: the unity of the German nation had not been written off at the Eighth Party Congress but had already ceased to exist long before; a socialist nation was developing in the GDR, but an internally divided bourgeois nation lived on in the Federal Republic; and the national question was as a 'class question', as Marx and Engels had claimed. In reality however, the class struggle in the Federal Republic, and the so-called 'national task of the German working class', had been given up in favour of *Abgrenzung*, once the two had become incompatible. One could almost say that the leadership of the SED had abandoned the West German proletariat in favour of the interests of the GDR, in other words, they had put their own state before proletarian solidarity, and accepted the notion of a separate 'GDR-nation'. Consequently, the West German working class was rarely mentioned, presumably to avoid complicating the issue with the idea of a unitary German proletariat. They themselves had to settle the as yet unresolved national question there.[81] In the GDR at least, the national question, in the sense of 'the historic mission of the working class', had apparently been resolved.[82]

Academic reactions to the new concept

For several years, theorists had privately contemplated the effects of political division on the nation, although they could not publicise their ideas so long as the SED leadership adhered to the old line associated with Ulbricht.[83] But they were not consulted prior to the Eighth Party Congress. Instead they were encouraged to address the question of the nation only after Honecker had declared that it had been resolved by history. Alfred Kosing thought this was not only a big mistake, but also an insult, and attributed it to Honecker's 'small-minded smugness' and his belief that he and his close associates knew best. Kosing and other theorists were shocked by the fact that a policy held for 25 years was given up in three sentences, without sufficient preparation or regard for the consequences, and merely stressing the political aspects of the national question, while ignoring 'all the elements associated with the nation and everything national'.[84] However, such simplified and abrupt answers were typical of Honecker who could hardly be described as an intellectual.[85]

The usual control mechanisms which prevented deviation from the official line laid down at the Party Congress severely restricted scholars' freedom to devise imaginitive new theories regarding the state of the nation in the early 1970s. They were also obliged to incorporate not only quotes from classic works of Marxism-Leninism, but also ideas emanating from the Soviet Union.[86] However, at an international conference on socialism and the nation in Moscow in October 1973, the East German delegation merely consisted of functionaries who had previously paid little attention to the topic.[87] Some Soviet specialists on Germany were interested in the East German concept of the nation, for example, Portugalov and Dashishchev, although the latter was contemptuous of the notion that there was a GDR-nation and of what Honecker was trying to create. However, debate on the nation, nationality and ethnicity only really got going in the 1980s in the Soviet Union, and with the benefit of hindsight we can see that like the SED, both the CPSU and leading experts, such as Bromlei, severely underestimated the strength of nationalism in the Soviet Union.[88] In practice, East German theorists could borrow relatively few arguments from their Soviet counterparts because the GDR and the Soviet Union were attempting nation-building under very different circumstances: the population of the former was part of the previously unitary German nation, while that of the latter was composed of many different ethnic nations. While theorists at the Academy for Social Sciences also had access to western publications and gained ideas from thinkers such as Karl Deutsch, they were obliged to condemn 'bourgeois' theories in books and articles.[89] At a major conference on socialism and the nation in Moscow in October 1973, the East German delegation merely consisted of functionaries who had previously paid little attention to the topic.[90]

A few days after the Eighth Party Congress, the Department of Sciences decided to consult social scientists from state-run institutions such as the Academy of

Sciences (AdW) and universities to discuss the 'tasks of the social sciences' arising from the congress.[91] A month later, the secretariat of the politburo examined the implications of the congress for both theoretical research and for agitation and propaganda. The Department of Sciences and social science institutes were to sort out 'problems with the further evolution of the socialist nation in the GDR' and the Ministry of Culture, the Academy of Arts, and artists' organisations were to develop 'socialist national culture in the GDR as an objective process of *Abgrenzung* from the imperialist philistinism of the Federal Republic'.[92] A publication plan for a series of theoretical articles evaluating the Eighth Party Congress in the central press organs aimed to address 'the class content of the national question and the role of nationalism in the ideological subversion of imperialism'. It stated that in articles:

> ...the nationalistic theories of the Federal Republic's imperialism - 'inner-German relations' and the 'unity of the nation' - are to be exposed, and the objective process of *Abgrenzung* that is taking place between the socialist GDR and the imperialist FRG, the class character of the national question, the inevitable demise of the bourgeois nation and the rise of the socialist nation are to be elaborated upon. In so doing it should be clearly stated that between the GDR and the FRG, only relations of peaceful coexistence, like those between sovereign states with different social orders, are possible.[93]

A new 'Central Research Plan for the Marxist-Leninist Social Sciences' was produced by the Department of Sciences in January 1972. It stated that the task of social science research was 'to develop the theoretical content of the Eighth Party Congress and to make it usable in the work of the party', although there was no direct mention of the topic of the socialist nation. This omission is rather hard to explain. Perhaps so soon after the party congress the shortcomings of the oversimplified concept of the socialist nation had not yet emerged, or maybe Honecker's comment that history had resolved the national question had been taken quite literally. Whatever the reasons, there was soon enough evidence to prove that this was not the case and that clarification was necessary. Theorists were given the task of explaining why the nation in the GDR was just socialist and no longer German, a policy shift which met with incomprehension among ordinary people, especially since the desirability of a united socialist Germany, led by the German working class, had been drummed into them for over 20 years.

The case of Alfred Kosing was typical of the situation for theorists working in this area at the time. Like others, he could not openly contradict the line represented by Honecker at the Eighth Party Congress without jeopardising his career prospects, but he has recently claimed that he did question the validity of the official line,[94] although this is not immediately apparent from his work. However, unlike the brief pronouncements of the leadership, his arguments were at least theoretically justified, though often rather convoluted and laboured due to the obligation to adapt Marxist-Leninist principles to the unique East German situation and to incorporate recent quotes from the First Secretary of the SED. Privately he objected to the concept of the socialist nation because it was overtly political, lacking in historical foundation, and had clearly not been thoroughly considered before the Eighth Party Congress.[95]

Apart from the speeches by functionaries mentioned earlier, little was published on the subject of the socialist nation until 1974. This may have been due to lack of encouragement from above and to the sensitive nature of the subject. However, in 1974, an influential article by Kosing and the historian, Walter Schmidt, appeared in the theoretical journal *Einheit* which noticeably contradicted Kosing's article in the same journal in 1962 (examined here in the second chapter).[96] Then Kosing had argued that the unitary German nation still existed, but at two different levels of development, and criticised the West German Karl Jaspers for suggesting that two separate nations were forming in the same way as had occurred in Germany and Austria.[97] Now, by claiming that a socialist nation existed in the GDR, while the old bourgeois nation continued in the Federal Republic, and that the two were totally irreconcilable, he and Schmidt were more or less accepting Jaspers' position, albeit supported by Marxist-Leninist arguments.[98] The article included a description of the factors which apparently determined the substance and character of the socialist nation in the GDR: socialism; socialist conditions of production; political power in the hands of the working class (under the leadership of their Marxist-Leninist party); the authority of Marxist-Leninist ideology; and integration into the community of socialist states, led by the Soviet Union.[99] The removal of class antagonism within the nation was supposed to lead to friendly co-operation for the common good and the homogenisation of thought, desires, actions and goals, while at the same time a convergence of socialist nations would occur.[100]

To readers unaccustomed to Marxist-Leninist theory regarding nationhood, many of the arguments used by Kosing and Schmidt might sound somewhat contrived and seem to have little in common with western perceptions of nationhood. The question of the 'Germanness' of the GDR continued to be a problem, and the authors used the adjective 'German' rarely and somewhat inconsistently. While they did not totally ignore the awkward question of ethnicity, to dismiss it as relatively insignificant compared with social factors was hardly a satisfactory explanation. Although one might accept the claim that the 'social-psychological components of national life' were changing as a result of the 'new economic, social, political and ideological conditions' of socialism in the GDR,[101] the assertion that 'ethnic components' were also changing was dubious and clearly an attempt to counteract the idea of a *Zusammengehörigkeitsgefühl* linking the two German states, which had been advocated by Brandt. Even so, the fact that Honecker himself had raised the question of a future all-German socialist nation, in the (unlikely) event of a socialist transformation of the Federal Republic, once again highlighted the problem of the GDR's German heritage.[102] It was also unclear what evolutionary stage the socialist nation in the GDR had reached -

whether it was established or still developing, although Kosing and Schmidt seemed to imply the latter. Certainly later articles tried to paint a more credible and realistic picture, making it clear that a new nation could not be created overnight. Finally, exactly what was meant by the convergence of socialist nations was not explained. According to the authors, with the further development of mature socialism and its gradual transition to communism, the importance of proletarian internationalism would increase, though this would not sideline or eliminate 'the national element'.[103]

Kosing has since justified his U-turn with the argument that in 1962 he could not have foreseen the changes that would take place on German soil by the mid-1970s, in particular, the further integration of the two German states into hostile alliances and their consolidation as states with conflicting political and economic systems. Apparently he wanted to reflect on the state of the nation to the best of his ability, even if that meant admitting he had previously been wrong. In spite of the subsequent reunification of Germany, Kosing does not claim to have been right in the first place, but blamed the inner contradictions and weaknesses of the social system for the collapse of the GDR.[104] Close associates suspect that he gave up his original theory very reluctantly,[105] which suggests that he and his colleagues were obliged to devise a justification for the new official line, however implausible it was, and even if this caused the embarrassment of having to retract a previous position.

The second edition of the reference book, the *Kleines politisches Wörterbuch* was published in 1973, and Kosing's entry for 'nation' was considerably altered. Stalin's definition of the general characteristics of a nation was still used, namely a common economy, territory, language, culture and social psychology, and certain specific references to the German situation were omitted.[106] Gone was the reference to 'the German nation that is currently composed of the populations of two states', the GDR as the representative of the entire German nation, and how the division could be overcome.[107] Instead, the new edition stated:

> Since the socialist and the bourgeois nation are based on conflicting social, political, economic and ideological foundations, there can be no unity of the nation between the GDR and the FRG, instead only a relationship of peaceful coexistence, the prerequisite for which is the diplomatic recognition of the GDR. The claims of an apparently still existing 'unity of the German nation' are directed against the unavoidable diplomatic recognition of the GDR, and are in pursuit of the goal of the subjugation of the masses of the GDR to the rule of the imperialist forces of the FRG.[108]

Over the next few years, the subject of the socialist nation rarely featured in documents regarding academic research at state-run institutions. The Central Research Plan for 1976-80, drawn up in 1974, did not mention the concept of the nation specifically, but reports from certain disciplines showed how the new line on the nation had far reaching consequences for many other areas of East German scholarship. In its report for 1973, the Council for Linguistic Research stated, 'The linguistic processes resulting from the transformation of the bourgeois nation into the socialist nation were emphasised as a topical and new problem for linguistics in the GDR'.[109] Overall, theorists and other scholars had to adapt to the new line on the nation, but among experts on nation-theory there was clearly little enthusiasm for the concept of a non-German, socialist nation in the GDR.

The 'de-Germanisation' of the GDR

Honecker's declaration of the development of a purely socialist nation in the GDR immediately raised the question of whether the state and its population were still German. Many functionaries tended to take the words of the First Secretary quite literally, and as a consequence, a highly unsubtle purge of the words 'German' and 'Germany' from official usage was implemented. While certain name changes were logical, for example, in the case of institutions unique to the GDR, the schizophrenic application of this 'de-Germanisation' policy highlighted the fact that it was purely a political tactic with no credible argument behind it. This extreme form of *Abgrenzung* continued until 1975, when the party leadership began to distinguish between nationality and citizenship.

The consequences of the new line were far reaching. At official functions, the East German national anthem was only played and no longer sung due to the fact that the lyrics written by Johannes R. Becher in 1949 had referred to 'Germany, united fatherland'.[110] In July 1971, the State Secretariat for West German Affairs was abolished because it suggested the relationship between the two states was different to that between any other two states. In the Federal Republic, this was interpreted as a further indication of the SED's desire for *Abgrenzung* and a reflection of 'the consistent continuation along the road towards a total separation of both parts of Germany pursued by the GDR'.[111] In November 1971, the radio station *Deutschlandsender* was renamed 'Voice of the GDR'. In this case, the change was not just cosmetic, but coincided with a change of role. A report from the Central Committee's 'West Department' stated that in view of the GDR's policy of *Abgrenzung* from the FRG and the prospect of diplomatic relations between the two, it was no longer appropriate for the station to try to influence the West German population, although ideological work directed at the Federal Republic should not be given up altogether, since West German communists apparently relied on it. It was also decided to cease production of publications which had dealt with internal developments in the Federal Republic for distribution there, although material about the GDR would still be distributed.[112] Following criticism and ridicule from Bonn, the SED later attempted to justify these changes, arguing that, 'We did not replace the *Deutschlandsender* with the "Voice of the GDR" because the word "Germany" disturbed us. Like the termination of broadcasts by the forces' channel, this step was more an expression of the fact that we do not want to interfere in the internal affairs of the FRG.'[113] The following February, the television corporation *Deutscher Fernsehfunk* became *Fernsehen der DDR*.

In May 1972, Honecker himself suggested that the *Deutsche Akademie der Wissenschaften zu Berlin* (DAW) should be renamed to express 'the increased social standing of the academy in the GDR'. As a result, it became the *Akademie der Wissenschaften der DDR* (AdW) in September. This made sense since it was not a pan-German institution. The ruling council of the Academy stated, 'This new name is in accordance with the social developments of recent years.' According to a report of a plenary session of the academy, 'the discussion expressed the great duty towards socialist society that the Academy has taken on with its new name'.[114] In some cases, the renaming of institutions was also an opportunity for 'de-Ulbrichtisation', for example, the *Deutsche Akademie der Staats- und Rechtswissenschaft Walter Ulbricht* dropped both the adjective 'German' and the name of the man it had originally honoured.[115] In connection with this policy, academic manuscripts were scrutinised before publication to check that the word 'Germany' did not crop up too often.[116]

The hard-line Interior Minister, Friedrich Dickel, decreed that on official forms and documents such as passports, people should give their nationality as 'GDR' as opposed to German (or *sorbish* in the case of members of the slavonic Sorb community based around the river Lausitz who numbered around 100,000[117]). As was typical of the power structure in the GDR, those at middle levels tended to enforce the Party line particularly rigidly, always fearful of antagonising their superiors, hence they strictly implemented the ban on the word 'German'. Even the *Hotel Deutschland* in Leipzig was renamed *Interhotel Leipzig*, and from January 1974 East German vehicles were obliged to carry the letters 'DDR' in place of 'D'.

Such extreme measures confused and alienated the population, who felt their national identity was under threat. They also handed the Federal Republic a great propaganda victory, reinforcing the latter's claim to sole representation of the German nation, since the SED appeared to be rejecting everything German including culture, literature and music. Ultimately, in spite of the political divide, the populations of the two German states were still related to each other, and not surprisingly considered themselves and their relatives 'over there' to share the same nationality, namely German, and to deny this fact laid the leadership open to ridicule. Finally, it was impossible to deny that the populations of the GDR and FRG both spoke German, although some functionaries claimed that a *Sprachspaltung* or linguistic divide had developed, though in practice, this seems to have been confined to political vocabulary,[118] and regional dialects predated the political division of Germany.

The 'de-Germanisation' campaign could be interpreted as a sign that the SED leadership was now sufficiently confident to present the GDR purely as a socialist state which no longer relied on its German credentials to prove its legitimacy. However, the fact that the SED later reversed this policy and began to draw heavily on the 'progressive' elements of German history seems to disprove this theory. A more likely explanation is that the leadership still regarded the 'Germanness' shared by both the GDR and the Federal Republic as a threat to the legitimacy of the state and as a propaganda weapon for the West German government.

In retrospect it is obvious that the German connection clearly did undermine the GDR, but the leadership of the SED was naive to believe that the cosmetic removal of words would be sufficient to break the subjective bond of German nationhood felt by the population. Interestingly however, there was no question of changing the name of the state (though usually only the abbreviated form 'DDR' was used, obscuring the adjective 'German'), nor of the Party, which was, after all, the *Sozialistische Einheitspartei Deutschlands*, nor of the newspaper *Neues Deutschland*. The inconsistent implementation of this policy proves the SED wanted to keep the historic link when it suited them. Furthermore, the fact that the word 'German', still sometimes cropped up in official speeches, especially with reference to 'the two German states', revealed continuing uncertainties even among the ruling elite themselves.

Unfortunately records of a top-level decision explicitly ordering the deletion of the words 'German' and 'Germany' is not to be found, but the idea must have originated from members of Honecker's close circle who were naive enough to believe that a complicated issue involving the deep-rooted, subjective feelings of the population, could be solved with word games, and must have had his blessing. Since Honecker was himself born on West German soil, this is perhaps rather surprising, although it is an indication of his willingness to subordinate the German national cause to that of socialist internationalism. Theorist Alfred Kosing did not believe the head of the Department of Sciences, Kurt Hager, was responsible because he was too intelligent and is known to have derided the idea, saying 'We are not Zulus, we are still Germans', but he lacked the courage to challenge Honecker on the issue.[119] Jürgen Hofmann suspected that it may have originated with Joachim Herrmann in the Propaganda Department, a close colleague of Honecker, and certainly no intellectual. Others may also have had reservations, but were silenced by the East German virtue of obedience to authority,[120] since we now know enough about how the politburo functioned not to expect any debate, let alone disagreement with a policy suggested or at least approved by the First Secretary.

Public opinion and propaganda

One of the primary reasons for the SED's sudden denial of the Germanness of the GDR and its people was the need to put an end to 'all-German illusions' among the population. In the early 1970s, the party leadership continued to monitor public opinion regarding the state of the nation, especially the level of popular identification with the socialist nation in the GDR. As before, this was not because they wanted to ensure that the new concept was in line with popular sentiment, but in order to identify areas where the Party's message was not getting across and where propaganda needed to be improved. Presumably if people did identify with the socialist nation, they would also feel a sense of allegiance to

GDR and be more willing to help increase its prosperity and international standing, instead of looking westwards and dreaming of German reunification. During the negotiations with Bonn, which culminated in the Basic Treaty of 1972, this was particularly important, since there was a risk that ordinary people would interpret the negotiation process as a sign that the two states were growing together, whereas the regime saw it as proof that the two were now totally separate. Also, any indications of popular dissent might discourage other states from recognising the GDR. A further reason why public opinion was monitored was the fact that within the politburo, agitation and propaganda was the responsibility of Werner Lamberz, who recognised that in order to produce successful propaganda, it was necessary to know what people actually thought.

Information about popular opinion was gathered in several different ways. For example, secretaries from each administrative district or *Bezirk* would regularly send reports of views articulated by the public to the Agitation Department; polls were undertaken by the IMF and also by the Academy for Social Sciences; discussion at academic institutions, such as the Academy of Sciences, was monitored and reported back to the Department of Sciences on a monthly basis. Research revealed a serious degree of incomprehension regarding the nation following the Eighth Party Congress. Reports indicated that although many people accepted the existence of two German states, they failed to see how this affected the unitary German nation.[121] An assessment by the Academy of Sciences acknowledged that with regard to the national question, people over-valued historic, linguistic, and cultural factors and failed to appreciate the significance of class.[122] In addition, opinion polls into historic consciousness conducted by the AfG revealed that even people who accepted the GDR as their fatherland failed to understand why the GDR should cut itself off from the Federal Republic.[123]

Such doubts were not confined to the working-class. Reports from the Humboldt University in East Berlin from 1971 confirmed that 'all-German illusions' persisted, particularly among non-Party members, who were always singled out in such reports.[124] A major investigation conducted for the Department of Sciences criticised the 'bourgeois ideas about the nation' which prevailed at the AdW, apparently as a result of 'insufficient attention to the theory of Marxist-Leninist tradition'. It stated that emotions were getting in the way, and some academics were trying to work out a definition of a nation that was 'politically value-free', hence they uncritically accepted the idea that 'We are all Germans'.[125] It was noted that some academics and researchers at the Academy still adhered to a traditional bourgeois concept of the nation, while others mixed bourgeois and Marxist concepts, though it was hoped that these misconceptions could be dispelled. Several members were also raising awkward questions such as why there were nations within socialism at all, and why it was necessary to discuss the topic, now that the Federal Republic had more or less recognised the GDR. Some scientists had even suggested that the socialist nation was just a temporary and functional concept, specifically designed to reinforce the SED's policy of *Abgrenzung*,[126] which was essentially true.

Research also revealed that the purge of the word 'German' had not altered the self-perception of the population as the regime had hoped. The virtual ban on the word was in fact more likely to turn people against the regime because they felt they were being denied their national identity and heritage. This was especially true of the Sorbs, who feared they would be forced to become simply 'citizens of the GDR' along with everyone else. Members of the Academy of Sciences wondered why the word 'Germany' was suddenly taboo, but also noticed how inconsistent the purge was.[127] While many institutions were renamed, *Deutsche Post, Deutsche Reichsbank* and *Neues Deutschland* remained unchanged. The case of a group of students who were reported for singing patriotic songs such as the *Deutschlandlied, Die alten Germanen* and *Kurfürst Friedrich von der Pfalz* during a party in a hall of residence illustrates just how far the 'de-Germanisation' campaign was taken. They were reported by an FDJ official, who claimed to have dutifully challenged them regarding the nationalistic content of the songs.[128]

One particular event that warrants attention due to its impact on popular opinion is the negotiation of the Basic Treaty in 1972, which defined the basis of the relationship between the two German states. The treaty was agreed after 60 meetings between the two sides and over 1,000 hours of negotiations.[129] Exactly why the SED agreed to negotiate at all is open to speculation. Four reasons have been identified: the desire for international recognition and greater access to world markets; Soviet pressure; increasing West German intrusions into the Eastern Bloc; and increased confidence in the socialist mentality of East German citizens on the part of the regime.[130] With the signing of the Basic Treaty, the Federal Republic had almost recognised the GDR, but not quite, hence Honecker could claim that it more or less had, while the Federal Government could appease its critics and claim that a special relationship still existed. The SED's chief negotiator, Dr Michael Kohl, used the line on the national question articulated by Honecker at the Eighth Party Congress as the basis for his arguments, and dismissed Bonn's attempts to allude to the SED's former pro-unification stance.[131] While details of the negotiations and the resulting treaty have been adequately described elsewhere,[132] the accompanying 'Letter on German Unity' from the West German government warrants attention.

During negotiations, Honecker had stated clearly that the GDR would not sign a treaty which made reference to the nation or to reunification. Consequently, Bonn attached a letter which stated that the German question remained open, that the treaty did not amount to diplomatic recognition of the GDR as a foreign country, and that the question of citizenship had not been settled.[133] Afterwards however, the SED stated, 'No mention is made of the unity of the nation or the unity of Germany or of Germany as a whole in the treaty, or in any supplementary document.'[134] The acceptance of permanent representations as opposed to full embassies was officially explained as 'in the interest of a constructive outcome of the negotiations'.[135] Whether the Basic Treaty amounted to recognition by the Federal Republic or not hardly mattered to Honecker, since for him it was a means to an end, namely to achieve his ultimate objectives - international recognition and membership of the UN. According to some commentators, this was sufficient to make Honecker temporarily relax his policy of *Abgrenzung*,[136] although as we shall see, the new constitution of 1974 reverted to a separatist line.

Although the SED leadership interpreted the Basic Treaty as proof that the two German states were entirely separate from each other, research showed that many East Germans interpreted it as a sign of rapprochement between the two states, and hoped that it might lead to greater things. During the negotiations, the SED's continuation of *Abgrenzung* caused confusion, since it seemed to contradict the aim of improving relations.[137] Indeed, polls revealed that even those who accepted that a unitary German nation no longer existed did not understand the need for *Abgrenzung* or for a stronger bond with the Soviet Union.[138] Contrary to the SED's wishes, the establishment of permanent representations as opposed to embassies was interpreted as a sign that a special relationship between the two states still existed.[139] In addition, most people were not interested in Marxist-Leninist arguments as to why there was no longer one German nation or a special relationship, or why *Abgrenzung* was a necessary aspect of the class struggle. They were more concerned with the practical consequences that directly affected them, for example, their inability to visit relatives 'over there'. Many had hoped that the Basic Treaty would bring freedom to travel to the Federal Republic, but were disappointed because the party soon found ways to reduce contact between the populations of both states, such as the dramatic increase in the minimum amount of money West Germans had to exchange to visit the GDR in November 1973. Clearly the leadership had very different reasons for celebrating the ratification of the Treaty to the population of the GDR and the West German government. However, in spite of the SED's claims to the contrary, the unusual practical measures and regulations agreed proved that the relationship between the two states was still far from ordinary.

Research also revealed yet another hindrance to the SED's propaganda campaign, namely the fact that Brandt was very popular among East Germans, in spite of the SED's attempts to portray him as a dangerous imperialist. A report from the Humboldt University acknowledged 'widespread illusions about Brandt and his policies' and the fact that the party had not yet succeeded in convincing people that the conflict with the Federal Republic was a class-conflict.[140] In a note to Honecker, Hans Modrow, then head of the Agitation Department, specifically referred to the population's failure to recognise what the SED claimed were Brandt's true intentions.[141] In 1972, Modrow wrote to Lamberz to draw his attention to the marked increase in answers the regime did not want to hear regarding the German question in opinion polls.[142] Overall, the Basic Treaty had revived ideas of one German nation which arched over the two states like a huge umbrella, with the result that 1973 marked the 'high point of illusion' regarding the German nation.[143] Although the treaty did pave the way for international recognition of the GDR, which had apparently revived the 'state consciousness of the citizens of the GDR',[144] this was no replacement for national consciousness, and the susceptibility of East Germans to the attractions of the Federal Republic was obvious, as was the need to create a stronger emotional bond between citizen and state.

Another event which provoked all-German sentiment during this period was the 1972 Olympic games in Munich. The regime saw it as an opportunity for the GDR to prove itself on the world stage, to strengthen patriotism at home and to outshine the Federal Republic; the fact that there were now two separate teams from the GDR and Federal Republic would be a clear sign to the rest of the world that they were separate states, and in the eyes of the SED, two separate nations. But did the population share this view? Apparently not, since the Agitation Commission recorded as typical the statement: 'Whether GDR or FRG - we're keeping our fingers crossed for all Germans and will celebrate every one of their victories', and the belief that since both states had good chances of winning medals, if they had a united team, Germany could win the most medals overall. The games also raised the sensitive issue of who would be permitted to travel to Munich.[145]

In summary, we can draw two conclusions from these reports of public opinion from the early 1970s. Firstly, that there was widespread confusion regarding the state of the German nation, in spite of Honecker's hope that the issue was over and done with, and secondly, that the leadership was aware of this. Archive material shows that Honecker himself received and read regular reports on public opinion from Modrow, thus he was personally aware of the level of incomprehension on this issue.[146] Reports proved that people still felt part of the German nation, even if they had come to terms with living in a socialist state. However, such information only made the regime try harder to promote its own version of the socialist nation in the GDR, in particular by continuing the blatant 'de-Germanisation' campaign. But the SED was wasting its time claiming that the unitary German nation no longer existed and that the nation in the GDR was no longer German, when the opposite message was emanating from the Federal Republic, to which the majority continued to be bound via family ties.

Undeterred the SED launched a major campaign to get the basic idea of the socialist nation across to the masses, which indicates how important it was that the new concept was accepted. The Department of Propaganda was responsible, assisted by the Department of Sciences on so-called 'ideological and theoretical questions'. According to a report from the Department for Propaganda:

> ...extensive theoretical and ideological work must be undertaken so that every citizen completely understands the class content of the national question, its historic development, the objective process of *Abgrenzung* by the socialist GDR from the imperialist FRG, leading to the formation and development of a socialist nation on the soil of the GDR as a result of a hard and unavoidable class struggle spanning several decades.[147]

The development of the socialist nation in the GDR within the community of socialist nations and states was also to be emphasised. In November 1972, a conference was held on the 'Tasks of Agitation and Propaganda for the further Implementation of the Resolutions of the Eighth Party Congress', organised by Werner Lamberz. The conference is interesting because there, problems arising from the propagation of the socialist nation were admitted. It was recognised that the concept of the socialist nation needed to be explained better and that insufficient theoretical work had been produced. For the first time it was acknowledged that the main hindrance to effective propaganda was West German television which kept the hope of German reunification alive, caused 'illusions' about a special relationship between the two states, and led to incomprehension regarding the need for *Abgrenzung*. This was apparently particularly prevalent among people who frequently watched sport and who continued to see victories for West German athletes as 'our victories'.[148]

To counteract such thoughts, propaganda was devised which would encourage identification with the socialist GDR as 'fatherland' and would turn the agreements between the GDR and Federal Republic to the SED's advantage. According to Lamberz:

> Tourism, family visits and other regulations take place not because we have given away part of our sovereignty or the democratic character of our society for the benefit of something or other common to us. Rather, it is because the FRG has had to recognise our sovereignty and our independent development as a socialist state... Even if Hans from the Heckert factory in Karl-Marx-Stadt and Fritz von Conti from Hanover visit each other, that does not alter any power relationships. Hans works in and for socialism, while Fritz remains exploited until the day when the West German working class liberates itself.[149]

However, it was obvious that the problem was not just that people were still thinking in all-German terms, but also that they were not convinced that socialism best served their interests, particularly when they could see the alternative on their television screens.

Events were organised by local branches of the SED, where socialist patriotism, proletarian internationalism and the socialist nation were stressed in an attempt to immunise the population against 'West German imperialism'. Honecker sent top functionaries to such gatherings to represent and justify his stance, for example, Hermann Axen gave an important speech at a 'theoretical conference' organised by the SED in Berlin in June 1973 which was later published. That two years had already passed since the Eighth Party Congress suggests that it was taking a long time for the population to get the message. Axen attempted to draw on classic works of Marxism-Leninism to support the SED's claim that a socialist nation was developing in the GDR. Here and on several other occasions, he argued that the solution of the national question was subordinate to the interests of the revolution and of socialism: 'What we call "national" *(Das Nationale)* does not stand above the class struggle - instead class relations and the class struggle determine the nature of the development of the nation and the national question.'[150]

His arguments were in stark contrast to those used during the 1960s. The development of two separate nations was now portrayed as an inevitable consequence of the division of Germany into two states. Gone were the references to the bond of the working class on both sides of the inner-German border and their task of reuniting what imperialism had divided, since as far as the GDR was concerned, the national question had been settled. In retrospect it seems ironic that Axen (and others) pointed to the Soviet Union as a shining example of how national problems could only be overcome via 'the solution of the social question by the working class',[151] in view of the brutal methods used to achieve this, and the fact that they ultimately failed, as the disintegration of the Soviet Union and recent ethnic conflicts show.

Axen accused the West Germans of 'bourgeois nationalism' and 'neo-revanchism' manifested by their attempts to use ethnic factors to prove that a unitary German nation still existed.[152] Although he said Marxist-Leninists did not, indeed should not underestimate ethnic factors, 'they do not determine the nature of the nation and its social, economic and class-based structure'.[153] The common language was a particular problem, firstly because it was hard to deny (although some functionaries tried to), and secondly because language was considered an important factor in the development of nations by Engels, Stalin and Lenin. Like Norden, Axen also took advantage of the numerous examples of separate nations who shared a common language to support his argument that they did not automatically have to form a unitary nation, not even if they had similar economic and political systems:

> The historic fact of the existence of the socialist GDR and the capitalist FRG differentiates these two German-speaking states according to class, and therefore in a more principled way than is the case between the FRG and other German-speaking states, for example, between the FRG and Austria.[154]

In case people did not accept the argument that ethnic factors did not determine nations, he added that they too would gradually evolve and change as a result of the political and social transformation in the GDR.[155] Finally Axen refuted Bonn's accusation that the socialist nation in the GDR was *geschichtslos* (lacking in history), describing it as firmly rooted in the history of the German people, and by implication, legitimate.[156] However, like other functionaries, including Honecker, he was inconsistent in his use of the adjective 'German'. Until the bitter end, Axen adhered to the line that he had written for Honecker's speech at the Eighth Party Congress, and only admitted that he might have got it slightly wrong after the 1989 revolution.[157]

It should be noted that compared with other issues, the amount of attention paid to the nation in official propaganda was relatively small. It was very much a subject that Honecker wanted to sweep under the carpet so that he could concentrate on economic and social consolidation. Even so, public acceptance of the socialist nation was an important element of the SED's campaign for legitimacy, and they clearly realised that people would work harder to strengthen the state if they felt a sense of allegiance to it.

The new constitution of 1974

One of the most illuminating examples of Honecker's leadership style, compared to that of his predecessor, was the revision of the constitution in 1974. As we saw in the previous chapter, the original constitution of 1949 was changed in 1968 after consultation with the population, followed by a referendum, and resulted in significant changes to the section on the nation. This time, the leadership's intention to change the constitution was announced at the 12th plenum of the Central Committee in July 1974. It had been drawn up by Honecker and a few of his close colleagues, and was then presented for ratification by the *Volkskammer* as a *fait accompli*. No academics were consulted, and, according to Alfred Neumann, even the majority of the politburo simply received the finished article.[158] The result was the ultimate example of the purge of references to the German nation, even the word 'German' itself. In Article 1, the GDR was no longer described as the 'socialist state of the German nation', but simply as a 'socialist state of workers and farmers'. The aim of overcoming the division of Germany in Article 8 was completely removed. Finally, the new Article 6 stressed that the GDR was 'for ever and irrevocably bound to the Soviet Union'.[159]

Officially these amendments were justified by the tangible changes which had taken place in the GDR since the beginning of the decade, and by changes in its 'international relationships'.[160] The most obvious reason, however, was that the old constitution clearly contradicted Honecker's stance at the Eighth Party Congress, and other statements - indeed, one wonders why it was not altered earlier. It is likely that this precise moment was chosen to coincide with the 25th anniversary of the founding of the GDR.[161] In an extremely brief speech to justify the change, Honecker merely expressed the need to bring the constitution in line with 'the life and the level of political and social development of our socialist state of workers and farmers, and with the basic ideological position of our people.' Although certain specific articles were mentioned, no reason was given for the dramatic change to Article 8, and the only time Honecker used the word 'nation' was with reference to the socialist nations drawing closer together. The emphasis was placed on the GDR as a developed socialist society, though Honecker did add that its people were continuing the 'revolutionary traditions of the German workers' movement'.[162]

No doubt there were also other reasons for the changes, for example, to counteract the effects of increased personal contact between East and West Germans following the Basic Treaty, and as a response to the West German Federal Constitutional Court's recent ruling that the treaty did not violate the idea of one German nation and the aim of reunification enshrined in the Basic Law.[163] While it made sense to bring the constitution in line with Honecker's stance, the removal of the word 'German' provided ammunition with which the West German government could attack the SED, and reinforced its claim to the sole right of representation of the German nation. Bonn accused the SED of 'abdication from the nation', 'taking flight from German history', and of making the GDR a 'socialist non-entity'.[164] The West German minister for Inner-German Relations stated that a nation could neither be founded nor abolished simply via a specification in the constitution.[165]

Unlike in 1968, the public had no opportunity to participate in the drafting of the constitution. One likely reason for this was that the leadership knew that they would not have supported the removal of all references to the German nation.[166] Certainly reports of public reaction to the change seem to support this theory, and show that the notion of a purely socialist nation in the GDR was still causing problems, especially since the SED's previous adherence to the unity of the German nation had not been forgotten.[167] At the Academy of Sciences, members were wondering whether the division of Germany had become permanent, why efforts were being made to reunite Korea but not Germany, how the GDR related to German history, and finally whether or not they were still Germans.[168] These were all valid questions for which the SED had failed to provided satisfactory answers - a situation which would have to be remedied, if the Party was to achieve what it had set out to do by denying the unity of the nation, namely to legitimise the GDR as an independent sovereign state.

Conclusion

In this chapter we have seen how the SED attempted to enhance the legitimacy of the GDR and its right to international recognition via the claim that the population constituted a nation in their own right, which was socialist and completely separate from the bourgeois nation in the Federal Republic. Thus the long-standing notion of the national bond of the German working class had finally been abandoned. Political objectives clearly determined the official line on the state of the nation during this period, and theories had to be adapted accordingly.

However, the extreme concept of the non-German socialist nation in the GDR was domestically untenable and reinforced the Federal Republic's claim to be the legitimate representative of the German nation. The fact that the SED reversed its policy of 'de-Germanisation' the following year indicates that even they eventually realised that the policy was destructive and had the opposite effect to what was intended. What was required was an argument that would both avoid accepting West German claims that one German nation still existed, and a loss of face for the leadership. However, as we shall see, the ruling elite did not manage to find a way out by itself.

Notes

1. Peter Przybylski, *Tatort Politbüro*, 2 vols. (Berlin, 1992), vol. 2: Honecker, Mittag und Schalck-Golodkowski, p.26.
2. SAPMO-BArch J IV 2/2A/1481 (30 November 1970).
3. SAPMO-BArch J IV 2/2A/1484 (8 December 1970).
4. *Dokumente der SED*, 22 vols. (East Berlin, 1972), vol. 13, pp.71-75.
5. Moreton, *East Germany*, pp.169, 174.
6. Erich Honecker, Bericht über den Umtausch der Parteidokumente, 14. Tagung des ZK der SED, 9-11. Dez. 1970. Cited in Naumann and Trümpler, *Der Flop*, pp. 194-196.
7. See chapter 3. Some commentators fail to recognise that *Abgrenzung* was not invented by the SED, for example, Naumann and Trümpler, *Der Flop*, pp 69-70.
8. SAPMO-BArch IV 2/1/416 (11 December 1970)
9. *Neues Deutschland*, 12 December 1970.
10. SAPMO-BArch IV 2/1/415
11. SAPMO-BArch IV 2/1/415
12. SAPMO-BArch J IV 2/2A/1489 (15 December 1970)
13. Vormerkung der SED Führung über Gespräche mit Breshnev in Moscow vom 20. August 1970. IfGA, ZPA 41656, cited in Przybylski, *Tatort* vol. 2, p.348.
14. Hofmann, *Ein neues Deutschland*, p.252.
15. Ulbricht, Sitzung der Kommission zur Vorbereitung des 25. Jahrestags der SED am 17. Dezember 1970, cited in Naumann und Trümpler, *Der Flop*, pp. 197-199.
16. Naumann and Trümpler, *Der Flop*, p.72.
17. For example, at a party conference in Berlin shortly after his removal from office, according to Helmut Meier, Berlin, 15 March 1993.
18. Letter from the politburo of the CPSU - unofficial translation for Honecker dated 21 January 1971. IfGA, IPA NL2/31, my italics.
19. Ilse Spittmann, 'Warum Ulbricht stürzte', *Deutschland Archiv* 4 (1971): p.568.
20. Moreton, *East Germany*, pp.177-178.
21. According to McAdams, *East Germany*, p.113.
22. SAPMO-BArch J IV 2/2A/1488 (15 December 1970)
23. SAPMO-BArch IV 2/1/419
24. SAPMO-BArch IV 2/1/419
25. Willy Brandt, 'Bericht zur Lage der Nation', 28 January 1971. *Europa Archiv* 26, (1971): pp.264-268.
26. Brandt, 'Bericht', my italics
27. 'Die ideologischen Probleme bei den weiteren Auswertung der 14. und 15. Tagungen der ZK', SAPMO-BArch IV A2/9.04/13.

28 'Die ideologischen Probleme', SAPMO-BArch IV A2/9.04/13.
29 'Die ideologischen Probleme', SAPMO-BArch IV A2/9.04/13.
30 SAPMO-BArch IV A2/9.04/13
31 Naumann and Trümpler, *Der Flop*, p.79.
32 Moreton, *East Germany*, p.183.
33 SAPMO-BArch J IV 2/2A/1497. (15 February 1971) The same phrasing was used by Ulbricht in a speech at the 24th conference of the CPSU in March 1971, and again in April on the 25th anniversary of the formation of the SED. See SAPMO-BArch NL182/798 and SAPMO-BArch J IV 2/2A/1509
34 SAPMO-BArch IV VIII/17
35 SAPMO-BArch J IV 2/2A/1504 (16 March 1971)
36 Letter from the politburo of the SED to Brezhnev, 21 January 1971, IPA NL2/32
37 Przybylski, *Tatort*, vol. 1, p. 304.
38 Alfred Neumann, Berlin, 7 April 1993.
39 See Przybylski, *Tatort* vol. 2, p.32.
40 Melvin Croan, 'Meinungen zum Führungswechsel in der SED', *Deutschland Archiv* 4 (1971): p.575.
41 Lippmann, *Honecker*, p.221.
42 Spittmann, 'Warum Ulbricht stürzte', p.569.
43 Moreton, Wettig and Lippmann agree. For a detailed analysis of the dispute over Berlin see Moreton, *East Germany*, pp.160-174, 179-193, and p.198, note 62; Gerhard Wettig, *Community and Conflict in the Socialist Camp* (London, 1975), pp.82-114.
44 Most commentators believe the decision was made in Moscow at the 24th CPSU conference at the end of March 1971, and then accepted by the majority of the SED in April. Spittmann opts for early April, (Spittmann, 'Warum Ulbricht stürzte', p.568), while Moreton and Wettig believe the decision was only made towards the end of the month. (Moreton, *East Germany*, p.185; Wettig, *Community and Conflict*, p.94). See also Martin McCauley and Stephen Carter, eds., *Leadership and Succession in the Soviet Union, Eastern Europe and China* (London, 1986), pp.64-65.
45 McAdams, *East Germany*, p.115.
46 SAPMO-BArch J IV 2/2A/1509 (15 April 1971)
47 Lippmann, *Honecker*, p.224.
48 Spittmann, 'Warum Ulbricht stürzte', p.569.
49 SAPMO-BArch J IV 2/2A/1514 (20 May 1971)
50 Manfred Uschner, Berlin, 21 July 1993.
51 SAPMO-BArch IV VIII/123
52 SAPMO-BArch J IV 2/2A/1515 (1 June 1971)
53 SAPMO-BArch IV 2/1/427 (10 June 1971)

54 Numerous articles on the subject appeared in journals, including: Ilse Spittmann, 'Honecker und die nationale Frage', *Deutschland Archiv* 5 (1972): pp.1-2; Jens Hacker, 'Der Begriff der Nation aus der Sicht der DDR', *Gegenwartskunde* 4 (1972): pp.391-403; John Sturrels, 'Nationalism in the GDR', *Canadian Review of Studies in Nationalism* 10 (1974): pp.23-37; Peter-Christian Ludz, 'Zum Begriff der Nation in der Sicht der SED - Wandlungen und politische Bedeutung', *Deutschland Archiv* 5 (1972): pp.17-27; Dettmar Cramer, 'Einheitspartei und Nation', *Deutschland Archiv* 5 (1972): p.457-64.
55 *Protokoll der Verhandlungen des VIII Parteitages der SED*, 2 vols. (East Berlin, 1971), vol. 1, p.49, my italics.
56 Zieger, *Die Haltung*, p.136.
57 McAdams, *East Germany*, pp.142-143.
58 SAPMO-BArch J IV 2/2A/1519
59 SAPMO-BArch J IV 2/2A/1500
60 SAPMO-BArch J IV 2/2A/1500
61 An article on the socialist German nation in the GDR appeared in the Soviet journal *Communist* in 1971, author unknown. A copy is located in SAPMO-BArch NL 182/1362.
62 For example, Hofmann, *Eine neues Deutschland*, p.251, although he is well aware that this was not the case. Jürgen Hofmann, Berlin, 11 May 1993.
63 SAPMO-BArch IV VIII/18
64 McCauley, *Leadership and Succession*, p.65.
65 Przybylski, *Tatort*, vol. 2, p.32.
66 Alfred Neumann, Berlin, 4 May 1993.
67 Ludz, 'Zum Begriff,' pp.21, 26.
68 Zeiger, *Die Haltung*, p.137.
69 SAPMO-BArch IV 2/1/471
70 Albert Norden, 'Zwei deutsche Nationalstaaten', *Deutschland Archiv* 5 (1973): p. 417.
71 Albert Norden, *Fragen des Kampfes gegen den Imperialismus* (East Berlin, 1972), pp. 22-23. Cited in Zimmermann, ed., *DDR Handbuch*, vol. 2, pp. 924-926.
72 Norden, *Fragen des Kampfes*, pp. 22-23.
73 Albert Norden, 'Fragen des Kampfes gegen den Imperialismus', speech given at the Partei Hochschule 'Karl Marx', July 1972, cited in *Deutschland Archiv* 4 (1972): p. 122. See also Norden, *Fragen des Kampfes*, p. 23.
74 Erich Honecker, 'Zügig voran bei der weiteren Verwirklichung der Beschlüsse des 8. Parteitages', *Reden und Aufsätze*, 12 vols. (East Berlin, 1975), vol. 2, pp. 239-242.
75 Honecker, 'Zügig voran', p.241

76 SAPMO-BArch IV 2/1/473
77 Honecker, 'Zügig voran', p.241.
78 Helmut Meier, Berlin, 15 March 1993.
79 Kurt Hager, 'Die entwickelte sozialistische Gesellschaft, Aufgaben der Gesellschaftswissenschaften nach dem 8. Parteitag', *Einheit* 26 (1971): p. 1231.
80 SAPMO-BArch IV A2/2.024/55
81 SAPMO-BArch NL281/85
82 125th anniversary of the Communist Manifesto, *Neues Deutschland*, 15 March 1973.
83 Helmut Meier, Berlin, 28 May 1993.
84 Alfred Kosing, Berlin, 11 February 1993.
85 Jürgen Hofmann, Berlin, 11 May 1993.
86 For example, the members of the AfG consulted P.N. Fedosseyev, *Leninism and the National Question in the Current Circumstances* (Moscow, 1972), (SAPMO-BArch NL182/922), and Jürgen Hofmann mentions Bromlei and Kaltachtschjan. Hofmann, Berlin, 11 May 1993.
87 Papers from the conference were published in *Sozialismus und Nation* (East Berlin, 1976).
88 The author is grateful to Martin McCauley for his helpful comments on this subject.
89 Jürgen Hofmann, Berlin, 11 May 1993.
90 Papers from the conference were published in *Sozialismus und Nation* (East Berlin, 1976).
91 SAPMO-BArch J IV 2/3A/2035
92 SAPMO-BArch J IV 2/3A/2035
93 SAPMO-BArch J IV 2/3A/2049
94 Alfred Kosing, Berlin, 5 February 1993.
95 Alfred Kosing, Berlin, 7 July 1993.
96 Alfred Kosing and Walter Schmidt, 'Zur Herausbildung der sozialistische Nation in der DDR', *Einheit* 29 (1974): pp.179-188.
97 Kosing, 'Illusion und Wirklichkeit', pp. 15-22.
98 Alfred Kosing and Walter Schmidt, 'On the Evolution of the Socialist Nation in the GDR', in McCardle and Boenau (eds.), *East Germany*, pp.4-5.
99 Kosing and Schmidt, 'On the Evolution', p.13.
100 Kosing and Schmidt, pp.8-9.
101 Kosing and Schmidt, p.11.
102 Kosing and Schmidt, p.12.
103 Kosing and Schmidt, p.14.
104 Alfred Kosing, Berlin, 5 February 1993 and 7 July 1993.
105 Jürgen Hofmann, Berlin, 11 May 1993.
106 Koenen, *Nation und Nationalbewußtsein*, p.18.

107	*Kleines Politisches Wörterbuch*, 1st ed., p.428.
108	Karl-Wilhelm Frick, 'Kleines Politisches Wörterbuch politisch revidiert', *Deutschland Archiv* 6 (1973): p.756. Kosing's contribution to another reference book, *Philosophisches Wörterbuch*, 8th ed., 2 vols. (East Berlin, 1971), is almost identical. Cited in Koenen, *Nation und Nationalbewußtsein*, pp.18-19.
109	SAPMO-BArch IV B2/9.04/115
110	*DDR Handbuch*, 3rd ed., Vol. 2, p.939.
111	SAPMO-BArch IV A2/2.028/122
112	SAPMO-BArch IV A2/2.028/42
113	SAPMO-BArch IV 2/1/460
114	SAPMO-BArch IV B2/9.04/43
115	Harry Krisch, 'Official Nationalism', in Lyman H. Legters (ed.), *The GDR a Developed Socialist Society* (Boulder, Colerado, 1978), p. 116.
116	Jürgen Hofmann, Berlin, 5 February 1993.
117	Very little has been written about the Sorbs. For an official East German history see Klaus J. Schiller and Manfred Tiemann, *Geschichte der Sorben*, 4 vols., (Bautzen, 1979). (Vol. 4 covers the GDR period). For a western account see Gerald Stone, *The Smallest Slavonic Nation. The Sorbs of Lusatia* (London, 1972).
118	See Elise Riesel, *Der Stil der deutschen Alltagsrede* (Moscow, 1964), p.7, cited in Erhard Hexelschneider and Erhard John, *Kultur als einigendes Band?* (East Berlin, 1984), p. 66; Schweigler, *National Consciousness*, pp. 46, 79; Zimmermann, ed., *DDR Handbuch*, vol. 2, pp. 1261-1265.
119	Alfred Kosing, Berlin, 11 February 1993.
120	Jürgen Hofmann, Berlin, 1 March 1993.
121	SAPMO-BArch IV A2/9.02/158. See also IfGA, ZPA 14350.
122	SAPMO-BArch IV B2/9.04/13
123	Helmut Meier, Berlin, 15 March 1992.
124	SAPMO-BArch IV B2/9.04/20
125	SAPMO-BArch IV B2/9.04/13
126	SAPMO-BArch IV B2/9.04/13
127	SAPMO-BArch IV B2/9.04/13
128	SAPMO-BArch IV B2/9.04/29
129	Hofmann, *Ein neues Deutschland*, p. 277.
130	Identified in Carl Pletsch, 'The "Socialist Nation in the GDR" or the Asymmetry in Nation and Ideology between the Two Germanies', *Comparitive Studies in Society and History* 21 (1979): p.344.
131	Hofmann, *Ein neues Deutschland*, p. 27.
132	For details see Kupper, 'Political Relations', pp.298-308; Zieger, *Die Haltung*, pp. 141-158.
133	Diemer, ed. *Kurze Chronik*, p.91.

134	Werner Lamberz, 16 November 1972, IfGA, ZPA 11527.
135	Hofmann, *Ein neues Deutschland*, p. 282-283.
136	McAdams, *East Germany*, p.147; Helmut Meier, Berlin, 15 March 1993.
137	SAPMO-BArch IV A2/9.02/158
138	IfGA, ZPA 14350
139	IfGA, ZPA 14350
140	SAPMO-BArch IV B2/9.04/29
141	IfGA, ZPA 14350
142	IfGA, ZPA 14350
143	According to Lamberz, SAPMO-BArch IV 2/2.033/24
144	SAPMO-BArch IV 2/2.033/24
145	SAPMO-BArch IV 2/2106/20; also SAPMO-BArch IV B2/9.04/29
146	IfGA, ZPA 14350
147	SAPMO-BArch IV A2/9.03/5
148	IfGA, ZPA 11533
149	IfGA, ZPA 11533
150	Axen, *Zur Entwicklung der sozialistischen Nation in der DDR*, (East Berlin, 1973), p. 18.
151	SAPMO-BArch IV 2/2.035/170
152	Axen, *Zur Entwicklung*, p. 26.
153	Axen, p. 15.
154	Hermann Axen, 'Zwei Staaten - zwei Nationen; Deutsche Frage existiert nicht mehr', *Deutschland Archiv* 5 (1973): p. 415; Axen, *Zur Entwicklung*, p.24.
155	SAPMO-BArch IV 2/2.035/170
156	Helmut Meier, in a review of Hermann Axen's 'Zur Entwicklung der Sozialistischen Nation in der DDR', *Einheit* 28 (1973): p. 1378.
157	Manfred Uschner, Berlin, 21 July 1993.
158	Alfred Neumann, Berlin, 4 May 1993.
159	Zeiger, *Die Haltung*, p.188-189.
160	Hofmann *Ein neues Deutschland* p.263
161	SAPMO-BArch IV B2/9.04/13
162	Erich Honecker, 'Errungenschaften und tiefgreifende Veränderungen im Leben des Volkes müssen in der Verfassung Ausdrück finden', Rede zur Begründung des Gesetzes zur Ergänzung und Änderung der Verfassung der DDR, 27 September 1974, *Reden und Aufsätze* (East Berlin, 1976), vol. 3, pp. 105-110.
163	Zieger, *Die Haltung*, p.187.
164	Hofmann, *Ein neues Deutschland*, p.265
165	Zieger, *Die Haltung*, p.188.
166	Zieger, p.190.
167	SAPMO-BArch IV B2/9.04/21
168	SAPMO-BArch IV B2/9.04/13

5 The 'socialist German nation' – from consolidation to crisis

The concept of a GDR-nation that was socialist but not German had clearly been a desperate attempt to prove that nothing linked the state to its western neighbour, and that the GDR was a legitimate entity in itself. It is hardly surprising that such a bizarre and sudden change of policy was greeted with dismay by the East German population and mocked by the West German government. In the first section of the following chapter, we shall see how the SED was provided with an 'ideological loophole'[1] by theorists which remedied the situation. This took the form of a distinction between nation, nationality and citizenship, resulting in the replacement of the notion of a purely 'socialist nation' in the GDR with the more credible 'socialist *German* nation' in official parlance, which appeared to be the most acceptable solution available: the SED was satisfied because the 'socialist German nation' was still socialist, while the population was relieved to know that it was still German. The party leadership believed it had finally found a *Nationskonzept* which would put an end to public uncertainty regarding the nation and which would therefore prove the legitimacy of the state.

The second section of this chapter examines the consequences of the new concept during the early 1980s, including the leadership's reluctance to reopen debate on the nation once an apparently acceptable solution had been found, and the official re-evaluation of the GDR's relationship to German history, which became both possible and necessary due to the acknowledgement of the Germanness of the GDR and its people. However, as the decade progressed, it was not only the past which was to raise questions regarding the relationship between the two German states and the condition of the German nation. Widespread concern regarding the threat posed to world peace by the nuclear arms race highlighted the artificial division of Cold War Europe, and of Germany in particular, and placed all Germans in a uniquely dangerous situation.

The third section examines the sudden return of the nation to the political agenda in the late 1980s, and as a result, to the academic agenda. The issue had been simmering away beneath the surface during the early 1980s, and the advent of

President Gorbachev to the Kremlin changed the SED's attitude towards socialist internationalism, although the final turning point appears to have been Honecker's highly symbolic official visit to the Federal Republic in 1987. The period is an example of how the SED attempted to suppress the problem of the German nation, while simultaneously attempting to use certain aspects of it to enhance the legitimacy of the GDR and for economic gain. It also shows that although the party controlled academic activity, it also relied on scholars to provide the arguments to back up dubious policies. In reality, however, the SED had merely brushed the idea of the German nation under the carpet, where it continued to erode the legitimacy of the GDR, until the opportunity arose for it to resurface, due to events beyond the SED's control.

Nationality: German; citizenship: GDR

At the 13th plenum of the Central Committee in December 1974, Honecker first distinguished between nation, nationality and citizenship, which finally put an end to the paranoia regarding the word 'German'. This has been interpreted as an attempt to distinguish the GDR from the Federal Republic without abandoning all of its heritage,[2] and as a sign of a more relaxed position regarding *Abgrenzung* on the part of Honecker,[3] although it is unlikely that he devoted much attention to the concept of the nation, merely adopting this convenient distinction because the denial of the Germanness of the GDR and its citizens had become untenable.

In fact the distinction between nation, nationality and citizenship, which appeared to make them compatible, was originally devised by the theorists, Alfred Kosing and Walter Schmidt. They argued that in spite of the fact that people were first and foremost citizens of the GDR, their nationality remained German (with the exception of the Sorbs), and that since nations were defined by class, both German and Sorb citizens belonged to the socialist nation in the GDR. Although they favoured a class-based definition of a nation, they had been outraged by the 'de-Germanisation' of what was, after all, still the German Democratic Republic, hence they took it upon themselves to work out a sensible concept of the socialist German nation. However, since they wanted to retain their academic positions, they were careful not to contradict the stance of the Eighth Party Congress. Their new theory was first published in the in-house journal of the Academy for Social Sciences, which was then brought to the attention of the ruling elite. According to the theorists:

> The socialist nation in the GDR is without doubt of *German nationality*, and it goes without saying that it encompasses those ethnic and social-psychological peculiarities that have arisen from the history of the German people, which goes back more than a thousand years. Due to specific historical circumstances, it is forming on one part of the territory of the former unitary capitalist German nation.[4]

This seems to be the first occasion where the distinction was made between the nation, which was essentially a socio-political concept, and nationality which was ethnically determined. In this way it was hoped that official paranoia regarding the word 'German' would cease. According to Kosing, German nationality was to the socialist nation in the GDR, what Russian or Ukrainian nationality was to the Soviet socialist nation. While the socialist nation in the GDR was relatively young, its nationality had a history stretching back over 400 years.[5] The authors also warned against underestimating the strength of ethnic factors, including language, origin, background, customs, practices and traditions.

Adopting this argument, Honecker told the Central Committee:

> Our socialist state is called the German Democratic Republic because the vast majority of her citizens are of German nationality. Therefore, there is no cause for confusion when filling out the forms that are necessary now and then, for example, for marriages and the reunion of families. The answer to such questions is simple, clear and unambiguous: citizenship: GDR; nationality: German.[6]

After maintaining a policy of 'de-Germanisation' for several years, Honecker now claimed, 'As Germans we have a claim to German history in the same way that as Europeans, we have a claim to European history'. However, he added, 'In our socialist German state, there is naturally no place for excessive Germanness *(Deutschtümelei)*.' He predicted that socialism would not make a detour around the Federal Republic, but did not go as far as to forecast the eventual establishment of a united socialist Germany.[7]

Kosing and Schmidt were asked by politburo member, Hermann Axen, to write a popular version of their article for *Neues Deutschland*,[8] and it may have been no coincidence that they were both awarded the prestigious National Prize of the GDR in 1975. Even though it was their idea, the obligation to quote the First Secretary's remarks from the recent session of the Central Committee gave the impression that he had devised the theory himself.

On this occasion they tackled the awkward issue of ethnicity:

> Shared ethnic characteristics certainly do play an important role in the formation of nations, but it is not they which integrate the classes and strata of a population into a nation, but economic, social, political and ideological relationships... This whole complexity of ethnic characteristics, traits and features of a population is described as 'nationality.' Therefore the concept of nationality is narrower than the concept of the nation, because it includes only one of the components of the nation, and what is more, not the most decisive. The concept of the nation is essentially more comprehensive because it includes the totality of socio-historic factors, together with ethnic ones.[9]

The authors even claimed that with the consolidation of the socialist nation, ethnic characteristics would change over time and develop 'socialist content'.[10]

Although no precise data can be found on the level of popular acceptance of the distinction between nationality and citizenship, the new theory appears to have been generally well received, and people were relieved to know that they were still allowed to be Germans, especially those who had no desire for a stronger bond with the Soviet Union and Warsaw Pact states. The Sorb minority were also relieved to hear that they would not be forced to give up their nationality, thereby losing generous minority rights on matters of culture and education. The distinction put an end to the crazy 'de-Germanisation' campaign which had done so much harm to the regime's credibility both at home and in the eyes of the world, and people could now use the word 'German' freely again, without fear of the consequences. According to information from the West German authorities, two-thirds of East Germans still refused to label the Federal Republic a foreign nation.[11]

In 1976, Kosing's book *Die Nation in Geschichte und Gegenwart* (The Nation in History and the Present) was published, which remained the most comprehensive East German work on the subject until 1989, securing Kosing's position as the leading authority on the subject, hence it warrants attention. The book expanded on Kosing's recent articles[12] and was an attempt to explain both general Marxist-Leninist nation theory and the evolution of the 'socialist German nation' in the GDR. However, it did not go unnoticed that Kosing had earlier been a 'vehement advocate of Ulbricht's confederation plan', but now appeared to be a 'relentless champion of Honecker's course of *Abgrenzung*'.[13] This was presumably due to the fact that Kosing, a party member since 1946, held a chair in Marxist-Leninist philosophy at the AfG and wanted to keep it.

The basic hypothesis of Kosing's book was that according to a Marxist-Leninist definition of a nation, the two halves of the German nation had grown so far apart, both socially and politically, and their international relationships so diametrically opposed, that two separate and irreconcilable nations now existed. Furthermore, these developments could not have been foreseen by the author, by the SED leadership, nor indeed by anyone during the early 1960s. Kosing acknowledged the fact that the SED had earlier sought the reunification of the nation in a unitary state, and admitted that he himself had written that the division of Germany as a state would not lead to the establishment of two separate nations. His justification for this dramatic U-turn was that historic development often changed circumstances, making previously realistic goals unrealistic, and making it necessary to reconsider theories, even to correct them. After all, had not leading West German politicians altered their stance regarding the status of the GDR as an independent state? He believed that the time would come when they would also have to accept the existence of an independent socialist German nation, which was a permanent member of the community of socialist nations.[14]

Kosing made it clear from the start that the idea that the GDR was not a German state was absurd, but aware of the consequences of negative comment about the regime, he carefully directed his criticism at Bonn's accusations that the SED was taking leave of the German nation,[15] as opposed to criticisms of actual policies, which had indeed aimed to 'de-Germanise' the GDR. Any elements undeniably shared with West Germans, such as culture, language, etc., were conveniently explained as aspects of nationality, which was of secondary importance to the social and economic factors which defined nations. Stalin's definition of a nation was considered inadequate because it was merely a list of fixed characteristics and paid no attention to 'the social function and historic role of the nation'.[16] Instead, Kosing concentrated on the work of Engels and Lenin in an attempt to prove that the classic writers of Marxism-Leninism had also distinguished between membership of a nation on the one hand (which was socially determined), and of an ethnic community on the other, that is to say, between nation and nationality.[17]

Turning to the awkward question of language, Kosing pointed out that according to Lenin, common languages had played a particularly important role as facilitators of trade within limited areas long before the establishment of nations, but had been superseded by economic, social and political factors which currently determined nations.[18] Kosing interpreted Engels' theory that the borders of nations should be determined by 'language and sympathies' to mean that wherever possible, the borders of nations should coincide with the borders of nationality or ethnicity, citing Engels' example of the inhabitants of Savoy, who had opted to join the Italy instead of France, and also the case of the people of Alsace and Lorraine, who, in spite of their German nationality, chose to join the French nation for social and political reasons.[19] On the subject of ethnicity, Kosing stated, 'Ethnic factors, which have arisen from German history in its entirety, have joined forces with the qualitatively new social content of the nation. They alone cannot justify a national unity, although they are decisive for nationality, which should not be confused with nation.'[20] All in all, Kosing's treatment of ethnicity was not entirely convincing, and his attempts to adapt theories by Engels and Lenin to fit the unique case of the GDR seemed somewhat laboured, and in his treatment of ethnicity, he ignored the question of race or blood.

'Socialist national consciousness', according to Kosing, arose from the social system of the socialist nation in the GDR, as opposed to being based on identification with the ethnic German nation, and continued to combine socialist patriotism with proletarian internationalism. Kosing criticised West German attempts to nurture an all-German consciousness, and, obviously aware of the dangers they posed, stated:

> In view of such attempts to undermine the socialist community with the help of a flexible nationalism, extremely careful ideological work to deepen socialist German national consciousness (which unites patriotism and internationalism, and knows neither national arrogance nor national

nihilism), is a permanent task of the Marxist-Leninist Party, all social organisations and especially of educational institutions in the GDR.[21]

He cited several western commentators who had identified a unique GDR-consciousness since the late 1960s, including Gebhard Schweigler, John Dornberg and Jean Edward Smith.[22]

However, as has been noted elsewhere,[23] Kosing never adequately explained the relationship between the working class in the GDR and their counterparts in the Federal Republic, and whether or not two nations were developing there, one socialist and the other bourgeois. In his conclusion, Kosing stated, 'The question of whether in the future, when a socialist revolution has triumphed in the FRG and a socialist nation arisen, a unitary socialist German nation could again develop, cannot be positively or negatively answered from the present situation.'[24] This contradicted what he had argued throughout the book, although Honecker himself had dropped a similar hint in 1973,[25] and would do so again. In conclusion, it has been noted that Kosing's theories were essentially 'a combination of historic materialism and communication theory',[26] 'designed to fashion a concept of the nation to suit the domestic functions of legitimacy and political stabilisation'.[27] However, in his defence, he did his best to justify the unjustifiable, a task that most leading functionaries were either intellectually incapable of or saw little need for. He had to perform a theoretical juggling act with party statements, Marxist-Leninist principles and ideas of his own, and as a result, personified the dilemma between the interests of the party and scholarship in the GDR.

The new Party Programme of 1976

By 1976, the Party Programme was 13 years old, and both the party's objectives and the reality of socialism in the GDR had changed dramatically. The existence of two seemingly irreconcilable German states had been confirmed by their full participation in the CSCE in 1975 and their acceptance of the Helsinki Final Act. Also that year, the SED had signed a Treaty of Friendship, Co-operation and mutual Assistance with the Soviet Union, which according to Hermann Axen, 'strengthened the objective process of growing together among socialist nations, and the evolution of the socialist nation and the irrevocability of the victory of socialism in the GDR.'[28] Clearly there was a need to bring the Party Programme in line with the Eighth Party Congress and with subsequent developments, indeed one wonders why this was not done earlier, since it was first suggested in July 1972.[29]

A Commission chaired by the First Secretary himself was formed to draw up a proposal and there appears to have been little input from the rest of the politburo. However, in contrast to the hurried, undemocratic way in which the new constitution had been rushed through in 1974, a draft Party Programme was published in *Neues Deutschland*[30] and readers were invited to submit suggestions as to how it might be improved in order to give an impression of democracy, albeit on a limited scale. Party representatives visited work places and local organisations to answer questions about the draft and to propagate the Party line.[31] The Secretary for Agitation, Werner Lamberz, monitored public reactions to concepts such as the socialist German nation, and concluded that the 'state consciousness' of the citizens was now secure, and that a 'socialist national consciousness' was developing. He added that the international recognition of the GDR had increased citizens' pride in the GDR and their identification with it, and that it had been possible to dispel the notion of a unitary German nation. However, Lamberz was realistic enough to recognise that due to a 'mass nationalistic campaign by the enemy', illusions concerning the things common to both German states persisted, and that more propaganda addressing the 'two irreconcilably conflicting class-lines in German history' was required 'to counteract imperialistic claims of a common German history'.[32] Public discussion of the proposed new Party Programme had highlighted the prevalence of what Lamberz called 'woolly ideas' regarding the socialist nation. Thus a clearer explanation of its nature and future was necessary, even though the socialist German nation was apparently 'developing according to plan'. It was recognised that ideological work needed to stress the increasingly close relationships between socialist nations, and would have to counteract West German claims that the socialist nation was merely invented by the SED to cause conflict between the GDR and the Federal Republic.[33]

Of 1,695 submissions from the public to the Programme Commission, 38 related directly to the question of the nation, 30 of which were in some way incorporated into the finished item.[34] As was the case with the drafting of the new constitution in 1968, it seems unlikely that people responded of their own initiative, and more likely that local party organisations encouraged them to do so. From these, and from reports of public discussion, four problem areas connected to the concept of the socialist German nation were identified. Firstly, the sentence in the Party Programme 'By taking power, the working class establishes itself as the nation', had caused confusion regarding the position of other social strata. Since the SED always portrayed the bourgeois nation in the Federal Republic as class-divided, it was understandable that they should portray the socialist nation in the GDR as free from all class antagonism, hence in the final version, the sentence was changed to: 'By taking power the working class, to which other strata are allied, have created the decisive prerequisites for the formation of the socialist nation.'[35]

Secondly, there was concern about the claim that the socialist nations were growing together, and some people even asked whether this meant that the GDR would eventually become a republic of the Soviet Union.[36] The leadership does not appear to have had an answer to this, but it seems inconceivable that even Soviet sympathisers such as Honecker would have advocated a total merging of all the socialist nations in Eastern Europe and the Soviet Union.

Thirdly, in spite of the distinction between nationality and citizenship, people still noticed inconsistencies in the use of the word 'German' in the names of institutions, etc. It was suggested that the SED should be renamed 'Communist

Party of the GDR' because 'if there is no such thing as "Germany," there cannot be a "Socialist Unity Party of Germany".'[37] However, this was rejected by the Programme Commission on the grounds that 'the name has arisen historically, therefore it would be politically incorrect to change it.'[38] The issue arose so often that a detailed article was published in *Neues Deutschland* to clarify the Party's stance:

> Whoever has a good name does not want to lose it or give it up... The name SED preserves the memory of a historic event in the history of the German workers' movement... 'Socialist' is fitting because we are forming a developed socialist society. 'Unity Party' is correct because the SED is the united party of the working class in our land. 'Of Germany' is right, because our party represents the socialist Germany... But our name does not only mean something to us - it also enjoys recognition and prestige far around the world... The organ of the Central Committee also has precisely the right name: *Neues Deutschland*. It is the leading newspaper of the leading party in the socialist Germany, the GDR, which is the new Germany in comparison to the FRG, the old Germany, which remains on the level of capitalism.[39]

Furthermore, the suggestion that the 'German Democratic Republic' should be renamed 'German Socialist Republic' was also rejected on the grounds that it had arisen historically and expressed the socialist character of the state. In addition, it was suggested that 'socialist German nation' should be replaced by 'socialist nation of the GDR', but this was dismissed, as were all examples of 'national nihilism', which showed that the SED was keen to retain the benefits of national sentiment when it suited them.[40]

Finally, the goal of overcoming the division of the German nation which appeared in the 1963 programme appeared to cause confusion, and the Programme Commission decided that this objective had been overtaken by history.[41] However, since the proposal mentioned the inevitable transformation of all countries to socialism, some people assumed this included the Federal Republic and that a chance for reunification still existed.[42]

Although academics were given the opportunity to contribute to the new Party Programme, their main task was to examine and explain the document only after it had been accepted by the next Party Congress.[43] Even Kosing and Schmidt's proposal for the section on the socialist German nation was not used.[44]

The finished article incorporated the changes to the GDR's status and to the concept of the nation which had occurred during the 1970s. The German nationality of the majority of the population (with the exception of the Sorbs), was acknowledged and the socialist German nation was said to be historically rooted in the struggle of the German people for social progress over several centuries. A socialist national culture, which incorporated the progressive and humanist heritage of German history and the achievements of world culture, especially those of the Soviet Union, was said to be growing, as was a socialist national consciousness, composed of socialist patriotism and proletarian internationalism, organically bound together. Furthermore, the party itself was allegedly 'leading the process of the further development of the socialist nation in the GDR according to plan, which is flourishing on the social foundation of socialism and growing towards the other socialist nations.'[45] The Party Programme was accepted by the Ninth Party Congress in May 1976. There Honecker himself used the phrases 'socialist *German* nation' and 'two independent sovereign *German* states'. But with reference to the German question, he stated 'Nothing about it is open - history had her say a long time ago.'[46]

The GDR certainly had come a long way since the Eighth Party Congress, and people were beginning to come to terms with the socialist nation now that it was officially still German. Even so, this maintained a link with the FRG, and however much the SED tried to deny it, the two German states were clearly not as foreign to each other as other states. For the time being, it seemed that the issue was closed, although even Honecker continued to make ambiguous remarks about possibilities in the event of the socialist transformation of the Federal Republic. The increase in official contact between the two German capitals during the 1980s suggested that he too accepted that a unique relationship did exist between the two states, a relationship which could be exploited to the SED's advantage.

The leadership and the 'socialist German nation'

From the late 1970s, the leadership of the GDR rarely addressed the question of the nation, suggesting that the line represented in the new Party Programme of 1976 was the last word on the subject. Honecker himself said that terms such as 'nation' and 'fatherland' had acquired new meanings through socialism.[47] Even so, after three decades, the legitimacy of the GDR still could not be taken for granted due to the absence of democracy and personal freedoms, in addition to its economic short-comings. Furthermore, during the 1980s, the state was to become increasingly susceptible to events in neighbouring countries to the East and West which threatened to reopen the question of the GDR's *raison d'être*.

In 1980, Honecker's 'Gera demands' for the normalisation of relations between the two German states, including the transformation of their respective Permanent Representations into proper embassies and the recognition of GDR citizenship by the Federal Republic, marked a hardening of the SED's attitude towards relations with the Federal Government from 1980.[48] However, compared with the previous decade, the General Secretary's frequent use of the adjective 'German' was striking, for example, at the tenth party congress he referred to 'the two German states' and 'German soil',[49] and a few months earlier, he had aroused the attention of the West German media when he warned Bonn, 'One day socialism will knock on your door, and when the day comes when the workers of the Federal Republic set about the socialist transformation of the FRG, the question of the unification of the two German states will be a different matter.'[50] These apparent inconsistencies are hard to explain. While it has been suggested that Honecker's bizarre reference to unification was a sign that the SED still harboured all-German designs,[51] it seems more likely that Honecker was just being provocative since the warning to Bonn was not repeated, whereas the uncompromising 'Gera demands' were.

From the early 1980s, the tactical nuclear weapons debate made the link between the two German states even more difficult to ignore. It created the sense of a shared fate, but also of a joint responsibility for peace, and led to a commitment to ensure that war would never again break out on German soil,[52] which implied that 'German soil' still meant something. Honecker himself spoke of the need for the two German states to form a 'coalition of sense' *(Koalition der Vernunft)* in the interest of peace.[53] In fact, the leadership was forced to confront the issue due to the growth of an unofficial peace movement in the GDR.[54] Such groups were illegal and unprecedented in East Germany, but were encouraged by the rise of the West German peace movement, visible on their television screens. As a result, contact between prominent representatives of the GDR and the Federal Republic increased considerably, culminating in a meeting between Honecker and Helmut Schmidt in 1981, which inevitably raised hopes regarding détente. During the early 1980s, various subjects were discussed on many separate occasions by representatives from both sides, including credit for the GDR, the inner-German border, humanitarian questions and the proliferation of nuclear weapons in Europe.[55]

Such contacts highlighted the fact that the relationship between the two German states was far from normal, although their reasons for entering into dialogue were completely different. The SED denied the unity of the nation to support its claim that the GDR was an independent sovereign state. Bonn, on the other hand, almost recognised the GDR as a means to improve relations, which it hoped would preserve the national bond.[56] Honecker was willing to take advantage of Bonn's offer to pay substantial amounts of money to the GDR in order to achieve this, though he insisted that the German question was closed for good. Ironically, it was the veteran critic of the GDR, Franz-Josef Strauß, who negotiated an increased credit limit for the GDR in 1983. This apparent betrayal of his principles encouraged a handful of outraged CSU politicians to form a new far-right party, the *Republikaner*.

By this time, Honecker seemed to believe that the 'GDR-nation' was sufficiently secure and socialist that its Germanness was now no longer a threat, but an asset. In 1983, he demanded a Europe without nuclear weapons 'in the name of the German people',[57] and in a speech in 1984, addressed the population as Germans, as opposed to 'Citizens of the GDR'.[58] And not only were they Germans - the leadership seemed intent on proving that they were the best Germans. For example, in 1983, a headline in *Neues Deutschland* proudly proclaimed 'First German in space is a citizen of the GDR!'[59] This reversion to 'national argumentation' reminiscent of the 1950s and 1960s has been interpreted as a means for a more offensive *Deutschlandpolitik*, made possible by new circumstances which were more favourable for the GDR.[60] At the end of the day, it is most likely that the leadership of the GDR was well aware that the relationship between the two German states was bound to be abnormal, and therefore decided to exploit the situation for the GDR's financial gain, in return for fairly minor humanitarian concessions. The instability in neighbouring Poland at the beginning of the decade may also have encouraged the SED to prioritise patriotism over internationalism. Until this point, the regime had tirelessly stressed the need for solidarity with the working classes in other Eastern Bloc states, but it was a different matter when those workers were striking and organising themselves to demand better conditions, and were on the GDR's doorstep.

Theoretical debate on the 'socialist German nation'

The early 1980s were characterised by a constant battle between theorists who believed that it was dangerous to neglect the problem of the nation, and their superiors, who did not wish to antagonise the leadership of the SED by raising awkward questions. The politburo had not expressly stated that the issuewas closed, but their silence was sufficient to make minor functionaries fear the consequences if academics attempted to reopen it. Therefore, to keep the subject alive, members of the Academy for Social Sciences tried to win the support of its director, Otto Reinhold, who was a member of the Central Committee. Even though he is reputed to have been sympathetic to their cause, his deputies posed a major obstacle between Reinhold and scholars at the institution, though he in turn had to conform to the wishes of the head of the Department of Sciences, Kurt Hager.[61]

The best way to guarantee the future of research was to ensure that the subject featured in the Department's 'Central Research Plan for the Social Sciences'. By chance, the Propaganda Department requested more material on socialist patriotism, socialist national consciousness and on the conflict between so-called 'counter-revolutionary theories' such as the 'openness of the German question' and the 'continued existence of the unity of the German nation' in the plan for 1981-86.[62] This suggests that the Department was aware that the message regarding the 'socialist German nation' had not yet gained popular acceptance. As a result, a new field of research *(Forschungsbereich)* on 'The Socialist Nation and History' was established at the Academy for Social Sciences, which facilitated new research.

The campaign to keep the nation alive as a subject for academic discourse was taken up by Jürgen Hofmann, a relatively young member of the Academy for Social Sciences and potential successor to Alfred Kosing as the leading authority on the nation in the GDR. In 1983, he completed a doctoral thesis on the evolution of the 'socialist German nation' and the national policies of the SED, supervised by the very individuals who had been responsible for the enhancement of the official line on the nation, Kosing and Schmidt. The same year, an academic committee was formed by individuals with an interest in the problem of the nation, chaired by Hofmann. Such committees had to be affiliated to a state-run academic institution and required the approval of its senior directors, which was a lengthy process. In this case, official permission was only granted due to politburo member Hermann Axen's personal interest in the subject. However, even after its formation, the future of the committee was uncertain due to the sensitivity of the topic concerned, and it was dissolved twice, resulting in the withdrawal of resources. Kosing and Hofmann hoped that the formation of the committee would enable them to conduct empirical research into the level of acceptance of the concept of the 'socialist German nation', but permission was refused.[63]

In spite of the lack of encouragement, behind the scenes, certain theorists retained an interest in the subject, although few publications appeared after the adoption of the new Party Programme until the late 1980s, shortly before the end of the GDR itself. Due to the lack of incentives, scholars turned their attention to less controversial subjects, in particular, those currently favoured by the leadership such as the reinterpretation of German history. During this period, only one article devoted to the 'socialist German nation' appeared in the theoretical journal *Einheit*[64] and one short book addressed the subject.[65] However, several articles did appear in the in-house journal of the Academy for Social Sciences,[66] and handful of doctoral dissertations were submitted.[67] A group from the AfG, which included all the big names on the subject of the nation - Kosing, Schmidt, Hofmann and Meier - produced a confidential paper outlining problems hindering the development of the Socialist German Nation in the GDR which was sent to Kurt Hager shortly before the Tenth Party Congress in 1981.[68] They also produced a paper during preparations for the 11th Party Congress in 1986, in which they expressed the opinion that ignoring the issue of the nation would lead to public uncertainty. However, because of this comment, it never reached the upper echelons of power - even Axen never received it - and Hofmann believed it was locked away because the deputy director of the institution feared the consequences of passing on material that could be interpreted as criticism of those responsible for agitation and propaganda.[69]

All these pieces of work contained similar ideas, partly because the same individuals (or students under their supervision) were responsible for them and also because the basic line on the nation had already been defined and incorporated into party documents, leaving little room for variation, and absolutely none for criticism. Leading theorists were reasonably happy with the party's current stance (which they had of course influenced during the mid-1970s), though most felt that certain qualifications were required, and attempted to slip them into their work. They were generally pleased that the regime had finally accepted that the socialist nation in the GDR was German, having denied this fact for several years, which they believed had had a damaging effect on national consciousness. They believed it would be useful to find out just how strongly German ethnic elements and socialist elements had become fused, and to assess the impact of customs and events unique to the GDR on national consciousness, such as anniversary celebrations and secular replacements for marriage and confirmation ceremonies.[70] But one problem remained, namely how to convince those responsible for public opinion research within the party leadership to agree to this.

The most important innovation in academic work on the concept of the nation in the GDR during the early 1980s was the recognition of the fact that the evolution of the nation was a long process, and that the distinction should be made between the foundation *(Konstituierung)* and consolidation *(Konsolidierung)* of the nation.[71] Theorists argued that the consolidation process would only be completed several generations later, and admitted that it was hindered by the presence of a bourgeois German nation next door,[72] though it was noted that the Austrian nation had been very quickly consolidated during the post-war period.[73] Here it can be seen that theorists were taking a more realistic view than party functionaries, who for political reasons, tended to state that a socialist nation had already developed in the GDR. But it also provided a convenient explanation for the weaknesses of the 'socialist German nation' which would apparently be resolved in time since the socialist nation was more of a goal or vision, than a description of the current situation.[74]

Theorists believed that without some form of 'socialist German national consciousness', the 'socialist German nation' was incomplete, and that it was essential that the population of the GDR perceived itself as a separate nation in view of the state's unique and vulnerable position. This suggests that they may have been influenced by the work of western scholars, although publicly they were obliged to criticise 'bourgeois ideologues' who attempted to prove the existence of a nation based exclusively on national consciousness.[75] However, official party material continued to define national consciousness in highly unemotional terms as an amalgamation of socialist patriotism and proletarian internationalism, and although Honecker talked about 'national pride' and 'the national honour of our socialist fatherland',[76] for him, 'national' was synonymous with socialist or GDR-wide.

Theorists were particularly concerned about the lack of empirical data on national consciousness but, as mentioned earlier, permission to undertake empirical research was hard to obtain. Until the mid-1980s, historians at the AfG, led by Professor Helmut Meier, investigated historical consciousness among the population, including their knowledge of German history and perceptions of the Federal Republic. While this research was officially sanctioned, there remained the problem of how to make the leadership take notice of the findings.[77] The Institute for Youth Research in Leipzig continued to monitor the views of young people, in particular, students, but again, the results were not sufficiently favourable for publication.

Furthermore, it was around this time that the Institute for Public Opinion Research was abolished following the sudden death of Werner Lamberz in 1978, who was one of the few politburo members to recognise its importance. Joachim Herrmann, Lamberz' successor, disbanded it, arguing that it had fulfilled its purpose, and anyway, 'We form public opinion ourselves.'[78] No doubt the real reason was that the findings rarely corresponded to what the leadership wanted to hear. Even though the findings showed that two-thirds of the population identified with the socialist nation in the GDR, this was not sufficient to satisfy the party leadership.[79]

In short, the main point theorists hoped to impress upon the leadership of the SED was that the nation was a living and developing organism, which required constant attention and should not be dropped from political and research agendas. Furthermore, effective propaganda was only possible if the current level of acceptance of the socialist German nation was known. The problem was that on the whole, the leadership did not want to hear suggestions which implied that there was a problem, or more often than not, minor functionaries assumed that they did not, and intercepted material before it could reach the decision-makers. All the leading theorists on the concept of the nation in the GDR have since complained of the frustration of wanting to help but not being listened to. However, a major development was the leadership's sudden interest in the GDR's relationship to German history, which was an attempt to dispel the charge that the 'socialist German nation' was rootless and therefore illegitimate, and was seen as a way to strengthen national consciousness among the population. By telling the story of the socialist revolution on German soil, from its origins in the days of feudalism till its ultimate triumph in the GDR, it was believed that the 'national pride' of the population as citizens of the GDR would be strengthened.

The SED: 'heir to everything progressive in the history of the German people'

The new Party Programme of 1976 not only acknowledged that the socialist nation in the GDR was German, but also emphasised that its 'socialist national culture' had a moral duty to 'uphold the rich heritage created during the entire history of the German people'. The state was no longer to be portrayed as a complete break with the past but as the climax of German history, and the SED itself was described as 'the heir to everything progressive in the history of the German people'.[80] While it is not necessary to examine all the publications, rehabilitations and celebrations which resulted, since an extensive literature on the subject already exists,[81] it is important to understand why this occurred and how it was then used to enhance the image of the 'socialist German nation'. Several reasons lay behind the re-assessment of German history.

Firstly, it appears that at long last, the SED recognised that every nation should have a 'national biography' and a 'historic personality'.[82] Until this point, the official concept of the nation had been based on an idealised version of the present, which did not match the reality of the situation in the GDR, and on a utopian vision of the future, which few believed the regime could deliver, indeed, a small group within the ruling elite itself knew it could not. West German governments had constantly accused the SED of 'taking leave of German history' to re-enforce the Federal Republic's own claim to be the only legitimate representative of the German nation. Thus by reclaiming German history, the SED aimed to prove not only that the GDR was German and historically legitimate, but also that it was more legitimate than the Federal Republic - a position reminiscent of the 1950s.

Secondly, as we have seen, the SED had finally accepted the fact that the population of the GDR and the FRG shared the same nationality. However, it was claimed that this did not alter the fact that a socialist nation existed in the former and a bourgeois nation in the latter, hence the leadership believed they could safely take advantage of selected aspects of German nationality such as German history, without undermining the claim that a separate GDR-nation had evolved.

Thirdly, the regime may well have been motivated by a desire to distinguish the GDR from other members of the Warsaw Pact, particularly during the unrest in Poland in the early 1980s, to deter people from copying their socialist brothers and sisters there. Later in the decade, even the Soviet model would be played down in favour of GDR-style socialism in an attempt to avoid reform.

Fourthly, even though the Institute for Public Opinion Research had been abolished, the party could still assess the public mood by examining applications to emigrate to the west and reports from the *Stasi*. Information on the unofficial peace movement in particular provided an indication of the strength of all-German feeling aroused by the nuclear debate. As a consequence, the regime may have recognised that the 'socialist German nation' lacked appeal, and identified its ambivalent relationship with the German past as both a cause, and a potential solution. Alternatively they may have believed that GDR-consciousness was by this time sufficiently strong that a revival of interest in the state's German heritage would enhance it as opposed to undermining it. While it is difficult to establish which of these was the true scenario on the evidence available, the leadership clearly believed that the advantages of linking the GDR to its German heritage outweighed the disadvantages, as the lavishness of the subsequent celebrations and architectural renovation showed. After all, the only other option was to ignore the GDR's German roots, a strategy adopted during the early 1970s which had failed spectacularly. Even so, later events, such as Honecker's sentimental behaviour while in the Federal Republic in 1987, and the SED's sudden panic about the German nation in the late 1980s, suggest a considerable degree of uncertainty regarding the validity of the concept of the 'socialist German nation', even among the ruling elite.

Finally, it appears that there was considerable enthusiasm for a more comprehensive examination of German history from historians themselves.[83] Until this point, German history had been divided into two traditions: the authoritarian aspects of Prussian history which had culminated in the Third Reich and were apparently continued by the Federal Republic; and the traditions of the peasant wars, the revolution of 1848, the KPD of the Weimar Republic and the anti-fascist resistance which supposedly lived on in the GDR.[84] During the 1970s, East German historians in the GDR had portrayed figures and events very much in black and white, either as totally good or totally bad, and without mention of the positive results of events considered essentially bad. This limited the range of subjects historians could write about, and encouraged them to stick to 'safe topics', fearing the consequences of tackling more controversial events, for example, being labelled 'bourgeois' and thus ostracised from the mainstream academic community. They had tended to concentrate on 'progressive' figures including Thomas Müntzer, Ernst Thälmann, Karl Liebknecht and Rosa Luxemburg, while controversial characters such as military heroes were effectively left to West German historians. Party bosses hoped that this would reinforce the claim that two separate nations with little in common existed on German soil. However, due to the tragic course of German history, this meant that the SED had rejected rather a large portion of that history.

In contrast, from the early 1980s, the new task of historians at state institutions such as the AdW's Institute for History, the AfG and the Institute for Marxism-Leninism (IML) was to portray 'the whole of German history as the national history of the GDR', though a significant distinction was made by historians between 'heritage' *(Erbe)*, which was shared by both German states and included both good and bad episodes, and 'tradition', which referred only to aspects considered to be progressive, and which supposedly only lived on in the GDR.[85] By paying attention to both the good and the bad strands of German history, it was hoped that the GDR could be shown to be the climax of the progressive strand, the triumph of good over evil, whereas the Federal Republic was portrayed as continuing the mistakes and injustices of the past.

The result was a sudden abundance of books and articles which for the first time covered events and personalities other than the workers' movement and the class struggle in Germany, including new biographies of Bismarck, Frederick the Great and Kaiser William I.[86] In the theoretical journal *Einheit,* one of the most popular topics during the early 1980s was the GDR as the highpoint of German history. In a typical article, the author recognised the need to uncover the roots of the 'socialist German nation', which were buried deep in the past, the need to publicise them, and to make them relevant to the present and the future.[87] However the writer was clearly aware of potential 'all-German illusions' that might arise from a more extensive treatment of German history:

> Between the GDR and FRG there exists neither a shared relationship with the past, nor some sort of historical 'all-German parentheses' around them. As Kurt Hager explained, '...the German question is not open. The GDR stands in the line of continuity of everything progressive, humanist and revolutionary in earlier German history. The ruling exploitative class in the FRG has no right to refer to the traditions of those forces and movements...'[88]

The 30th anniversary of the GDR in October 1979 was a demonstration of the SED's enthusiasm for the idea that the 'socialist German nation' was firmly rooted in German history in its entirety. However, the SED appeared to want it both ways, claiming, 'Our socialist state embodies the continuation of everything good in German history, while at the same time embodying a radical break with everything reactionary.'[89] Particularly striking was the personal involvement of Honecker, who was in fact born in the West German Saarland, close to the French border. During celebrations to mark the 30th anniversary of the GDR, he used language reminiscent of his predecessor, calling the state 'the new, socialist Germany'. The foundation of the state was proclaimed as 'the turning point in the history of the German people and of Europe' and 'the beginning of the triumphal march of socialism in the country of birth of Marx and Engels'![90] He even accepted that socialist national consciousness would be strengthened 'if we uphold and tend the progressive historical traditions of the entire history of the German people'.[91] In short, Honecker seemed to have reverted to the argument that the GDR was *the* legitimate German state, in competition with the Federal Republic with which it retained a special historic connection.

Martin Luther was the key figure in the SED's campaign to provide the 'socialist German nation' with a history, and subsequently to legitimise the GDR, in spite of the fact that he had previously been denounced for subservience to the princes. The intention was both to win over the population, particularly Christians, who were becoming increasingly involved in the peace movement, and also to enhance the international reputation of the GDR and its leader. Honecker personally set up the Martin Luther Committee in 1980, and claimed the GDR was realising 'the ideals of the best sons of the German people'.[92] The celebration of the quincentenary of Luther's birth in 1983 almost became a competition between the two German states as they both claimed Luther as their own, though here the GDR had a distinct advantage because the most important historical sites of the reformation were on East German territory. Suddenly the Federal Republic's claim to German history in its entirety was under threat. Chancellor Kohl called the lavish celebrations in the GDR 'a subtle attempt by the SED to use Luther to bind the concept of nation with that of socialism, as if there were a direct line of continuity from Frederick the Great to Erich Honecker',[93] which was precisely what the party was trying to do.

Honecker was challenged on this total reversal of official opinion regarding figures such as Luther and Clausewitz in an interview with Robert Maxwell in 1980. In response, the General secretary explained:

> When we acknowledge the historic achievements of Martin Luther and Carl von Clausewitz, it is quite in keeping with the traditions of Marx, Engels, Lenin, the German workers' movement and our history since 1945. However, we in no way ignore the limitations of these and other personalities of German history, their negative traits, their contradictory behaviour, or the historic tragedy in which they became entangled. An understanding of the objective, factual course and entire dialectic of history

conforms with our view of the world. A view of the greatness and the limitations of prominent personalities in history is part of that.[94]

Asked whether or not there was an element of risk involved when both the GDR and FRG celebrated the same national heroes, Honecker replied:

> Our approach to history and the past is quite different to that of the Federal Republic... We cannot possibly run the risk of celebrating the same national heroes as the FRG since you will search in vain for institutions bearing the names of Nazi greats in our country.[95]

In retrospect we can question the wisdom of the SED's decision to portray the 'socialist German nation' as a product of German history in its entirety. Unfortunately there was no longer an institute which monitored public opinion, therfore no precise data on the resonance of the new approach among the population exists. Research into historic consciousness was continued by historians at the AfG until 1984, but even if the results were available, they may well have been 'improved' to make them more palatable to the authorities.[96]

On the positive side, the new approach did provide the GDR with the 'national biography' and 'historic personality' which it had previously lacked. It gave people the same opportunity to celebrate their historical roots as their West German cousins and provided new opportunities for historical research. Furthermore, it helped make identification with the ethnic German nation compatible with allegiance to the East German state,[97] although this somewhat contradicted the SED's earlier claim that ethnicity was insignificant compared to class. Finally, it was very obvious that little had been gained by denying the German heritage of the socialist nation in the GDR, hence the party had little to lose.

However, there were clearly risks involved with the new approach, in particular, the danger that the population would be reminded of things they shared with West Germans, thus reinforcing the national bond, and arousing a latent desire for reunification. Furthermore, the SED's U-turn regarding figures such as Luther was highly unsubtle, as was the political motivation of the new approach. But for the party, offering its own version of events was preferable to letting Bonn get away with influencing the citizens of the GDR via West German television, and to being accused of having 'taken leave of history', since the GDR could hardly be the greatest achievement in the history of the German people if it bore no relationship to that history.

Ultimately, the intended effects of the GDR's new relationship with its past were bound to be limited, because the party was trying to prove something illogical, something that a substantial proportion of the population did not believe, namely that there were two separate German nations, one socialist, the other bourgeois, with certain things in common but nothing of real significance because their social and political systems determined their relationship. Even so, once it had accepted that the GDR was a German state, as was the Federal Republic, the SED had little choice but to address the issue of the state's relationship to its history. The episode highlighted the fact that in spite of the regime's claims that the GDR was an independent, sovereign state, with a (socialist) nation of its own, the ethnic German nation continued to undermine the legitimacy of the GDR. Also, while it had retained certain rather old-fashioned German traits which had been diluted by Americanisation and cosmopolitanism in the Federal Republic, the GDR could never be the 'best' German state when the yardsticks were economic success and genuine democracy. Thus the existence of the Federal Republic continued to challenge the GDR's *raison d'être,* while the reverse was never the case. Meanwhile, the leadership was about to be attacked on a second front, with the beginning of a new era in Moscow, which we now know marked the beginning of the end for the socialist German state.

The return of the nation to the political agenda

In the early and mid-1980s, the SED had stubbornly adhered to the line that the nation was not negotiable, in spite of the undeniable links between the two German states, which had intensified due to the peace issue. While a great deal of attention had been paid to the GDR's relationship to German history, the concept of the nation itself had lain dormant, in spite of theorists' attempts to keep it alive as a subject for debate. It was not mentioned at all at the 11th Party Congress in April 1986. However, in 1988, an internal working party was convened on 'the question of the nation', chaired by a member of the politburo, followed a year later by a new 'Interdisciplinary Academic Committee for Research on the Nation' at the Academy for Social Sciences, resulting in a sudden increase in publications addressing the topic. This officially sanctioned attention was in stark contrast to the leadership's indifference towards the issue for over a decade, and as before, it was no accident. It proves not only that the SED was aware that the problem of the nation still threatened to destroy the GDR, but also that the leadership believed it could be the state's salvation if handled correctly.

Three reasons for the return of the subject to the political agenda can be identified: Gorbachev's reforms and new hopes for détente across Europe; Honecker's official visit to the Federal Republic in 1987; and internal problems, especially the deepening economic crisis.[98] While the German aspect of the 'socialist German nation' had always raised doubts about the legitimacy of the GDR, both when it was emphasised and when it was denied, suddenly even its socialist character, until now taken for granted by the leadership, was becoming a liability due to unwelcome changes within the socialist bloc and the increasingly obvious short-comings of the centrally planned socialist economy. But it was socialism which differentiated the 'socialist German nation' from the 'bourgeois German nation' in the Federal Republic - indeed it was the only real justification for the existence of the GDR at all. In short, the very foundations on which the

GDR-nation had been constructed were suddenly being eroded by forces beyond the SED's control, hence a response was unavoidable, though ultimately in vain.

The challenge of perestroika and glasnost

The SED disapproved of both Gorbachev's internal reforms and his ideas for the future of Europe. The concept of a 'common European home' was particularly worrying, both because it raised questions about the sovereignty of the states concerned, and because it implied that Moscow was questioning the status quo in Europe, including the current solution to the German question. As the only guarantor of the future of the GDR, it was feared that Gorbachev might be willing to do a deal with the West against the wishes of the SED leadership.[99] Therefore the latter portrayed the 'common European home' as merely a mechanism for security and peace-keeping, which consisted of sovereign states, and which would always have a socialist wing and a capitalist wing.[100]

However, the one aspect of Gorbachev's approach that the party did approve of was the idea that each socialist state was free to determine its own brand of socialism, and that what was right for the Soviet Union would not necessarily be right for others.[101] This was christened the 'Sinatra doctrine' by Gennardy Gerasimov, i.e. doing it 'my way'.[102] For 15 years, Honecker, an ardent believer in proletarian internationalism, had proclaimed that 'To learn from the Soviet Union, is to learn to win', and that the Soviet model was the only model. But that was in the days of the communist old guard, with whom Honecker felt akin. Now he was keen to take up Gorbachev's offer of socialism *à la carte*, claiming that the development of socialism in individual states needed to be appropriate for 'national conditions'.[103] Precisely what these conditions were is unclear, but the intention was to avoid reform. As Kurt Hager put it: 'Just because your neighbour puts up new wallpaper in his flat, would you feel obliged to put up new wallpaper in your own flat?'[104]

Another problem was the impact of the charismatic Gorbachev on the East German population. He was regarded by many as a bringer of hope, rather like Brandt had been 15 years earlier. His popularity was demonstrated during the 750th anniversary of the founding of Berlin, celebrated on both sides of the Wall in June 1987, when a large group of young East Germans gathered near the Brandenburg Gate, chanting 'We want Gorbachev' and 'The wall must go'.[105] By stressing patriotism over internationalism, the SED aimed to discourage people from looking eastwards for hope, just as they had previously looked westwards. This strategy was also conceived as a means to distance the state from other socialist countries, particularly Poland, in order to reduce the risk of unrest spreading to the GDR, which had worried the leadership since the beginning of the decade. Merely to play down the events would not be sufficient because, 'all negative occurrences in socialist countries immediately enter the GDR via West German television', as Honecker himself acknowledged with unusual candour.[106]

In spite of continued verbal adherence to the principle of socialist internationalism, the SED responded to these developments with a more nationalistic stance based on the rather simplistic concept of 'socialism in the colours of the GDR'. The phrase had been introduced by Honecker at the seventh plenum of the Central Committee in 1988, and was often used during the final year of the GDR's existence. There he admitted that 'developments in the socialist world are more varied than many people previously believed'[107] (himself included presumably). The concept was not his own invention, but was adapted from an idea introduced by the leader of the French communist Party, Georges Marchais. Ironically, the SED had criticised Marchais during the mid-1970s for his advocation of 'socialism in French colours', but Honecker may have been persuaded to adopt a similar idea by his personal adviser and script-writer, Frank-Joachim Herrmann.[108] The concept was also reminiscent of Anton Ackermann's idea of a 'German road to socialism' dating back to 1946, which was subsequently condemned by the pro-Soviet leadership of the SED. However, whereas Ackermann had intended to keep out Stalinism, the new concept was 'a phrase to repel reform... in which reality and fiction became increasingly blurred'.[109]

These so-called 'colours' were in fact little more than the self-proclaimed achievements of the state (such as free education, scientific and technological innovation, full employment, adequate housing, and equality for women), combined with the traditions and experiences of the German workers' movement.[110] As Kurt Hager rather dishonestly explained, 'When we speak of "socialism in the colours of the GDR", what we mean is that we have gone our own unmistakeable way, that we have adapted Marxism-Leninism to fit our conditions, and that here, socialism bears the hallmark of characteristics that conform to our traditions, preconditions, experiences and possibilities.'[111] Responding to ridicule from the West, one writer argued:

> When we talk about establishing socialism in the colours of the GDR, the intention is not to fence ourselves off from other socialist countries... but actively to introduce our own unmistakable contribution for the greatest benefit of all in the community of socialist states, entirely in the sense of the unity between socialist patriotism and proletarian internationalism. Thus the colour red, and the red banner of the working class, always was, is and remains vital and imperative for the political identity of the GDR.[112]

The transparency of the notion of 'socialism in the colours of the GDR' sheds light on the motives behind the revival of interest in the concept of the nation. However, as was the case with the SED's attempt to reclaim German history, whether or not it was a good idea is debatable. The word 'colours' was somewhat inappropriate, suggesting the black, red and gold of the German flag with its all-German connotations. While theorists on the nation believed that the unique characteristics of the GDR should be emphasised, including its Germanness, they remained unconvinced of the validity of this particular concept due to its overreliance on achievements which could not be guaranteed, as opposed to the subjective elements of GDR identity.[113] Essentially it was little more that an attempt to arouse a state consciousness divorced from (German) nationalism. The very next year it became clear that even in 'the colours of the GDR', it was socialism that was the problem, and soon there was no socialism and no GDR, and only the emotive colours *schwarz-rot-gold* remained.

Honecker's visit to the Federal Republic

In spite of the fact that the SED did not pay direct attention to the concept of the nation during the first half of the 1980s it is clear that the national question had still been simmering in the background. According to the last communist leader of the GDR, Egon Krenz, what finally caused the pot to boil over was Honecker's highly symbolic official visit to the Federal Republic in September 1987.[114] For two reasons, contact with the Federal Republic was becoming vital for the survival of the GDR itself. The first was that those in the highest echelons of power in the GDR knew that it was economically bankrupt, and that only financial assistance from the very state that disputed its right to exist could bail the GDR out, and thus guarantee its continued existence in some form.[115] This would inevitably lead to increased contact and co-operation between the two states, but there was a shortage of alternatives, especially at a time when the party leadership was playing down its commitment to the socialist bloc. It has recently emerged that a very select group within the ruling elite, led by the head of 'Commercial Co-ordination' *(KoKo)*, Alexander Schalck-Golodkowski, had been contemplating greater economic reliance on the FRG and even a future confederation if it was the only means of salvaging something of the GDR.[116] This put the 'developed socialist society' in doubt, which had been the essential framework within which the 'socialist German nation' had evolved.[117] But, as mentioned earlier, without socialism, there would be no 'socialist German nation', and no justification for a separate socialist German state.

The second reason behind the increase in official contact was the widespread fear among the population that if the two German states did not actively strive to prevent a nuclear war, they would be the victims of it, but as Honecker himself pointed out, 'Neither can have their peace in isolation'.[118] A historic paper was jointly produced by representatives of the SED and the West German SPD, entitled 'The Conflict between Ideologies and Common Security'. It aroused much interest within intellectual circles on both sides of the divide, and was unofficially referred to in the GDR as 'the new thinking' since it questioned the notion that only socialism could guarantee peace. However, this sent a confused message to the masses, who had been led to believe that the West German SPD were imperialists just like the CDU/CSU, and because talk of 'no more wars on German soil' once again suggested that 'German soil' meant something. Unfortunately the 'new thinking' was short-lived and although the paper was published in *Neues*

Deutschland in 1987, it was then quickly and intentionally forgotten before it could have very much impact beyond political and academic elites.[119]

Increased contact with Bonn had both benefits and drawbacks for the East German regime. On the positive side it was perceived by the ruling elite as a great propaganda opportunity, aimed both at domestic and international audiences, which would highlight the fact that the GDR was actively striving for peace, that its status was equal to that of the Federal Republic, and that it was a more important international actor than other members of the socialist bloc. The drawback was that any official contact between the two German states would inevitably revive the German question, both at home and abroad.

The culmination of this bilateral contact was Honecker's visit to the Federal Republic in 1987 which was an odd demonstration of what linked the two German states and what divided them, with Bonn naturally stressing the former and the SED the latter. The party portrayed the visit as the ultimate indication that the GDR was a separate sovereign state from the Federal Republic, demonstrated by the fact that Honecker was to receive the same treatment and honours as the head of any other foreign country. Beforehand, Hermann Axen called the visit 'one of the strongest blows against revanchism in history'.[120] The first blow had been the foundation of the GDR in 1949, the second the erection of the so-called 'protective wall' in 1961, and the third had been the signing of the Basic Treaty in 1972, followed by the admission of the GDR into the UN. Honecker's visit would constitute the fourth blow, and was billed as undeniable proof that two German states now existed, whose relationship could only be one of peaceful coexistence.

In his after-dinner speech at a state banquet in Bonn, Honecker adhered to the line that socialism and capitalism (and by implication, the two German states), were as hard to combine as fire and water.[121] In contrast, Chancellor Kohl expressed Bonn's commitment to the unity of the German nation, and the continued openness of the German question. The latter referred to 'both states within Germany', and stressed his hope that the division could be overcome peacefully. The Federal President, Richard von Weizsäcker had welcomed Honecker 'as leader of the GDR, but also as a German among Germans who have a history under which he himself had suffered as a German'.[122] The joint communiqué issued by both heads of state emphasised the equality and independence of both states and concentrated on the further development of 'normal, good-neighbourly relations in accordance with the Basic Treaty', while at the same time acknowledging that there were still differences of opinion, including regarding the national question.[123]

Afterwards, the SED portrayed the visit as a great victory, and as Bonn's acknowledgement that the GDR was a sovereign state, just like any other. Much was made of the use of protocol as was customary during an official visit by a foreign head of state, such as the raising of the East German flag and the sound of its national anthem on West German territory. These symbolic acts were portrayed as a sign of Bonn's recognition of the GDR's sovereignty and equal status, and of the normality of their relationship in accordance with international law. They apparently highlighted the discrepancy between the 'all-German illusions' contained in the Basic Law, and the reality of the situation.[124] According to the East German side, Kohl's references to the 'unity of the nation' would do nothing to change this,[125] and it was the need to secure peace as opposed to some sort of 'national bond' that formed the basis for the relationship between the two German states.[126] However, subsequent attention paid to the state of the German nation suggested that Honecker had been considerably unnerved by Kohl's comments, especially since it was clear that the GDR literally could not afford to fence itself off from its western relation.

How much truth was there in the SED's claims regarding the visit? While Honecker was superficially treated like any other visiting head of state, many of the gestures were purely symbolic, and while not insignificant, they could not hide the fact that the relationship between the two German states was still far from normal. Due to their shared history, the range of subjects discussed went far beyond those discussed by two states who just happened to be neighbours. It included undeniable matters of common interest, such as peace and environmental protection, but also voluntary co-operation in many areas, indicating both parties' willingness to increase contact - not just at a governmental level but also between citizens. Topics discussed included communications, travel arrangements, cultural exchanges, sporting events, Berlin, AIDS, and town-twinning.[127] According to the West German interpretation, the agreements that resulted from the visit were both a sign that the two states were still linked by a national bond and a means to preserve it.

While it goes without saying that economic motives lay behind Honecker's willingness to co-operate, the opportunity to do so only existed due to the national connection, regardless of whether or not the SED acknowledged it as such. Furthermore, his nostalgic visit to his birthplace in the Saarland totally discredited the claim that nothing linked the two German states.[128] The leadership appeared to recognise that it was pointless, even destructive, to deny the national bond, when it could be put to good use to benefit the GDR. This realisation finally ended the party's policy of silence on the nation and gave the green light for renewed discussion on the subject.

Theorists in demand

In February 1988 an internal working party was set up by politburo member Hermann Axen to address 'the question of the nation', which had not been debated at an official level since the publication of the Party Programme in 1976. All the theorists who had previously been involved with the topic were called upon to participate. The 15 members included Alfred Kosing, Walter Schmidt, and Jürgen Hofmann, other social scientists and historians, and representatives from the Department of Sciences and Ministry for Foreign Affairs.[129] Honecker sanctioned the formation of the working party, which suggests that the issue was to be prioritised, although exactly how interested he really was is debatable. Some commentators claim he took a personal interest in the group's activities,[130] but insiders say the project was very much Axen's own initiative, and that Honecker may have had an ulterior motive for giving the group his blessing. Axen's personal adviser, Manfred Uschner, has claimed that his boss, who was officially responsible for foreign affairs, had been 'shunted into a siding' by Honecker, who had more or less taken over foreign policy. Therefore he needed to carve out a new niche for himself, and offered to tackle the problem of the nation in the light of Bonn's challenge. This offer was accepted by Honecker, not least because it would give Axen something to do and thus serve as a consolation prize for excluding him from foreign affairs.[131] The topic provided an ideal opportunity for Axen to re-assert himself, not only because it had been in urgent need of attention since Honecker's official visit to the Federal Republic, but also because his interest in the subject dated back to the early 1970s.

There is no evidence to suggest that any other members of the politburo were interested in the subject. Though Axen sent them copies of the paper produced by the working party, according to Egon Krenz, it was never formally discussed, because it was still a sensitive issue and the others did not want to be bothered with it.[132] In a special edition of the party journal *Einheit* to commemorate the 40th anniversary of the GDR in October 1989, which included articles by many senior functionaries, only Hermann Axen even mentioned the word 'nation'.[133] Others, including Honecker, chose to emphasise the concept of 'socialism in the colours of the GDR', which was a poor substitute for a real national identity, especially since the shortcomings of socialism were becoming apparent not only in the GDR, but in the Eastern bloc as a whole.

The academic members of the working party had several reasons not to expect it to achieve much.[134] Although they had been called upon for their expertise, this was so that it could be put to good use to serve the party. While Axen was reputed to be less dogmatic than other members of the leading elite, he too was old and out of touch with reality in the GDR. He still adhered to the class-based definition of the nation, dating back to the Eighth Party Congress in 1971, which he himself had formulated. Furthermore, he was afraid to rock the boat by confronting Honecker with unfavourable findings or appearing to criticise those closest to him due to an inferiority complex and due to his reliance on elite privilege for health provision for his ailing wife.[135] While it was possible to have a reasonably frank discussion within the working party, for the usual reasons, the reports that were passed on to the Central Committee were inevitably modified.[136]

During its first meeting in February 1988, the working party recognised that the SED's increased contact with Bonn during the early 1980s had led to uncertainties regarding the state of the nation, and made people question the validity of the line expressed in party documents. This was not only true of the masses, but also of party functionaries and propagandists.[137] Therefore plans were made for a new offensive with two main components - an increase in academic work on the state of the nation at party institutions, and more effective propaganda to enhance people's 'national self-perception' *(nationales Selbstverständnis)* as citizens of the GDR.[138]

To achieve the former, a new field of research into the nation at the Academy for Social Sciences was proposed, and the topic was included in the Department of Sciences' 'Central Research Plan for the Social Sciences' for 1991-1995. Subjects in need of attention included the relationship between the 'socialist German nation' and the 'capitalist German nation' (an indication that this remained a problem), and their historic 'community of responsibility' *(Verantwortungsgemeinschaft)*, and also the dialectic between national and European elements in the light of the concept of the 'common European home'. This suggests that the SED recognised the GDR's predicament, caught between developments in the Eastern Bloc on the one hand, and the advances of the Federal Government on the other.

To improve the population's identification with the socialist German nation, an extensive list of journal and newspaper articles was planned, particularly to coincide with the 40th anniversary of the GDR. The intention was to ensure that the population not only understood that the unitary German nation no longer existed, but also who was responsible for the division (i.e. 'West German imperialists'). It was hoped that this would dispel illusions that the two German states were growing closer together again, which had arisen as a result of the increased contact between their leaders during the 1980s. Furthermore, the question of the nation was to be introduced in foundation courses in Marxism-Leninism and addressed in the forthcoming ideological indoctrination programme or *Parteilehrjahr* in preparation for the next party congress.[139]

A detailed paper was produced by academic members of the internal working party in the spring of 1988.[140] In spite of constraints, it was relatively realistic and the theorists managed to include most of their main points. Unlike published work, which described the socialist German nation that the party desired, as though it was already a reality, it highlighted several problem areas, including the need to formulate better arguments to ensure the masses understood the concept of the 'socialist German nation', and the need to counteract West German claims regarding the unity of the nation and 'the openness of the German question'. Proletarian internationalism was mentioned, although for the first time, the point was made that while socialist nations were growing closer together economically, it did not follow that national distinctions would merge or that national structures would dissolve.[141] Privately the theorists still wanted to find out whether or not a national consciousness unique to the GDR had evolved. With thousands of citizens applying for permission to leave for the Federal Republic, the evidence suggested otherwise.[142]

The paper was sent to Honecker by Axen with a letter stating that it was time to expand on the line expressed at the Eighth Party Congress in 1971 and in the Party Programme, because a large proportion of the population was too young to remember the SED's alleged struggle on behalf of the entire German people for a 'united, peace-loving, democratic Germany' and a unitary socialist German nation. It was also necessary to ensure that the history of the GDR and the SED was portrayed in a professional and coherent manner. Axen added that the working party sought the General Secretary's approval and that it would adhere to the line he had recently taken in Bonn.[143]

The second, and, as it turned out, last meeting of the working party in September 1988 concentrated on 'socialist national consciousness' in the GDR, and how theoretical work on the subject of the nation could be encouraged. At last empirical research was planned in order to identify the most common misunderstandings. The intention was to collect data on popular opinion by examining letters to the press and applications by those wishing to leave the country, and by conducting a proper opinion poll. In this way they hoped to establish which factors furthered the development of a national consciousness unique to the GDR and which hindered it. Factors to be taken into consideration included German history and culture, family ties, ethnic and linguistic factors, the foreign policy of the GDR, and last but not least, the impact of Bonn's claim that the unitary German nation still existed. Research in the early 1980s had shown that the population had failed to grasp the SED's explanation as to why Germany was divided. A better understanding of the party's earlier efforts to preserve the unity of the nation (which had been played down since the 1970s), was also considered necessary in order to justify the current stance on the national question.[144] Unfortunately, official approval at various levels was required for such a project which was a lengthy process, and the members of the working party could not have known just how little time they, and the state itself, had left.

A questionnaire on national consciousness was drawn up and later reworked by both Axen and the Department of Sciences before the latter approved it in April 1989. It then had to be registered with the Central Authority for Statistics, which only gave the green light in September 1989,[145] by which time it was already the beginning of the end for the GDR, and events answered many of the questions regarding popular consciousness in the GDR before they could even be asked. The questions concerned the extent of respondents' identification with concept of the 'socialist German nation' and of their acceptance of the SED's account of how Germany came to be divided. They were also to be asked whether they believed the German question was still open, for their opinion of the Federal Republic and its people, and of the GDR's relationship with the Soviet Union. They were to be questioned about what made them proud to be citizens of the GDR, what they understood by national culture and *Heimat,* what aspects of history most interested them, and even their views on the efforts made to preserve Sorb culture.[146] Although the poll was never conducted, which is unfortunate as the responses would have been interesting, the fact that it was permitted at all can be interpreted as an indication that the leadership had finally recognised the seriousness of the threat posed by the revival of the national question to the legitimacy of the GDR.

The working party on the nation also agreed that the issue required more theoretical attention. The best way to guarantee this was to set up an officially recognised committee at a party institution, therefore it was agreed that an 'Interdisciplinary Academic Committee for Research on the Nation' should be established at the Academy for Social Sciences, and a new field of research into the 'socialist German nation' at the Institute for the History of the Workers' Movement (IfGA). The need for such bodies was apparently all the more pressing due to the recent increase in international interest in the 'so-called German question' and its role in the long-term strategies of the West German government.[147]

Due to its unusual interdisciplinary nature, the new academic committee was greeted with enthusiasm by those who had been trying for years to keep the nation alive as a subject for research and debate. Along with several familiar names, such as the chair, Jürgen Hofmann, it included experts on the Sorb community and Korea.[148] The first meeting in May 1989 was also attended by Hermann Axen and Otto Reinhold, the director of the AfG - an indication of its importance. Hofmann has claimed that the committee was far more academic than the earlier working party, which had been formed with the specific purpose of producing more effective propaganda.[149] However, while the discussion may have been freer and more intellectual, the possibilities should not be overestimated. The usual constraints applied, and the leadership had not permitted the committee simply out of kindness. But by the summer of 1989, there was little point in theorising about how long the consolidation of the 'socialist German nation' would take when the opposite process was happening on the streets of Leipzig and East Berlin.

Numerous publications on the subject of the nation appeared in 1988 and 1989, in accordance with the plan drawn up by the working party. The fact that both specialist journals and the popular press were targeted highlighted the intention of reaching as many sections of the population as possible. Most of the articles were written by members of the interdisciplinary committee and/or the working party. Even the veteran theorist, Alfred Kosing, was called upon to address the subject for the first time since the beginning of the decade in a lengthy piece written in the spring of 1988. But by the time it was published in the autumn of 1989,[150] it had already become embarrassingly irrelevant due to events beyond the SED's control. Writers still had to conform to the line on the socialist German nation laid down in the Party Programme, which remained official policy. But the material produced was generally more realistic in tone, and drew on the ideas and problems outlined in the paper produced for the working party mentioned earlier. Though the Marxist-Leninist theory that nations were primarily determined by social factors was still maintained, this view was somewhat modified, even contradicted, by increased emphasis on non-Marxist aspects of nations, and considerable attention was paid to subjective factors such as national consciousness and identity,[151] and to the GDR as a product of German history in its entirety.[152] It was argued that the establishment of two separate states with incompatible social orders had led to the development of two completely separate nations,[153] and that increased contact between them was not an indication that the German question was still open,[154] but merely a device to secure peace.[155]

The most significant publication resulting from the renewal of interest in the nation was Jürgen Hofmann's *Ein neues Deutschland soll es sein*, the first major work on the subject since Kosing's 'The Nation in History and in the Present' published in 1976. Mass-produced as a paperback, the book served the requirements of the party before those of serious scholarship. Hofmann himself had difficulty getting permission for the title because the rector of the Academy for Social Sciences thought it might cause too much trouble, but the latter was overruled by Hermann Axen who allowed it.[156]

In 1988, the fifth edition of the official *Kleines Politisches Wörterbuch* appeared. As before, the entry for 'nation' appeared to have been penned by Alfred Kosing, though since the first edition in 1967, it had grown from four columns to eight. The basic line was still that of the Party Programme, with considerable detail on the relative insignificance of nationality in the development of nations, compared with social factors. According to the writer, 'The unitary German nation is a thing of the past. The socialist German nation and the capitalist German nation have a common history in the past, it is true, but no common present or future.' However, this was all somewhat contradicted by the lines, 'The question of whether at a later date, when the working class of the FRG, together with all working people, has won the socialist transformation of society and the capitalist nation, a unitary socialist German nation can arise, remains unanswerable at present.'[157] This appears to indicate that although the German question was officially settled, the dream of a united socialist Germany had not entirely faded away, however unlikely it was to materialise.

One further indication that the nation was a matter of concern for the leadership was that the subject was on the agenda for the 12th Party Congress, scheduled for May 1990. This was highly significant because the problem had not been directly addressed at a Party Congress since 1971. Members of Axen's working party were commissioned by the Department of Sciences to produce analytical material in preparation for it. Thus we can conclude that for the first time in nearly 20 years, the state of the nation would almost certainly have been addressed at the Party Congress, which is further evidence of the leadership's concern about the issue, during the later 1980s, especially after Honecker's visit to the Federal Republic. This assumption is supported by the prominence of the subject during the 1989/90 *Parteilehrjahr*, although at this stage, there was no plan for a radical alteration of the official line. Instead, propagandists were instructed to emphasise the stance on the nation expressed in the Party Programme and at the Eighth Party Congress, although the former had superseded the latter due to the acceptance that the socialist nation in the GDR was German. The undeniable existence of two German states and nations and their significance for the balance of power in Europe was also to be stressed.[158] Official contacts with the Federal Republic were to be portrayed as purely in the interest of peace, as opposed to being a result of any special relationship, and people were to be reminded of the fact that that socialism and capitalism were as hard to combine as fire and water, as Honecker had stated in Bonn in 1987.[159]

Conclusion

While a small group of functionaries and theorists contemplated how to improve the concept of the nation in order to make it more effective as a device to legitimise the GDR, other factors continued to gnaw away at the foundations of the state, in particular, the deepening economic crisis and the brutal methods employed by the regime to suppress dissent. Whereas economic shortcomings and the lack of democracy were nothing new, during the 1980s, the SED faced two additional problems in its attempts to legitimise the state and its system, namely the fact that Gorbachev seemed to be offering something better than the 'socialism in the colours of the GDR' endured by East Germans, and increasing popular interest in the shared past and uncertain future of the two German states.

Although the SED had denied that the German question was still open, for economic reasons, it was forced take advantage of Bonn's continued belief in the German national bond in the form of credit from the Federal Republic, which simultaneously sustained and undermined the GDR. The reinterpretation of history also showed how the party was willing to make U-turns, and to take advantage of the German roots of the state when there was more to be gained acknowledging them than by denying them.

The concept of the 'socialist German nation', originally conceived by theorists, had proved to be the most acceptable option, certainly more so than the purely 'socialist nation' of the early 1970s, even if it was rather a contradiction in terms. It was the ultimate example of how theorists had to produce work in accordance with the current needs of the party, but also how the latter relied on them to solve its ideological dilemmas.

But before conclusions about the state and future of the 'socialist German nation' could be drawn, the ailing GDR was suddenly released into the international community by its guardian, the Soviet Union, and left at the mercy of highly contagious capitalism, and what was more, capitalism with a German face. And without socialism, all that would apparently remain of the 'socialist German nation' would be part of the German nation lacking a justification for a state of its own.

Notes

1. Timothy Garton Ash, *In Europe's Name* (London, 1993), p.189.
2. McAdams, *East Germany*, p.146.
3. Fred Oldenburg, 'Blick zurück nach vorn. Zum 13. Plenum des Zentralkomitees', *Deutschland Archiv* 8 (1975): p.2.
4. Alfred Kosing and Walter Schmidt, 'Über die Dialektik von Internationalem und Nationalem', *Thematische Information und Dokumentation* 32 (1974): p. 80, my italics.
5. Alfred Kosing, Berlin, 11 February 1993.
6. SAPMO-BArch IV 2/1/495

7	SAPMO-BArch IV 2/1/495
8	Alfred Kosing and Walter Schmidt, 'Nation und Nationalität in der DDR', *Neues Deutschland*, 15/16 Feb 1975, p.10.
9	Kosing and Schmidt, p.10.
10	Kosing and Schmidt, p.10.
11	Ludz, 'The SED's Concept', pp.214, 208.
12	For example, Alfred Kosing, 'Theoretische Probleme der Entwicklung der sozialistischen Nation in der DDR', *Deutsche Zeitschrift für Philosophie* 23 (1975): pp.237-261.
13	Gunther Holzweißig, 'Der bestrittene Positionswechsel in der nationalen Frage', *Deutschland Archiv* 9 (1976): p.1189.
14	Kosing, *Nation in Geschichte*, pp.19-20.
15	Kosing, p.18.
16	Kosing, p. 39.
17	Kosing, pp. 169, 175.
18	Kosing, pp. 115-116.
19	Kosing, pp.169-171.
20	Kosing, p.152.
21	Kosing, *Nation in Geschichte*, p. 283
22	Kosing, p. 282. See chapter 2.
23	Ludz, 'The SED's Concept', p.223.
24	Kosing, p. 305.
25	Erich Honecker, 'Zügig voran bei der weiteren Verwirklichung der Beschlüsse des 8. Parteitages', *Reden und Aufsätze*, 12 vols. (East Berlin, 1975), vol. 2, p.241.
26	Meuschel, *Legitimation*, pp.280-283. Meuschel summarises Kosing's main points but does not evaluate his arguments or elaborate on the constraints of the system within which he worked.
27	Ludz, 'The SED's Concept', p.216.
28	Hermann Axen, 'Die Herausbildung der sozialistischen Nation in der DDR', *Probleme des Friedens und Sozialismus* 3 (1976): p.291, cited in Meuschel, *Legitimation*, p.279.
29	SAPMO-BArch J IV 2/2A/1606
30	*Neues Deutschland*, 14 January 1976.
31	Hofmann, 'Studien zur Entwicklung', p.106.
32	SAPMO-BArch IV 2/2.033/4
33	SAPMO-BArch IV 2/2.033/1
34	SAPMO-BArch IV B2/2.024/11. The submissions are examined in detail in Hofmann, 'Studien zur Entwicklung'. Hofmann has recently admitted that the submissions were of little significance, since people could no longer be bothered to oppose the leadership. Jürgen Hofmann, Berlin, 5 February 1993.
35	SAPMO-BArch IV B2/2.024/11

36 SAPMO-BArch IV 2/2.033/1
37 SAPMO-BArch IV B2/2.024/12
38 SAPMO-BArch IV B2/2.024/11
39 *Neues Deutschland*, 7/8 Feb 1976.
40 SAPMO-BArch IV B2/2.024/11
41 SAPMO-BArch IV B2/2.024/11
42 SAPMO-BArch IV 2/2.033/1
43 *Das Parteiprogramm und die Wissenschaft. Sitzungsberichte der AdW* (East Berlin, 1976), p.16.
44 Alfred Kosing, Berlin, 11 February 1993.
45 *Programm der SED* (East Berlin, 1976), pp. 56-57.
46 Protokoll der Verhandlungen des 9. Parteitages (East Berlin, 1976), p.42, my italics.
47 Erich Honecker, 'Die Aufgaben der Partei bei der weiteren Verwirklichung der Beschlüsse des 9. Parteitages', 17 February 1978, in Erich Honecker, *Die Kulturpolitik unserer Partei wird erfolgreich verwirklicht* (East Berlin, 1982), p.191.
48 For details see Zieger, *Die Haltung*, pp.207-210; Garton Ash, *In Europe's Name*, p. 164; McAdams, *East Germany*, pp.170-172.
49 *Protokoll des 10. Parteitags der SED* (East Berlin, 1981), pp. 28, 46.
50 *Neues Deutschland* 16 February 1981, cited in Zimmermann (ed.), *DDR Handbuch* vol. 2, p. 926.
51 Zieger, *Die Haltung*, p.211.
52 This idea was expressed by Schmidt and Honecker in 1981, and in a joint declaration by Kohl and Honecker on 12 March 1985. See Garton Ash, *In Europe's Name*, pp. 166, 170.
53 See Honecker's report to the 9th session of the Central Committee, November 1984. Honecker, *Reden und Aufsätze*, vol. 10, p.366. See also Hermann Axen, 'Sozialistische Klassenstandpunkt und Menscheninteressen - friedliches Koexistenz heute', *Einheit* 44 (1989): p.45.
54 For more information see John Sandford, 'The GDR and the German Question: the unofficial debate in the peace movement', in *Studies in GDR Culture and Society* 7, ed. Margy Gerber (Lanham, New York, and London, 1987), pp.221-236.
55 The content of the dialogue has been documented elsewhere, for example, Zieger, *Die Haltung*, pp.214-219; Garton Ash, *In Europe's Name*, Meuschel, *Legitimation*, pp.292-294. For a populist East German account, see Hofmann, *Ein neues Deutschland*, pp.289-294.
56 Garton Ash, *In Europe's Name*, p.163.
57 *Neues Deutschland*, 10 October 1983, cited in Zimmermann (ed.), *DDR Handbuch*, p. 926.

58	*Neues Deutschland,* 8 October 1984, cited by F. Trommler, 'The Creation of History and the Refusal of the Past in the GDR', in Harms, Reuter and Durr (eds.), *Coping with the Past,* p.79.
59	*Neues Deutschland,* 26 August 1983.
60	Zimmermann (ed.), *DDR Handbuch,* p. 926.
61	Jürgen Hofmann, Berlin, 11 May 1993.
62	SAPMO-BArch IV B2/9.04/67
63	Alfred Kosing, Berlin, 7 July 1993; Jürgen Hofmann, Berlin, 1 March 1993.
64	Alfred Kosing and Walter Schmidt, 'Geburt und Gedeihen der sozialistischen deutschen Nation', *Einheit* 34 (1979): pp.1068-1075.
65	Gerhard Riege and Hans-Jürgen Kulke, *Nationalität Deutsch, Staatsbürgerschaft DDR* (East Berlin, 1979).
66	For example, Dietmar Säuberlich, 'Das Problem der Nation in der Strategie und Taktik der SED in der ersten Hälfte der 60er Jahre', *Thematische Information und Dokumentation* 48 (1985); G. Benser, 'Sozialistische Nation und Nationspolitik in der Geschichte der DDR', *Thematische Information und Dokumentation* 47 (1984).
67	Including Hofmann's 'Studien zur Entwicklung' and theses by Peter Rentsch, Wilfried Trompelt and Marianne Braumann.
68	AfG/IfGA, 'Probleme der Entwicklung der Sozialistischen Deutschen Nation und der Auseinandersetzung mit neuen Tendenzen des Bürgerlichen Nationalismus in der Politik und Ideologie des Imperialismus in der BRD', (1980), located in SAPMO-BArch IV B2/2.024/4.
69	Jürgen Hofmann, 1 March 1993 and 11 May 1993; Helmut Meier, 28 May 1993, Berlin.
70	'Probleme der Entwicklung', p.33.
71	'Probleme der Entwicklung', p.29.
72	Hofmann, *Ein neues Deutschland,* p.300; Schmidt, 'The National Question', p.169.
73	Jürgen Hofmann, Berlin, 1 March 1993.
74	Jürgen Hofmann, Berlin, 1 March 1993.
75	Hofmann, *Ein neues Deutschland,* p.299.
76	17 February 1978. Honecker, *Die Kulturpolitik,* pp. 192-193.
77	Helmut Meier, Berlin, 15 March 1993. See also Marianne Braumann, 'Zum Bedeutung des sozialistischen Geschichtsbewußtseins für die Entfaltung des sozialistischen Nationalbewußtseins in der DDR', *Thematische Information und Dokumentation* 53 (1986): pp.43-52.
78	Alfred Kosing, 3 March 1993; Jürgen Hofmann, Berlin, 1 March 1993; Helmut Meier, Berlin, 15 March 1993.
79	Jürgen Hofmann, Berlin, 1 March 1993.
80	*Programm der SED,* pp. 52, 5.

81 An extensive literature exists both in English and in German, of which only a selection is included here. For example, Dorpalen, *German History;* Wolfgang Büscher, 'Geschichte als Denk- und Spielraum. Die DDR Historiker im Lutherjahr', *Studies in GDR Culture and Society* 4, ed. Margy Gerber (Lanham and London, 1984), pp.243-253; I.R. Mitchell, 'The Changing Image of Prussia in the GDR', *German Life and Letters* 37 (1983); Meuschel, *Legitimation,* pp.285-291; Jan Herman Brinks, *Die DDR Geschichtswissenschaft auf dem Weg zur deutschen Einheit* (Frankfurt and New York, 1992); Gert-Joachim Glaessner, 'Sozialistische Neohistorismus?' in Glaessner (ed.), *Die DDR in der Ära Honecker* (Opladen, 1988); Hasko Hüning, 'Geschichtswissenschaft zwischen Fachhistorik und Geschichtsphilosophie?' in Glaessner (ed.), *Die DDR,* pp.574-588; G. Iggers, *Marxist Historiography in Transformation. New Orientations in recent East German History* (New York and Oxford, 1991); Günther Heydemann, *Geschichtswissenschaft im geteilten Deutschland* (Frankfurt, 1980).

82 The term used in Shoup, 'The National Question', p.124, and Benedict Anderson, *Imagined Communities* (London and New York, 1983), p.124. On the relationship between nations and history see Mary Fulbrook, 'Introduction: States, Nations and the development of Europe', in Fulbrook (ed.), *National Histories and European History* (London, 1993), pp.1-20; Teich and Porter (eds.), *The National Question*; Anthony D. Smith, *National Identity* (London, 1991), pp.160-165; Leonard Krieger, 'Germany', in Orest Ranum (ed.), *National Consciousness, History and Political Culture in Early Modern Europe* (Baltimore and London, 1975), pp.67-97; F. Hertz, *Nationality in History and Politics* (London, 1944); Manfred Hättich, *Nationalbewußtsein und Staatsbewußtsein* (Mainz, 1966), pp.20-23.

83 That this was the case has been confirmed by Alfred Kosing, Berlin, 3 March 1993, Walter Schmidt, Berlin, 3 June 1993, and Helmut Meier, Berlin, 15 March 1993.

84 Iggers, *Marxist Historiography,* p.11

85 This distinction first appeared in Horst Bartel, 'Historische Erbe und Tradition', *Einheit* 34 (1981), pp. 272-278, and became standard practice.

86 For example, Ingrid Mittenzwei, *Friedrich II von Preußen. Eine Biographie* (East Berlin, 1979); K-H. Börner, *Wilhelm I: Deutscher Kaiser und König von Preußen. Eine Biographie* (East Berlin, 1984); E. Engelberg, *Bismarck: Urpreusse und Reichsgründer* (East Berlin, 1975); Horst Kühne, 'Die NVA: Legitimer Erbe aller progressiven militärischen Traditionen des deutschen Volkes', *Einheit* 36 (1981): p.156-62. The multi-volume *Grundriß der deutschen Geschichte* (East Berlin, 1979) also appeared and an official account was even published in English: H. Heitzer, *GDR. A Historical Outline* (Dresden, 1981).

87   Bartel, 'Historische Erbe', p.272.
88   Bartel, p.278. See also Kurt Hager, *Die Gesellschaftswissenschaften vor neuen Aufgaben* (East Berlin, 1981).
89   'Aufruf zum 30. Jahrestag der DDR', *Einheit* 34 (1979): p.637.
90   Erich Honecker, 'Der Siegeszug des Sozialismus auf deutschem Boden', *Einheit* 34 (1979): pp.899-900, my italics.
91   Erich Honecker, 'Die Aufgaben der Partei bei der weiteren Verwirklichung der Beschlüsse des 9.Parteitages', 17 February 1978, cited in Honecker, *Die Kulturpolitik*, p.192.
92   Erich Honecker, 'Martin Luther und unsere Zeit', 13 June 1980, cited in Honecker, *Die Kulturpolitik*, p.257.
93   Bulletin des Presse- und Informationsamts der Bundesregierung, 28 June 1983, p. 637, cited in R.F. Goekel, 'The Luther Anniversary in East Germany', *World Politics* 37 (1984): p.125.
94   Erich Honecker, *Aus meinem Leben* (East Berlin, 1981), p.436.
95   Honecker, p.437.
96   Helmut Meier, Berlin, 15 March 1993. For an 'improved' account, see also Braumann, 'Zum Bedeutung', For a West German view see Johannes Kuppe, 'Geschichtsbewußtsein in der DDR', in Werner Weidenfeld (ed.), *Geschichtsbewußtsein der Deutschen. Materialen zur Spurensuche eine Nation* (Cologne, 1987), pp.175-177.
97   This was reminiscent of the ideas of Johann Gottfried Herder, who had stated that identification with the German *Volk* was compatible with loyalty to the Prussian or Bavarian state. See Fulbrook, 'States, nations', p.6.
98   This question is briefly addressed in Gerd-Rüdiger Stephan and Daniel Küchenmeister, 'Die nationale Frage in der Politik der SED am Ende der 80er Jahre', (1993). The authors argue that the subject was revived due to the economic situation and as a response to Gorbachev's idea of a 'common European home'.
99   On Gorbachev's rethink of Soviet *Deutschlandpolitik*, see Mike Dennis, *Social and Economic Modernization in Eastern Germany from Honecker to Kohl* (London and New York, 1992), p.23.
100 Jürgen Hofmann and Gerhard Basler, 'Zwei deutsche Staaten und Nationen im europäischen Haus', *Einheit* 44 (1989): p.171.
101 27th Conference of the CPSU, March 1986, cited in Barbara von Ow, 'Der Vogel in Moscows Käfig', in Konrad Löw, ed., *Beharrung und Wandel: Die DDR und die Reformen von Michail Gorbatschow* (Berlin, 1990), p.10.
102 *The Guardian*, 26 October 1989, p.8, cited in Garton Ash, *In Europe's Name*, p.4.
103 SAPMO-BArch IV 2/1/685 (18 August 1988: Honecker in conversation with Oskar Lafontaine)

104 *Neues Deutschland*, 10 April 1987.
105 Zieger, *Die Haltung*, p.233.
106 SAPMO-BArch IV 2/2.039/64. Report of a speech between Erich Honecker and W. Medwedjew, 24 August 1988.
107 SAPMO-BArch IV 2/1/692.
108 Alfred Kosing certainly had a very low opinion of him. Kosing, Berlin, 3 March 1993.
109 Meuschel, *Legitimation*, p.304.
110 Bruno Mahlow, 'Patriotismus und Internationalismus in der Politik der SED', *Einheit* 44 (1989): pp.548-549. This article appeared in a special edition of *Einheit* devoted to 'socialism in the colours of the GDR'.
111 Kurt Hager, 'Die Geschichte und das Verständnis unserer Zeit', *Einheit* 44 (1989): p.599. Here Hager listed what he considered these 'colours' to be.
112 Mahlow, 'Patriotismus,' p.549.
113 Alfred Kosing, Berlin, 3 March 1993; Jürgen Hofmann, Berlin, 1 March 1993.
114 Egon Krenz, Berlin, 15 July 1993.
115 Alexander Schalk-Golodkowski in *Die Zeit*, 11 January 1991, p.11.
116 Schalk in *Die Zeit*, 11 January 1991. He claims to have discussed the idea with West German politicians Gerhard Schürer and Siegfried Wenzel.
117 Stephan and Küchenmeister, 'Die nationale Frage', pp.3-4.
118 Literally 'Keiner kann seinen Frieden allein haben', *Die Zeit*, 11 September 1987.
119 Meuschel, *Legitimation*, p.300.
120 SAPMO-BArch J IV 2/2A/3045, (report by Axen of a discussion with the CPSU, 4 August 1987).
121 Erich Honecker, *Reden und Aufsätze*, 12 vols., (East Berlin, 1988), vol. 12, p.518.
122 SAPMO-BArch J IV 2/2A/3054, (report to the politburo on Honecker's official visit to the FRG).
123 *Neues Deutschland*, 7 September 1987.
124 Hofmann, *Ein neues Deutschland*, p.291.
125 SAPMO-BArch J IV 2/2A/3054
126 Hofmann, *Ein neues Deutschland*, p.292.
127 SAPMO-BArch J IV 2/2A/3054.
128 For western accounts of the visit see Anne McElvoy, *The Saddled Cow. East Germany's Life and Legacy* (London and Boston, 1992), pp. 87-88; *Die Zeit*, 11 September 1987, pp.1,3; Dennis L. Bark and David R. Gress, *A History of West Germany*, 2 vols., (Oxford and Cambridge M.A., 1989), vol.2: Democracy and its Discontents 1963-88, pp. 489-490.

129 SAPMO-BArch IV 2/2.035/16
130 Stephan and Küchenmeister, 'Die nationale Frage', p.3.
131 Manfred Uschner, Berlin, 23 July 1993; Uschner, *Die Zweite Etage*, p.60.
132 Egon Krenz, Berlin, 15 July 1993.
133 Hermann Axen, 'Die DDR - fest verankert in der neuen sozialistischen Welt', *Einheit* 44 (1989): pp.814-815.
134 For example, Alfred Kosing was under no illusions about what could be achieved. Kosing, Berlin, 3 March 1993.
135 Manfred Uschner, Berlin, 23 July 1993.
136 Jürgen Hofmann, Berlin, 1 March 1993.
137 SAPMO-BArch IV 2/2.035/16. This meeting took place on 3 February 1988.
138 SAPMO-BArch IV 2/2.035/16
139 SAPMO-BArch IV 2/2.035/16
140 AfG/IfGA, 'Studie: Fragen der Entwicklung der sozialistischen Nation in der DDR und der Auseinandersetzung mit dem gegenwärtigen Nationalismus in der BRD', February 1988. SAPMO-BArch IV 2/2.035/16
141 SAPMO-BArch IV 2/2.035/16
142 Jürgen Hofmann, Berlin, 1 March 1993.
143 SAPMO-BArch IV 2/2.035/16
144 SAPMO-BArch IV 2/2.035/16
145 Jürgen Hofmann, Berlin, 1 March 1993.
146 SAPMO-BArch IV 2/2.035/16
147 SAPMO-BArch J IV 2/3A/4668
148 For a full list of participants see Stephan and Küchenmeister, 'Die nationale Frage', footnote 36.
149 Jürgen Hofmann, Berlin, 1 March 1993.
150 Alfred Kosing, 'Sozialistische Gesellschaft und Sozialistishe Nation in der DDR', *Deutsche Zeitschrift für Philosophie* 37 (1989): pp.913-924. He also produced several populist pieces for *Neues Deutschland*.
151 Hofmann, 'Zur Entwicklung', p.741; Kosing, 'Sozialistische Gesellschaft', p.920.
152 Kosing 'Sozialistische Gesellschaft', p.913. The excitement over the reassessment of German history had died down by this stage, and the claim that the GDR was rooted in German history in its entirety was commonplace. However, historians continued to discuss the idea among themselves, which resulted in the publication of Helmut Meier and Walter Schmidt (eds.), *Erbe und Tradition in der DDR. Die Diskussion der Historiker* (East Berlin, 1988).
153 Jürgen Hofmann, 'Zur Entwicklung der sozialistischen deutschen Nation in der DDR', *Einheit* 43 (1988): p.738.

154 See for example Klaus-Uwe Koch, 'Warum es keine offene deutsche Frage gibt', *Einheit* 44 (1989): p.274; Otto Reinhold, 'Zur Gesellschaftskonzeption der SED', *Einheit* 44 (1989): p.486; Hager, 'Die Geschichte', pp.,601-602.
155 Basler and Hofmann, 'Zwei deutsche Staaten', p.175.
156 Jürgen Hofmann, Berlin 11 May 1993.
157 Entry for 'Nation', *Kleines Politisches Wörterbuch* vol. 8, (East Berlin, 1988), pp.648-652.
158 See 'Guidelines for Propagandists', *Studien- und Seminarhinweise zur Entstehung und Entwicklung der DDR unter Führung der SED* (East Berlin, 1989), p.102.
159 *Studien- und Seminarhinweise,* pp.97-99.

6 Conclusion

The East German revolution of 1989 suggests that in spite of propaganda, lavish spectacles, U-turns, and convoluted arguments, the SED never found a concept for a GDR-nation sufficiently credible to arouse a stronger sense of attachment than the ethnic German nation, or appealing enough to enable East Germans to resist the attractions of West German capitalism once they were faced with a choice between it and 'socialism in the colours of the GDR'. Nor had the SED's earlier 'all-German' stance appealed to a nation which clearly did not see a Marxist-Leninist party as the embodiment of the German national interest. That autumn, the brave chants of *Wir sind das Volk!* (We are the people) during the first mass demonstrations, imploring the *Volkspolizei* (People's Police) and the NVA (National People's Army) not to shoot on them, the people, were replaced after a month by the more assertive *Wir sind ein Volk!* (We are *one* people), marking the point when reunification replaced reform as the ultimate objective for the majority of ordinary people.

It is tempting to assume that in the autumn of 1989 the East German population was motivated by the conviction that they and the citizens of the Federal Republic still formed one nation, and that they rejected their state precisely for this reason. However, before jumping to such a conclusion, it is important to remember that the collapse of the GDR occurred as a result of broader changes in the international order which originated elsewhere.[1] In fact, the main reasons why thousands of people demonstrated on the streets of East German cities that year were similar to those of their counterparts in other Eastern Bloc states, namely to demand basic rights, such as democracy and freedom of movement, which they had hitherto been denied. Indeed, it is questionable whether the first demonstrations had anything to do with German nationalism at all,[2] and initially the demand was for a new German Democratic Republic which lived up to its name. However, the fall of the Berlin Wall and freedom to travel to the West also meant freedom to window-shop, which generated a desire to possess the goods East Germans were seeing for themselves for the very first time. Furthermore, the revelations which followed the end of the SED-dictatorship, for example, the extent of *Stasi* surveillance and elite privileges, and the gravity of the economic crisis, showed that there had been even more wrong with the GDR than ordinary people realised. This provided the yeast which gave rise to the popular view that the GDR was unreformable, and that reunification with the Federal Republic was the only solution,[3] a view greatly encouraged by the fact that the West German government appeared willing to 'put its money where its mouth was' and to bring about the national unity that had been a constitutional objective for 40 years.

The paradoxes of official nationalism in the GDR

As we have seen, the SED's policy regarding the state of the German nation was always subordinate to other policy objectives, most notably regarding the international status of the GDR. In other words, it was a means to an end which the SED believed could be adapted to suit the needs of the moment, initially to support the claim that the GDR was the legitimate model for a future reunited Germany, and later to prove that it was an independent sovereign state. The key determinants were the SED's obligation to respect the wishes of the Soviet Union with regard to East-West relations, the need to respond to the actions and claims of the Federal Republic, and at times, the personal convictions and ambitions of the ruling elite. The party leadership also decided what should form the basis of national consciousness in the GDR and monitored popular feeling merely in order to identify areas where propaganda needed to be improved, especially regarding popular perceptions of the Federal Republic. Overall, the potency of ethnic nationalism was seriously underestimated by the SED and the nature of national identity misunderstood. Thus while Issac Deutscher argued in 1971 that socialists needed to understand the nationalism of the masses, but only in the way that doctors understand the illnesses of their patients,[4] it appears that the leadership of the GDR did not subscribe to this view.

Being politically motivated, the SED's contradictory positions regarding the German nation and unrealistic claims regarding the national consciousness of the population of the GDR had little in common with conventional theories of nationhood and national identity, and in spite of the efforts of theorists, they often contradicted the basic principles of Marxism-Leninism too. In fact, as a self-proclaimed Marxist-Leninist party, the SED should not have been concerned with the nation and nationalism at all since classical Marxist teaching viewed nationalism as a device used by the bourgeoisie to weaken the class consciousness of the working class and to disguise their own selfish interests as the interests of society as a whole.[5] Since there is a fundamental incompatibility between socialism and nationalism, even the most acceptable solution, the 'socialist German nation in the GDR' was a contradiction in terms. But the SED could point to the fact that Marx and Lenin had condoned the manipulation of national sentiment as a means to advance the revolution, providing it was vanquished once that objective had been achieved.[6]

In practice however, the SED and its loyal theorists tended to pick and choose only the aspects of Marxist-Leninist theory regarding the nation that fitted current objectives, hence their arguments often sounded distinctly contrived. For example, earlier emphasis on the unity of the German working class was soon dropped once the SED began to assert the legitimacy of the GDR as a complete state in its own right. Also, during the 1970s, the importance of factors such as a common language in the formation of nations had to be explained away by theorists, in spite of the fact that it was an important factor according to classical Marxist-Leninist teaching.[7] But they could always justify their actions with the argument that Lenin had advocated pragmatism where the national question was concerned.

In order to harness nationalism for their own purposes without appearing to do so, the SED utilised two strategies. The first was to make the national interest synonymous with the interests of the German working class, and the word 'national' synonymous with socialist. This was most visible during the first decade of the GDR's existence, when the SED used the word 'national' extensively in order to support its objective of a united socialist Germany. The second strategy was to rename what was essentially nationalism 'patriotism'. This was acceptable, even encouraged, providing it was 'socialist patriotism' which was inextricably linked to proletarian internationalism. This apparently prevented it from becoming the chauvinism or imperialism which developed from 'bourgeois nationalism'. However, far from being two sides of the same coin, as was claimed, the two clearly contradicted each other, and in practice, the SED's obsessive emphasis on the need for friendship and solidarity with the Soviet Union greatly undermined its national credentials. Furthermore, the SED always maintained that the socialist states were growing together, but precisely where this process was leading was never directly addressed.

Looking back, several factors explain why none of the SED's various policies regarding the nation achieved popular acceptance. Firstly, because the regime itself lacked democratic legitimacy, this inevitably undermined every policy declaration, especially regarding the status of the GDR and the German nation. If the regime and state had been legitimate in the first place, the former would not have had to resort to trying to invent a new nation, nor for that matter, to fencing the population in to prevent their defection. Other factors, such as the absence of civil liberties, the state's subservient relationship with the Soviet Union, and economic shortcomings further undermined the legitimacy of the GDR, both as the rightful representative of the entire German nation, and as a legitimate state in its own right, with a justifiable claim to the loyalty of the people.

Secondly, the SED's attempts to create a new GDR-nation failed because the alternative option, namely the ethnic and historical German nation, was associated with another state which appeared to deliver all the things the GDR did not, such as prosperity, freedom and liberal democracy. A key factor here was the fact that West German television penetrated practically all areas of the GDR, with the exception of a small area around Dresden, whose population were labelled 'the clueless' *(die Ahnungslosen)* as a result. West German TV showed East Germans that the grass was greener on the other side of the border, although it played a paradoxical role in the history of the GDR by satisfying a demand the SED could not meet and by improving the quality of life for ordinary East Germans. It also showed some of the negative aspects of capitalist society such as crime, hence the regime gave up the practice of dispatching members of the Free German Youth to turn round west-facing TV aerials.[8]

The final factor was the passage of time. While it is conceivable that a separate GDR-nation may have evolved over several generations, blood ties had always been a significant element of German identity and after a mere four decades, most East Germans were still directly related to citizens of the Federal Republic.

In short, it could be said that the German Democratic Republic was neither German, nor democratic, and that for various reasons, East Germans lacked incentives to identify with any form of GDR-nation.

The SED was not the only communist regime to attempt to use nationalism to legitimise an undemocratic, illegitimate regime however. Other regimes in the Communist Bloc also attempted to combine socialism with the vocabulary of nationalism to gain the allegiance of the population. Mao, for example, discovered that appealing on behalf of 'the nation' was a means to achieve the homogeneity that his highly centralised, totalitarian system required,[9] and similar tactics were employed by Ceausescu in Romania. Even the Kremlin appeared to have substituted Russian nationalism for Marxism-Leninism in the 1970s.[10] However, while all the Warsaw Pact states suffered from the delegitimising effects of heavy-handed control mechanisms and economic shortcomings, in particular, shortages of consumer goods and fresh foods, the GDR was engaged in 'an unusual national competition',[11] therefore using nationalism to legitimise the GDR was a risky strategy which could have completely the opposite effect to that which was intended by serving to reinforce the German national bond.

Although communist states claimed to have solved the 'national question', the case of the GDR epitomises the fundamental conflict between class solidarity and national loyalty that Marx and Engels themselves failed to resolve. Though faced with the opposite problem, being states trying to integrate many different nationalities, the fate of the former Soviet Union[12] and Yugoslavia highlights how other Marxist-Leninist regimes and ideologues also greatly underestimated the power of ethnic nationalism. As Walker Connor has concluded, 'When communism and nationalism have been wedded in the popular mind, communist movements have found broad acceptance. When communism and nationalism have been perceived as at odds, such movements have tended to be spurned.'[13] In other words, 'socialism has had to "nationalize" itself in order to gain political influence'.[14] In the East German case, the SED initially adopted this strategy, then in the 1970s, reversed it and tried to 'socialise nationalism', before reverting to 'nationalising socialism' during the 1980s by attempting to capitalise on the GDR's German heritage.

The four phases of the official line

As we have seen, the SED's attempts to use various concepts of the nation and national sentiment to legitimise an otherwise illegitimate state can be divided into four phases, which can be summarised as follows. The first phase begins with the transformation of the Soviet Occupied Zone into the GDR in 1949. The GDR was then described by the ruling party as the one true state of the German people, since power was (in theory) in the hands of the working class, and was somewhat idealistically portrayed as the basis or model for a future united socialist Germany. So soon after the war, the continued existence of the German nation was not yet in doubt, and during this period, the party proclaimed itself to be the defender of the unity of the German nation, and accused 'Western imperialists' of trying to destroy it, in order to support the assertion that the GDR was the only legitimate representative of the entire German nation. However, the Federal Republic was also making a similar claim, with several obvious advantages, such as western economic aid and a democratic political system.

By the beginning of the 1960s, it was clear that the SED had overestimated the appeal of the GDR - not just to the citizens of the other German state, but also to its own population, and in spite of the leadership's all-German words, its deeds, such as the building of the Berlin Wall, appeared to cement the division between the two German states. Consequently, the SED needed an argument to prove that socialism and national unity were compatible. The result, originally devised not by the party leadership, but by the theorist, Alfred Kosing, was that the nation was at two different stages of development in the two German states - united in the GDR, but still class-divided in the Federal Republic. Furthermore, in spite of the political division, it was claimed that the national bond was preserved by the unity of the German working class in both German states, who together constituted the nation. Using this argument, the SED could still portray itself as a national party with national, i.e. all-German objectives, and that the GDR was the model for a unified socialist German state, though 'national' was used to mean 'of the entire German working class'.

By the late 1960s, it had become increasingly obvious that the SED's vision of a united socialist Germany was unlikely to be realised, hence a reconsideration of what could realistically be achieved became unavoidable. During the second identifiable period, from 1967 until 1970, a contradictory dual policy evolved, consisting of continued official adherence to the notion of a unitary German nation on the one hand, and an escalation of the campaign for the recognition of the GDR as a sovereign state on the other, manifested by strict *Abgrenzung* or 'fencing off' from the Federal Republic. In fact, within the politburo itself, two conflicting views on the national question were emerging, with several members advocating a more 'GDR-centric' line, which emphasised the independent development of the GDR as 'our socialist fatherland', as opposed to the traditional all-German view. This raised doubts concerning the unity of the German nation. However, with the ageing Walter Ulbricht still at the helm, the GDR remained the 'socialist state of the German nation', as enshrined in the new constitution of 1968, and he continued to hope that the working class in the two German states would reunite what 'imperialism' had apparently torn apart.

But continued official adherence to the unity of the German nation and the inevitability of reunification was undermining the GDR's claim to be an independent sovereign state, and was becoming clear that a choice would soon have to made between reunification and recognition. The final catalyst for change was Chancellor Willy Brandt's new approach to relations with the GDR, based on the notion that there were 'two states of one nation', that nation being sustained by a 'feeling of belonging together' shared by the populations of both German states. Because Brandt would not grant full recognition of the GDR as a foreign country for this reason, the SED needed to prove his notion of 'two states of one nation' wrong, if they were to achieve their primary objective of international recognition of the GDR. The fact that both Brandt and his ideas were so warmly received by the East German population made clarification of the SED's position regarding the state of the nation a matter of urgency.

The most dramatic period in the history of the official concept of the nation runs from 1970 until 1974. At the Eighth Party Congress in 1971, the new First Secretary of the SED, Erich Honecker, declared that a purely *socialist* nation was developing in the GDR and that the national question had been resolved by 'history'. The reasons behind this total reversal of a policy officially held for 20 years were complex. In fact, contrary to popular belief, the turning point had occurred earlier, and it was actually Ulbricht who had first denied the unity of the German nation. That this so obviously contradicted his previous position suggests that Ulbricht was merely being pragmatic and trying to discredit Brandt's argument not only to support the SED's primary political objective of international recognition of the GDR, but also to reassert his own position. But for him it was too late, and we now know that Ulbricht's stance on the national question was the main reason why he was replaced in 1971.

By claiming that the population of the GDR now constituted a nation in itself, Honecker intended to reinforce the claim that it was a permanent, independent sovereign state. Furthermore, the 'GDR-nation' was merely described as socialist and no longer German, which was reflected in the revised constitution of 1974. A general purge of the word 'German' followed, which was clearly a desperate attempt to prove that the GDR was a complete and legitimate entity in its own right, following the SED's failure to defeat the Federal Republic's rival claim to be the sole legitimate representative of the German nation and to bring about reunification in the for of a socialist German state. However, the idea of a socialist nation in the GDR was an artificial concept, devised for political purposes, with no theoretical basis and no consideration of the feelings of the population.

However, it soon became apparent that the question could not be solved in a few sentences, and that a more detailed explanation of the concept would be required if it were to be comprehensible and credible to the population. Consequently, theorists and even some leading functionaries devised complex arguments which aimed to prove that nations were determined by class, and a major propaganda campaign was waged to get the message across to the population via public meetings and official publications. Carefully selected quotes from classic works of Marxism-Leninism were adapted to fit the SED's arguments and the East German situation. Awkward characteristics shared with the population of the Federal Republic, such as language, culture and traditions, were defined as ethnic factors, which were apparently of secondary importance, and therefore not decisive in the formation of nations.

By clearing up the problems arising from the earlier contradictory policy of adherence to the unity of the German nation, while simultaneously claiming that the GDR was a legitimate sovereign state in its own right, the SED was now effectively undermining the legitimacy of the GDR in another way, namely by denying its roots and appearing to deny people their national identity. This caused much confusion among the population and provoked ridicule in the West.

A way out of this dilemma was provided by theorists, who first made the distinction between nation, nationality and citizenship in 1975, marking the beginning of the fourth and final period, which ended with the demise of the state itself. They argued that according to class-based criteria, a socialist nation did indeed exist in the GDR, but this did not alter the fact that the majority of the population were of German nationality. In other words, while people were citizens of the GDR and therefore members of the socialist nation, their nationality remained German (or Sorb). As a result, ethnic factors shared with West Germans could be classed as aspects of nationality, and therefore of secondary importance to the nation, which was determined by class. Honecker himself adopted this distinction and in 1976, the phrase 'socialist German nation in the GDR' was enshrined in the Party Programme. Here was a classic example of the leadership's inability to formulate policy on the nation effectively without the assistance of theorists, although due to the constraints of the system, the latter could not actually contradict the basic party line.

Following the SED's acceptance of the distinction between nation, nationality and citizenship, the subject disappeared from the political agenda. The party gave up its paranoid fear of all things German, which led to a major reassessment of German history and a re-evaluation of the GDR's traditional roots in the early 1980s. However, theorists believed that due to the state's volatile position and the unstoppable flow of West German influence, it would be foolish to let the issue drop, but their concerns fell on deaf ears.

In 1987, the leadership suddenly renewed its interest in the nation in response to external events, which indicated that the national question had not been resolved after all. Since the early 1980s, the issue had been quietly simmering in the background due to the nuclear debate, which had highlighted the unique and dangerous position shared by both German states and their joint responsibility to preserve peace. However, the event which finally brought the issue to the boil was

Honecker's official visit to the Federal Republic in 1987, by which time the GDR had grown considerably economically reliant on its western neighbour. In addition, the leadership's desire to distance itself from the Soviet Union under Gorbachev led to the reassertion of the independence, and even the Germanness of the GDR. In response the SED suddenly called on theorists who had previously worked on the subject to take a fresh look at the 'socialist German nation' and national consciousness in the GDR.

However, by this stage, it was too late. The SED had failed to recognise that the key to successful nation-building was democracy and prosperity. Had they been able to provide these supports, then maybe a more viable 'GDR-nation' could have developed over a long period of time, but it was only the socialist economic and political system that had justified the continued existence of a second German state, and the Cold War that had maintained it, as its rapid demise from November 1989 appears to indicate.

The nature of East German identity

Since it is a historical fact that the population of the GDR rejected their state in its undemocratic, communist form, the question arises as to whether they were also rejecting the notion of a specific East German national identity, believing instead that they were still simply Germans like their western neighbours. While this may have been the case during the euphoric days and nights of 1989/90, there is ample evidence since reunification to suggest that East Germans had overestimated both the amount they and their West German cousins had in common, and the solidarity they could expect from them. In addition, it is clear that while a fully fledged GDR-nation had not yet evolved, a specific East German *identity* had, based on the unique experience of living in the SED-state. Since 1990, personal experience of the negative aspects of capitalism such as unemployment and high prices led many East Germans to recognise that there was more to the GDR than its corrupt political system and lack of freedom to travel abroad.[15] Indeed, post-unification hardship may even have strengthened their identity as East Germans,[16] manifested in nostalgia for the past *(Ostalgie)* and support for the post-communist PDS, who are regarded by many as the only voice of the East Germans in the Bundestag in distant Bonn.

Therefore, even if the population of the GDR did not embrace the official national identity prescribed for them by the SED, it is widely believed that an unofficial GDR-consciousness had become established, and the difficult process of reconciliation between the populations of the two German states appears to confirm this. While it was impossible for western researchers to acquire accurate data on national consciousness in the former GDR, even in the late 1960s, outside observers recognised a *Selbstverständnis* or self-perception peculiar to East Germans.[17] Rather than being based on the principles which had been ceaselessly advocated by the SED, such as socialist patriotism and proletarian internationalism (which had always been a euphemism for subservience to the Soviet Union both in the GDR and throughout the Eastern bloc), actual GDR-consciousness appears to have been based on the experience of day-to-day life in the GDR and solidarity in the face of hardship, combined with traditional Prussian values. However, while it did not correspond to the official version of GDR-consciousness advocated by the regime, it corresponded even less to the West German consciousness firmly established in the Federal Republic.

In fact, in the view of many outsiders, the GDR remained a typical German state in an old-fashioned, Prussian sense, and possessed an everyday culture that was very different from the materialistic, universal American culture which had flourished in the Federal Republic. Indeed, in the 1980s, the SED seemed to be winning the battle to prove which state was the most traditionally German, and German nationalism was demonstrated by a sense of superiority towards their socialist neighbours both on the part of ordinary East Germans and their leaders, in spite of all the rhetoric concerning proletarian internationalism. However, to the regime's credit, there was no attempt to 'Germanise' the Sorb minority, who numbered approximately 100,000 around the river Lausitz. On the contrary, the party went to great lengths to preserve their language and culture, maybe even beyond the call of duty, since the ability to speak *Sorbisch* was not much use to a young person in the GDR. This commitment may have been for propaganda purposes, i.e. to demonstrate how well the GDR treated minority groups, but probably originally arose from a genuine desire to make amends for the Nazis' treatment of minorities.

Some East German researchers have concluded that in the GDR, neither the notion of the unbroken unity of the nation, nor the policy of *Abgrenzung* found total acceptance during the 1970s and 1980s.[18] However, in the end, the desire on the part of East Germans for reunification as a means to achieve freedom, democracy and prosperity as soon as possible was so strong that they chose to overlook what differentiated the populations of the two German states. But the conflict East Germans experienced between their official citizenship and their subjective identity in the GDR may not have been resolved in the new enlarged Federal Republic. Indeed, it would be unrealistic to expect two communities to recover from 40 years of separation overnight. Nevertheless, it seems highly unlikely that they would want to go their separate ways again, not least because they did not choose to in the first place.

West German policy regarding the German nation

In contrast to that of the SED, West German policy regarding the state of the German nation was totally consistent over the years. Although it too formed only part of the geographical area and population of the former German Reich, the Federal Republic had several advantages right from the start, namely by being larger, by recovering from the war quicker thanks to Marshall Aid, and by gaining international recognition as 'Germany', even from her wartime enemies. These factors helped successive West German governments to pursue a far more subtle and consistent policy regarding the German nation than their East German counterparts.

The continued existence of one German nation was enshrined in the Basic Law, along with a commitment to the ultimate goal of reunification. The Federal Republic confidently claimed to be the sole legitimate representative of the nation, and this was accepted by the majority of the West German population, by the 'free world' and apparently even by a large proportion of the citizens of the GDR. By clearly stating the official position regarding the state of the German nation and then quietly but resolutely adhering to it, Bonn was able to minimise doubt and controversy regarding the issue, and could concentrate on making the Federal Republic a country people were happy to live in and to identify with.[19] Although Willy Brandt's recognition of the existence of 'two states of one nation' appeared to conservative West German politicians to challenge these assumptions which had been taken for granted for 20 years, this did not fundamentally alter the Federal Republic's own status, and the Federal Constitutional Court ruled that it did not contravene the Basic Law. In contrast, the SED's numerous policy changes encouraged confusion and reduced the credibility of the party's arguments.

Unlike in the GDR, there was no active policy designed to create a separate West German nation. Instead, a specific West German identity gradually evolved of its own accord. Far from being based on ethnic nationalism and chauvinism, which had been discredited by the experience of the recent past, this new, specifically *West* German identity was primarily based on allegiance to the constitution and a commitment to a strong currency, termed *Verfassungspatriotismus* and *Deutschmarkpatriotismus* by the West German thinker, Jürgen Habermas.[20] The nationalist element of West German identity was tempered by robust regional identities, reinforced by a federal system of government, and by a firm commitment to further integration among the countries of Western Europe.

However, while German nationalism of the pre-1945 variety was not encouraged, identification with the Federal Republic did not actually preclude identification with the ethnic or historical German nation. Indeed, the recent increase in racially motivated attacks and neo-nazi organisations demanding the resurrection of Germany's borders of 1937, and the electoral success of parties with an overtly nationalist programme suggests that a significant minority do hold strong nationalist views. Generally, however, they seem to be either disgruntled youths, in particular, under-achievers, who remain on the fringe of prosperous West German society, or elderly traditionalists. Furthermore, before making assumptions about the rise of German nationalism, it is worth mentioning that support for extreme right-wing parties increased elsewhere in Europe during the early 1990s.

Most people in the old *Länder* appear to have willingly identified with West German affluence and with the peace-loving, democratic character of the Bonn-state, although the materialistic, pro-American basis of West German political culture was questioned by radical students in the late 1960s, by left-wing terrorists in the 1970s, and again by the Greens from the early 1980s. However, most West Germans did not cease to view themselves as Germans, and although one can speak of a unique West German *identity,* it does not appear to have been the case that a West German *nation* was evolving as an alternative to the traditional German nation. Instead, traditional German elements and new characteristics arising from the post-war experience became fused together. Thus, what was actually meant in the Federal Republic by 'German' was considerably transformed over the years, and content with their lot, at least in a material sense, West Germans had less reason to concern themselves with the national question than East Germans, and the existence of an alternative German state did not affect their own self-perception.

Presumably, however, as the chances for reunification receded, whether or not the populations of two very different states, which called themselves German, still constituted one nation became rather irrelevant. Although difficult to prove, it is possible that West Germans of the post-war generation realised that the divide between the two German states was more than superficial. Many young West Germans may well have regarded East Germans as citizens of the Soviet bloc who just happened to speak German, and with whom they had considerably less in common than their contemporaries from France or the Netherlands. In short, the existence of the GDR was not nearly so much of a problem for West Germans as the existence of the Federal Republic was for East Germans and their rulers. However, in spite of the fact that the West Germans do not seem to have had a problem being both Germans and citizens of the Federal Republic, this did not mean that they had answered all the questions regarding what it meant to be German, some of which stemmed from the need to come to terms with the Nazi era, while others had concerned intellectuals for centuries. This was most clearly illustrated by the *Historikerstreit* of the late 1980s, which was essentially a bitter disagreement between conservative historians, who maintained that the Germans were not uniquely evil, and therefore had no reason to be ashamed of their national identity, and liberals, who regarded this as white-washing or justifying the Nazi period.[21]

The case of the GDR and nation-building theory

The mass rejection of the SED's claims regarding the German nation can shed some light on nationhood in general and on the problems facing rulers of states which are not nation-states. Firstly, it shows that nations neither appear nor disappear overnight, but develop gradually (a fact often ignored by the SED, though recognised by theorists). Therefore, while it would be extremely difficult to prove that a fully-fledged national identity had become established in the GDR, it is true that a social identity not shared by the West Germans had developed.

The example of Austria shows that in certain circumstances, it is possible for two separate 'civic-territorial nations' to evolve out of one 'ethnic-genealogical' nation,[22] which gradually acquire cultural characteristics of their own, and it is conceivable that a separate nation could have developed in the GDR in the same way, once blood ties had been weakened through generational change. However, precisely when the point of no return has been reached is difficult to establish. According to Walker Connor, four factors contribute to the problem: nationhood is a mass, not an elite phenomenon; it is a process; the process may not necessarily achieve nationhood; and it is not tangible or measurable.[23] If we accept Anthony Smith's general definition of a nation as being 'a named human population sharing a historic territory, common myths and historic memories, a mass public culture, a common economy and common legal rights and duties for all its members',[24] it appears that we can neither say that two separate nations had evolved on German soil, nor that the unitary German nation continued to exist unchanged by 40 years of geographical and ideological division. In view of the events of 1989/90, we must conclude that the embryonic nation in the GDR had not reached the point of no return, and that its citizens still believed that the German national bond had not been severed beyond repair, and that they and the West Germans continued to have plenty in common.

This brings us to our second point about nations, namely that they are defined by a combination of objective and subjective criteria. If one were to believe that objective criteria alone define nations, one could argue that two separate nations existed on German soil. If on the other hand, one is of the opinion that nations are primarily defined according to subjective criteria, then Brandt was right to claim that the most important factor in the German case was 'a feeling of belonging together' *(Zusammengehörigkeitsgefühl)*. With the benefit of hindsight, the German experience appears to confirm that nations are defined by both objective, tangible factors on the one hand, and subjective elements, i.e. national consciousness, on the other. However, objective factors change more quickly than subjective ones and can be altered artificially, as occurred in the German case. But because subjective elements change very slowly, they had not yet reached the point where one could talk of two completely separate and irreconcilable national identities, hence the German national bond had not quite been broken for good, although this might have occurred in time. The theory of a discrepancy between the nation, which in objective terms, had become deeply divided after 40 years, and a subjective national consciousness, that is to say, a consciousness of being German, which had not yet been totally eroded, is supported by evidence from the first few years since reunification, and today one could talk of a difference between the unity of the nation in theory and the disunity of the nation in practice. An analogy can be drawn with twins separated at birth, who are then brought up by very different adoptive parents and later reunited, and although directly related, they have very little in common.

The third point that can be made about nations in general is that national identity is by definition positive. It implies a sense of pride in the nation, perhaps even a feeling of superiority and that there are advantages in being a member of that nation. In 1989/90 the citizens of the GDR clearly had good (economic) reasons to identify themselves as Germans first and foremost, and at the time of reunification, had no desire to defend their East German identity, although recent experiences may have changed this. Had the GDR become more successful in satisfying the needs and desires of its people, within a few generations, it is possible that the situation would have been different.

A final point is that the East German case appears to support the notion that the nation-state, defined by Cornelia Navari as 'a polity of homogeneous people who share the same culture and the same language, and who are governed by some of their own number, who serve their interests',[25] continues to be regarded as the ideal political unit compared with the alternatives. Recent history shows that artificially created, multinational states such as the former Soviet Union and Yugoslavia, and politically divided nations such as Korea are generally considered unnatural and are less likely to attract the allegiance of all their citizens. Even though the two German states became well established and apparently permanent, the memory of the former unitary German nation-state lived on, and continued to be seen as natural, even though, in real terms, it was not, since the borders of the German nation and of the German state have never coincided exactly,[26] in spite of Hitler's attempts to achieve this. When the attributes of the nation and the state become fused, as opposed to being in conflict, and eventually a fusion of national and state consciousness occurs, the result is a highly resilient entity, a genuine nation-state, of which there are relatively few.[27] The case of the GDR shows what happens when people are torn between loyalty to a nation and a state, and when two states compete for the loyalties of that nation, namely that the most successful state wins.

As was discussed in the first chapter, most regimes have three devices at their disposal to enhance the legitimacy of the state, namely democracy, economic success, and by successfully appealing to a sense of nationalism. However, a deficiency in any of these three may have the opposite effect and may well undermine the state. Unwilling or unable to offer the first two of these factors, the SED attempted to make use of the third device, albeit in several different forms over the years. However, in the absence of genuine democracy and economic success, and due to the existence of two states on German soil, this strategy proved inadequate to achieve state legitimacy, defined earlier as a voluntary acceptance of the state by the majority of the population. It also showed that the nineteenth century German thinker, Johann Gottfried Herder, was right when he argued that the development of nations is essentially a natural process, not a policy imposed from above,[28] and proved how hard it is to create a nation from above without support from below. While both Germans themselves and the international community could hardly believe their eyes when the Berlin Wall came down, it is equally remarkable that an apparently artificial and unwanted state like the GDR could survive for 40 years, a scenario that few would have believed when the two German states were first created.

In the end, the party's various positions regarding the nation were not accepted by the population, in spite of the efforts of those whose task it was to make them credible. Not only was it too soon for a separate East German national identity to replace the fundamental sense of Germanness felt by the majority of the population of the GDR - the Federal Republic also scored more highly on the other criteria, namely democracy and economic success. Had the GDR been able to match these achievements, then maybe it would have survived and gradually gained legitimacy, particularly once those who preserved the ethnic national bond had died out. But as a copy of the Federal Republic, the GDR would have lacked a *raison d'être*,[29] therefore unlike other members of the Warsaw Pact which also lacked democratic legitimacy and failed to deliver in material terms, as a state, it could not survive the collapse of communism. As Otto Reinhold, the rector of the Academy for Social Sciences and a member of the Central Committee, conceded in the summer of 1989, 'The GDR is only conceivable as an anti-fascist and socialist alternative to the FRG. What justification would a capitalist GDR have next to a capitalist Federal Republic?'[30] In other words, in the absence of two artificially imposed, ideologically incompatible political systems on German soil, all that would remain would be one people and one nation.

Notes

1   For a useful bibliography see Roland Bleiker, *Nonviolent Struggle and the Revolution in East Germany* (Cambridge MA., 1993), pp.44-45, or Jonathan Osmond, ed. *German Reunification: a Reference Guide* (London, 1992).

2   That reunification was not an issue during the early days of the revolution is born out by empirical research conducted by former members of the AfG in Detlef Eckert, Jürgen Hofmann and Helmut Meier, *Zwischen Anschluß und Ankunft. Identitätskonflikte und Identitätssuche der Ostdeutschen auf dem Weg zum Bundesbürger* (Potsdam, 1992), pp.7-8. On this question see also John Breuilly, 'Nationalism and German Reunification', in Breuilly (ed.), *The State Of Germany*, pp.224-238; David M. Keithly, *The Collapse of East German Communism* (Westport and London, 1992), pp.41-58; Karl-Rudolf Korte, *Die Chance genutzt? Die Politik zur Einheit Deutschlands* (Frankfurt and New York, 1994), pp.82-88. In Ernst Plock, *East German-West German Relations nd the Fall of the GDR* (Boulder, Colerado, 1993), pp.93-123, the author looks at the strength of all-German consciousness in both German states.

3   Eckert et al., *Zwischen Anschluß*, p.10.

4   Cited in A.W. Wright, 'Socialism and Nationalism', in Tivey (ed.), *The Nation-State*, p.148.

5   Connor, *The Nation in Marxist-Leninist Theory*, p.7. See also Motschmann, *Sozialismus und Nation*.

6   Connor, pp.XIII, 7. See also Wright, 'Socialism', p.152.
7   For more detail on this issue, see McKay, 'The SED's Concept', pp.973-986.
8   A bibliography on the role of West German television in the GDR can be found in Bleiker, *Nonviolent Struggle*, pp.50-51
9   P. Shoup, 'The National Question and the Political Systems of Eastern Europe', in S. Sinanian, I. Deak, P-C. Ludz (eds.), *Eastern Europe in the 1970s* (London and New York, 1972), p.124.
10 Joseph Rothschild, 'Political Legitimacy in Contemporary Europe', in Denitch (ed.), *Legitimation of Regimes*, p.41.
11 Plock, *East German-West German Relations*, p.127.
12 A thorough account of the past and present is provided by Bremmer and Taras (eds.), *Nations and Politics*.
13 Connor, *The National Question*, p.584.
14 Wright, 'Socialism and Nationalism', p.152.
15 Eckert et al, *Zwischen Anschluß*, p.37. On East German attitudes during the immediate post-reunification period, see the section 'Ossi und Wessi - oder neue Gräben nach der Mauer', pp.28-35.
16 Numerous books address the complicated subject of East German identity in the 1990s, for example, Werner Weidenfeld (ed.), *Deutschland - Eine Nation, Doppelte Geschichte* (Cologne, 1993); Erwin K. Scheuch, *Wie Deutsch sind die Deutschen? Eine Nation wandelt ihr Gesicht* (Bergisch Gladbach, 1991); Christian Meier, *Die Nation, die keine sein will* (Munich and Vienna, 1991); Werner Weidenfeld and Karl-Rudolf Korte, *Die Deutschen - Profil einer Nation* (Stuttgart, 1991); Peter H. Merkl, *The Federal Republic at 45* (London and Basingstoke, 1995), part II; Hans-Joachim Veen and Carsten Zelle, 'National Identity and Political Priorities in Eastern and Western Germany', *German Politics* 4 (1985): pp. 1-26, especially note 3, p.25.
17 The best attempt to assess national consciousness in the GDR was Schweigler's *National Consciousness in Divided Germany*. Schweigler, a pupil of Karl Deutsch, accepted the limitations of his data but nevertheless believed that the question was no longer whether or not one German nation still existed, but whether or not it could be resurrected. Only with difficulty, he believed, since the answer to the German question appeared to be 'two Germanies, not one'. Schweigler, pp.277-281. For other views from the GDR period, see Chapter 2. For a retrospective evaluation of GDR-identity see Anne McElvoy, *The Saddled Cow. East Germany's Life and Legacy* (London, 1992); Dirk Verheyen, *The German Question. A Cultural, Historical and Geo-Political Exploration* (Boulder, Colorado, 1993), pp.79-97; Scharf, C.B. 'Necessity and Vision in East German Identity', in Harms, Reuter and Dürr (eds.), *Coping with the Past*, pp.94-103.

18   Eckert et al, *Zwischen Anschluß*, p.11.
19   For a bibliography on the basis of West German identity see Veen and Zelle, 'National Identity', p.25, note 3. See also Schweigler, *National Consciousness*, pp.141-231; Verheyen, *German Question*, pp.45-77; Harold James, *A German Identity. 1770 to the Present Day* (London, 1994), pp.187-209; Alan Watson, *The Germans. Who are they Now?* (London, 1992), especially chapter 7.
20   For an assessment see Howard Williams, Catherine Bishop and Colin Wright, 'German (Re)Unification: Habermas and his Critics,' *German Politics* 5 (1996): pp.214-239.
21   Mary Fulbrook, 'Nation-state and political culture in divided Germany 1945-90', in Breuilly (ed.), *The State of Germany*, p.127. For more detail on the *Historikerstreit* see among others, Richard J. Evans, *In Hitler's Shadow: West German Historians and the attempt to escape from the Nazi Past* (London, 1989); Christian Maier, *The Unmasterable Past: History, Holocaust and German National Identity* (Cambridge, M.A., 1986); Thomas Herz, 'Der Historikerstreit', in Christian W. Thomsen (ed.) *Aufbruch in die Neunziger* (Cologne, 1991),   pp.358-382; James Knowlton and Truett Cates, *Forever in the Shadow of Hitler? Original Documents of the Historikerstreit, the Controversy concerning the Singularity of the Holocaust* (New Jersey, 1993);
22   These two types of nation have been identified by the eminent scholar of nations and nationalism, Anthony D. Smith. See Smith, *National Identity* (London, 1991).
23   Connor, 'When is a nation?' *Ethnic and Racial Studies* 13 (1990): p.92.
24   Smith, *National Identity*, p.43. A similar though longer definition appears in Tivey (ed.), *The Nation-State*, pp.5-6.
25   Cornelia Navari, 'The Origins of the Nation-State', in Tivey, ed. *The Nation-State*, p.13. For an interesting discussion of the paradoxes of the nation-state see also Gordon Smith, 'A Future for the Nation-State?' in Tivey, ed. *The Nation-State*, pp.197-208.
26   Breuilly, 'Nationalism', p.229.
27   Only 10 per cent according to Walker Connor in the 1970s. Cited in Smith, *National Identity*, p.15.
28   See Isiah Berlin, *Vico and Herder* (London, 1976), pp.58-9.
29   A point also made by Jürgen Habermas, 'National Unification and Popular Sovereignty', p.6.
30   SAPMO-BArch IV 2/1/699. See also A. James McAdams, *Germany Divided. From the Wall to Reunification* (Princeton, 1993), p.194.

Bibliography

Published sources

Abusch, Alexander (1969), 'Das geistig-moralische Antlitz des neuen Menschen in unserer Republik', *Einheit*, Vol. 24, pp. 1078-1091.

Ackermann, Anton (1946), 'Gibt es einen besonderen deutschen Weg zum Sozialismus?' *Einheit*, Vol. 1, pp. 22-32.

Ackermann, Anton (1950a), 'Die Bedeutung der außenpolitischen Abkommen der DDR', *Einheit*, Vol. 5, pp. 689-693.

Ackermann, Anton (1950b), 'Der Kampf gegen den Nationalismus - für die Entwicklung eines deutschen Nationalbewußtseins', *Einheit*, Vol. 5, pp. 491-495.

Akademie der Wissenschaften (1976), *Das Parteiprogramm und die Wissenschaft*, Akademie Verlag: East Berlin.

Almond, Mark (1992), *The Rise and Fall of Nicolae and Elena Ceausescu*, Chapmans: London.

Anderson, Benedict (1983), *Imagined Communities. Reflections on the Origins and Spread of Nationalism*, Verso: London and New York.

Apel, Hans (1967), *DDR 1962 1964 1966*, Voltaire Verlag: West Berlin.

Axen, Hermann (1973a), *Zur Entwicklung der sozialistischen Nation in der DDR*, Dietz Verlag: East Berlin.

Axen, Hermann (1973b), 'Zwei Staaten - zwei Nationen. Die deutsche Frage existiert nicht mehr', *Deutschland Archiv*, Vol. 6, pp. 414-416.

Axen, Hermann (1989a), 'Die DDR - fest verankert in der neuen sozialistischen Welt', *Einheit*, Vol. 44, pp. 810-816.

Axen, Hermann (1989b), 'Sozialistische Klassenstandpunkt und Menscheninteressen - friedliches Koexistenz heute', *Einheit*, Vol. 44, pp. 45-50.

Baring, Arnulf (1965), *Der 17, Juli 1953*, Kiepenheuer und Witsch: Cologne.

Bark, Dennis L., and Gress, David R. (1989), *A History of West Germany*, 2 vols, Vol. 2: Democracy and its Discontents, Basil Blackwell: Oxford.

Bartel, H., Mittenzwei, I. and Schmidt, W. (1979), 'Preussen und die deutsche Geschichte', *Einheit*, Vol. 34, pp. 637-646.

Bartel, Horst (1981), 'Historische Erbe und Tradition', *Einheit*, Vol. 36, pp. 272-278.

Belitz-Demiriz, Hannelore, and Voigt, Dieter (1990), *Die Sozialstruktur der Promovierten Intelligenz in der DDR und in der BRD 1950-1982*, Universitätsverlag Dr Brockmeyer: Bochum.

Benser, G. (1984), 'Sozialistiche Nation und Nationspolitik der SED', *Thematische Information und Dokumentation*, No. 47, pp. 29-44.

Berlin, Isiah, (1976), *Vico and Herder,* Hogath Press: London.

Berthold, Lothar (1966), 'Unser nationales Geschichtsbild', *Einheit*, Vol. 21, pp. 225-231.

'Beschluß des Politbüros über die weitere Aufgaben der politischen Massenarbeit der Partei, 18. Mai 1977', (1978), *Einheit*, Vol. 33, pp. 779-791.

Bittighöfer, Bernd (1969), 'Das Menschenbild unserer sozialistischen Gemeinschaft', *Einheit*, Vol. 24, pp. 418-429.

Bleiker, Roland (1993), *Nonviolent Struggle and the Revolution in East Germany,* Cambridge M.A.: The Albert Einstein Institution, 1993.

Blumenwitz, Dieter (1989), *What is Germany? Exploring Germany's Status after World War Two*, Kulturstiftung der deutschen Vertriebenen: Bonn.

Böhme, Waltraud et al. (eds.) (1988), *Kleines politisches Wörterbuch*, 8th ed., Dietz Verlag: East Berlin.

Börner, K-H. (1984), *Wilhelm I. Deutscher Kaiser und König von Preussen. Eine Biographie*, Dietz Verlag: East Berlin.

Brandt, Willy (1971), 'Bericht zur Lage der Nation, 28 January 1971', *Europa Archiv*, Vol. 26, pp. 264-268.

Brandt, Willy (1993), *Was Zusammengehört. Reden zu Deutschland,* Dietz Taschenbuch Verlag: Bonn.

Bremmer, Ian and Taras, Ray (eds.) (1993), *Nations and Politics in the Soviet Successor States,* Cambridge University Press: Cambridge.

Breuilly, John (1992), 'Nationalism and German Reunification', in Breuilly, John (ed.), *The State of Germany,* Longman: London and New York.

Braumann, Marianne (1986), 'Zur Bedeutung des sozialistischen Geschichtsbewußtsein für die Entfaltung des sozialistischen Nationalbewußtseins in der DDR', *Thematische Information und Dokumentation*, No. 53, pp. 43-52.

Braun, Aurel (1978), *Rumanian Foreign Policy since 1965,* Praeger: New York.

Brinks, Jan Herman (1992), *Die DDR-Geschichtswissenschaft auf dem Weg zur deutschen Einheit,* Campus Verlag: Frankfurt and New York.

Buhr, Manfred and Kosing, Alfred (1974), *Kleines Wörterbuch der Marxistisch-Leninistischen Philosophie*, Dietz Verlag: East Berlin.

Burleigh, Michael (1988), *Germany Turns Eastwards. A Study of Ostforschung in the Third Reich,* Cambridge University Press: Cambridge.

Büscher, Wolfgang (1984), 'Geschichte als Denk- und Spielraum. Die DDR Historiker im Lutherjahr', in Gerber, Margy (ed.), *Studies in GDR Culture and Society 2*, University Press of America: Lanham and London.

Choue, Chung-Won (1985), *The Integration of Korea*, Koreaone Press: Seoul.

Christopher, Inge (1981), 'The GDR - a German nation or a socialist nation?' *GDR Monitor*, Vol. 6, pp. 80-89.

Churchward, L.G. (1973), *The Soviet Intellegensia. An Essay on the Social Structure and Roles of Soviet Intellectuals during the 1960s*, Routledge and Kegan Paul: London and Boston.

Committee for German Unity, (1959), *GDR: 300 Questions, 300 Answers*, Verlag der Wirtschaft: East Berlin.

Connor, Walker (1972), 'Nation-Building or Nation Destroying?' *World Politics*, Vol. 24, pp. 319-355.

Connor, Walker (1984), *The Nation in Marxist-Leninist Theory and Strategy*, Princeton University Press: Princeton

Connor, Walker (1990), 'When is a Nation?' *Ethnic and Racial Studies*, Vol. 13, pp. 92-103.

Cramer, Dettmar (1972), 'Einheitspartei und Nation', *Deutschland Archiv*, Vol. 5, pp. 457-464.

Croan, Melvin (1962), 'East Germany: a Lesson in Survival', *Problems of Communism*, Vol. 11, pp. 7-12.

Croan, Melvin (1969), 'Czechoslovakia, Ulbricht and the German Problem', *Problems of Communism*, Vol. 18, pp.1-7.

Croan, Melvin (1971), 'Meinungen zum Führungswechsel in der SED', *Deutschland Archiv*, Vol. 4, pp. 575-579.

Dennis, Mike (1993), *Social and Economic Modernization in Eastern Germany from Honecker to Kohl*, Pinter and St Martin's Press: London and New York.

Diemer, Gebhard (ed.) (1990), *Kurze Chronik der deutschen Frage*, Olzog Verlag: Munich.

Dokumentation zur Ostpolitik der Bundesregierung (1988), Presse- und Informationsamt der Bundesregierung: Leck.

Dokumente der SED (1951-88), 22 vols, Dietz Verlag: East Berlin.

Dörnberg, Stefan (1963), 'Zum nationalen Geschichtsbild', *Einheit*, Vol. 17, pp. 148-152.

Dörnberg, Stefan (1964), *Kurze Geschichte der DDR*, 1st ed., Dietz Verlag: East Berlin.

Dörnberg, Stefan (1969), *Kurze Geschichte der DDR*, 4th ed., Dietz Verlag: East Berlin.

Dornberg, John (1968), *The Other Germany*, Doubleday: Garden City.

Dorpalen, Andreas (1985), *German History in a Marxist Perspective*, Wayne State University Press: Detroit.

Eckert, D., Hofmann, J. and Meier, H. (1992), *Zwischen Anschluß und Ankunft. Identitätskonflikte und Identitätssuche der Ostdeutschen auf dem Weg zum*

Bundesbürger, Brandenburger Verein für politische Bildung 'Rosa Luxemburg' e.V.: Potsdam.

Engelberg, Ernst (1962), 'Vom Werden des nationalen Geschichtsbildes der deutschen Arbeiterklasse', *Einheit*, Vol. 18, pp. 110-121.

Engelberg, Ernst (1975), *Bismarck. Urpreusse und Reichsgründer*, Dietz Verlag: East Berlin.

Erbe, Günther (1982), *Arbeiterklasse und Intelligenz in der DDR*, WestdeutscherVerlag: Opladen.

Evans, Richard J. (1989), *In Hitler's Shadow. West German Historians and the Attempt to Escape from the Nazi Past*, I.B. Tauris: London.

Fischer, A. (1971), 'Außenpolitische Aktivität bei ungewisser sowjetischer Deutschlandpolitik', in Jacobsen, H-A., Leptin, G., Scheuner, U., and Schulz, E. (eds.), *Drei Jahrzehnte Außenpolitik der DDR*, 2nd ed., Oldenbourg Verlag: Munich.

Frick, Karl-Wilhelm (1973), 'Kleines politisches Wörterbuch politisch revidiert', *Deutschland Archiv*, Vol. 6, pp. 756-757.

Fulbrook, Mary (1991), *The Fontana History of Germany. 1914-1990*, Fontana: London.

Fulbrook, Mary (1992), 'Nation-state and Political Culture in divided Germany', in Breuilly, John (ed.), *The State of Germany*, Longman: London.

Fulbrook, Mary (1993), 'States, Nations and the development of Europe', in Fulbrook, Mary (ed.), *National Histories and European History*, UCL Press: London.

'Fünfzehn Jahre DDR: Thesen der ideologischen Kommission beim Politbüro der ZK der SED zum 15. Jahrestag der Gründung der DDR', (1964), *Einheit*, Vol. 19, pp. 3-29.

Gallin, Alice (1986), *Midwives to Nazism. University Professors in Weimar Germany 1923-33*, Mercer: Macon, G.A.

Garton Ash, Timothy (1981), *'Und willst du nicht mein Bruder sein...' Die DDR heute*, Spiegel-Buch Rowohlt: Hamburg.

Garton Ash, Timothy (1993), *In Europe's Name*, Randon House: London.

Gaus, Günther (1983), *Wo Deutschland liegt. Eine Ortsbestimmung*, Hoffmann und Campe: Hamburg.

Gebhardt, Birgit (1993), 'Reform, Evaluation, Abwicklung. GDR Science in the Process of Unification: the example of the Academy of Sciences', in Gerber, Margy, and Woods, Roger (eds.), *Studies in GDR Culture and Society 11/12*, University Press of America: Lanham and London.

Glaeßner, Gert-Joachim (ed.) (1988), *Die DDR in der Ära Honecker*, Westdeutscher Verlag: Opladen.

Goeckel, Robert F. (1984), 'The Luther Anniversary in the GDR', *World Politics*, Vol. 37, pp. 112-133.

'Die Gründung der SED - ein historischer Sieg des Marxismus-Leninismus', (1961) *Einheit*, Vol. 16, pp. 332-352.

Grunenberg, Antonia (1983), 'Die gespaltene Identität', in Weidenfeld, Werner (ed.), *Die Identität der Deutschen*, Hanser Verlag: Munich and Vienna.
Habermas, Jürgen (1996), 'National Unification and Popular Sovereignty', *New Left Review*, No. 219, pp.3-13.
Hacker, Jens (1972) 'Der Begriff der Nation aus der Sicht der DDR', *Gegenwartskunde*, Vol. 4, pp. 391-403.
Hager, Kurt (1971), 'Die Entwickelte sozialistische Gesellschaft. Aufgaben der Gesellschaftswissenschaften nach dem 8. Parteitag', *Einheit*, Vol. 26, pp. 1203-1242.
Hager, Kurt (1981), *Die Gesellschaftwissenschaften vor neuen Aufgaben*, Dietz Verlag: East Berlin.
Hager, Kurt (1989), 'Die Geschichte und das Verständnis unserer Zeit', *Einheit*, Vol. 44, pp. 595-610.
Hahn, Roland (1990) 'Die Idee der Nation und die Lösung der nationalen Frage', *Aus Politik und Zeitgeschichte*, Vol. 29, pp. 3-12.
Hale, Julian (1971), *Ceausecu's Rumania*, Harrap: London.
'Die Haltung der SED im Konflikt mit Prag', (1968), *Deutschland Archiv*, Vol. 1, pp. 620-646.
Hangen, Welles (1966), 'New Perspectives behind the Wall', *Foreign Affairs*, Vol. 45, pp. 135-147.
Hangen, Welles (1967), *The Muted Revolution*, Victor Gollanz: London.
Hanke, Irma (1990), 'Experiment Deutschland oder ein neues Nationalgefühl?' *Deutschland Archiv*, Vol. 24, pp. 154-164.
Hättich, Manfred (1966), *Nationalbewußtsein und Staatsbewußtsein*, Hase und Koehler Verlag: Mainz.
Heise, Wolfgang (1961), 'Um die Zukunft der Nation', *Deutsche Zeitschrift für Philosophie*, Vol. 9, pp. 1029-1037.
Heitzer, H. (1981), *GDR. A Historical Outline*, Zeit im Bild: Dresden.
Henrich, Dietrich (1993), *Nach dem Ende der Teilung. Über Identitäten und Intellektualität in Deutschland*, Suhrkamp: Frankfurt.
Henriksen, T. H. and Lho, K. (eds.) (1994), *One Korea? Challenges and Prospects for Reunification*, Hoover Institution Press: Stanford.
Herrmann, Detlef (1984), 'The Bitter Pills of the Politburo', in McCardle, Arthur W. and Boenau, A. Bruce (eds.), *East Germany: a New German Nation under Socialism?* University Press of America: Lanham and London.
Hertz, F. (1944), *Nationality in History and Politics,* Kegen Paul, Trench, Turner and Co.: London.
Hexelschneider, Erhard and John, Erhard (1984), *Kultur als einigendes Band? Eine Auseinandersetzung mit der These der 'einheitlichen deutschen Kulturnation'*, Dietz Verlag: East Berlin.
Heydemann, Günther (1980), *Geschichtswissenschaft im geteilten Deutschland*, Campus Verlag: Frankfurt.
Hofmann, Jürgen (1988), 'Zur Entwicklung der sozialistischen deutschen Nation in der DDR. Erfahrungen und Perspectiven', *Einheit*, Vol. 43, pp. 734-742.

Hofmann, Jürgen (1989), *Ein neues Deutschland soll es sein*, Dietz Verlag: East Berlin.
Hofmann, Jürgen (1989), 'Solange es eine Chance für die Einheit gab', *Berliner Zeitung*, 24 June.
Hofmann, Jürgen and Basler, Gerhard (1989), 'Zwei deutsche Staaten und Nationen im europäischen Haus', *Einheit*, Vol. 44, pp. 170-176.
Hofmann, Jürgen (1990), *Wie weiter mit der deutschen Nation?* Dietz Verlag: Berlin.
Holzweißig, Gunther (1976), 'Der bestrittene Positionswechsel in der nationalen Frage. Rezension', *Deutschland Archiv*, Vol. 9, pp. 1189-1192.
Homann, Heinrich (1965), 'Der 8. Mai 1945 und die Entwicklung des Nationalbewußtseins in Deutschland', *Einheit*, Vol. 19, pp. 30-41.
Honecker, Erich (1973-88), *Reden und Aufsätze*, 12 vols., Dietz Verlag: East Berlin.
Honecker, Erich (1979), 'Der Siegeszug des Sozialismus auf deutschem Boden', *Einheit*, Vol. 34, pp. 899-900.
Honecker, Erich (1981), *Aus meinem Leben*, Dietz Verlag: East Berlin.
Honecker, Erich (1982), *Die Kulturpolitik unserer Partei wird erfolgreich verwirklicht*, Dietz Verlag: East Berlin.
Horn, Werner and Vietze, Siegfried (1969), 'Die DDR - Krönung des Kampfes aller fortschrittlichen Kräfte des deutschen Volkes', *Einheit*, Vol. 24, pp. 188-197.
Hruby, Peter (1980), *Fools and Heroes: The Changing Role of Communist Intellectuals in Czechoslovakia*, Pergamon Press: Oxford and New York.
Hüning, Hasko (1988), 'Geschichtswissenschaft zwischen Fachhistorik und Geschichtsphilosophie?' in Glaeßner, Gert-Joachim (ed.), *Die DDR in der Ära Honecker*, Westdeutscher Verlag: Opladen.
Iggers, G. (1991), *Marxist Historiography in Transformation. New Orientations in recent East German History*, translated by Bruce Little, St Martin's Press: New York.
Institut für Marxismus-Leninismus (1966), *Geschichte der Deutschen Arbeiterbewegung*, 8 vols, Dietz Verlag: East Berlin.
James, Harold (1989), *A German Identity 1770-1990*, Weidenfeld and Nicholson: London.
Jaspers, Karl (1966), *Wohin treibt die Bundesrepublik?* Piper: Munich.
Kang, Myoung-Kyu and Wagner, Helmut (1990), *Korea and Germany: Lessons in Division*, Seoul University Press: Seoul.
Kegel, Gerhard (1968), 'Zur Deutschlandpolitik der beiden Deutschlands', *Einheit*, Vol. 23, pp. 734-43.
Keithly, David M. (1992), *The Collapse of East German Communism. The Year the Wall came down, 1989*, Praeger: Westport and London.
Kennedy, Michael D. (1991), 'Eastern Europe's Lessons for Critical Intellectuals', in Lemert, C. Charles (ed.), *Intellectuals and Politics. Social Theory in a Changing World*, Sage: Newbury Park, London, New Delhi.

Koch, Klaus-Uwe (1984), 'Die Vaterlandsdiskussion am Vorabend des 7. Parteitags', *Thematische Information und Dokumentation*, No. 42, pp. 99-105.

Koch, Klaus-Uwe (1989), 'Warum es keine offene deutsche Frage gibt', *Einheit*, Vol. 44, pp. 271-275.

Koenen, Reiner (1975), *Nation und Nationalbewußtsein aus der Sicht der SED*, Studienverlag Dr. Brockmeyer: Bochum.

König, G., Schütz, G. and Zeisler, K. (eds.) (1967), *Kleines Politisches Wörterbuch*, 1st ed., Dietz Verlag: East Berlin.

Kohlschütter, Andreas (1970), 'Sie sagen "ja" zu ihrem Staat', *Die Zeit*, 7 August, pp.3-4.

Korte, Karl-Rudoph (1994), *Die Chance genutzt? Der Weg zur Einheit Deutschlands*, Campus Verlag: Frankfurt and New York.

Kosing, Alfred (1962a), 'Illusion und Wirklichkeit in der nationalen Frage', *Einheit*, Vol. 16, pp. 15-22.

Kosing, Alfred (1962b), *Die nationale Lebensfrage des deutschen Volkes*, Dietz Verlag: East Berlin.

Kosing, Alfred and Schmidt, Walter (1974a), 'Über die Dialektik von Internationalem und Nationalem', *Thematische Information und Dokumentation*, No. 32, pp. 75-82.

Kosing, Alfred and Schmidt, Walter (1974b), 'Zur Herausbildung der sozialistischen Nation in der DDR', *Einheit*, Vol. 29, pp. 179-188.

Kosing, Alfred (1975), 'Theoretische Probleme der Entwicklung der sozialistischen Nation in der DDR', *Deutsche Zeitschrift für Philosophie*, Vol. 23, pp. 237-261.

Kosing, Alfred (1976), *Nation in Geschichte und Gegenwart*, Dietz Verlag: East Berlin.

Kosing, Alfred and Schmidt, Walter (1975), 'Nation und Nationalität in der DDR', *Neues Deutschland*, 15/16 February, p.10.

Kosing, Alfred and Schmidt, Walter (1979), 'Geburt und Gedeihen der sozialistischen deutschen Nation', *Einheit*, Vol. 34, pp. 1068-1075.

Kosing, Alfred (1989), 'Sozialistische Gesellschaft und sozialistische Nation in der DDR', *Deutsche Zeitschrift für Philosophie*, Vol. 37, pp. 913-924.

Krenz, Egon (1991), *Wenn Mauern fallen*, Paul Neff Verlag: Vienna.

Kreusel, Dietmar (1971), *Nation und Vaterland in der Militärpresse der DDR*, Seewald Verlag: Stuttgart-Degerloch.

Krieger, Leonard (1975), 'Germany', in Ranum, Orest, (ed.), *National Consciousness, History and Political Culture in Early Modern Europe*, Johns Hopkins University Press: Baltimore and London.

Krisch, Harry (1978), 'Official Nationalism', in Legters, Lyman H. (ed.), *The GDR - a Developed Socialist Society*, Westview Press: Boulder, Colerado.

Kühne, Horst (1981), 'Die NVA: Legitimer Erbe aller progressiven militärischen Traditionen des deutschen Volkes', *Einheit*, Vol. 36, pp. 156-162.

Kupper, Siegfried (1982), 'Political Relations with the FRG', in Schulz, E., Jacobsen, H-A., Leptin, G. and Scheuner, U., (eds.), *GDR Foreign Policy*, M.E. Sharpe Inc.: New York and London.

Kuhn, Ekkehard (1993), *Gorbatschow und die deutsche Einheit*, Bouvier: Bonn.

Larrabee, F. Stephen (ed.) (1989) *The Two German States and European Security*, MacMillan: London and Basingstoke.

Leonhard, Wolfgang (1957), *Child of the Revolution*, Collins: London.

Lippmann, Heinz (1973), *Honecker and the New Politics of Europe*, translated by Helen Sebba, MacMillan: London.

Löw, Konrad. (ed.) (1990), *Beharrung und Wandel: Die DDR und die Reformen von Mikail Gorbatschow*, Duncker und Humblot: Berlin.

Ludz, Peter-Christian (1972), 'Zum Begriff der Nation in der Sicht der SED - Wandlungen und politische Bedeutung', *Deutschland Archiv*, Vol. 5, pp. 17-27.

Ludz, Peter-Christian (1977), 'The SED's Concept of the Nation: deviations and political meanings', *Canadian Review of Studies in Nationalism*, Vol. 13, pp. 206-224.

Ludz, Peter C. (1979), 'Legitimacy in a Divided Nation', in Denitch, Bogdan (ed.), *Legitimation of Regimes. International Frameworks for Analysis*, Sage: London and Beverly Hills.

Mahlow, Bruno (1989), 'Patriotismus und Internationalismus in der Politik der SED', *Einheit*, Vol. 44, pp. 545-552.

Maier, Christian (1988), *The Unmasterable Past. History, Holocaust and German National Identity*, Harvard University Press: Cambridge MA.

Maier, Christian (1991), *Die Nation die keine sein will*, Carl Hanser Verlag: Munich and Vienna.

Marbach, Renate (1968), 'SED Nation', *Stuttgarter Nachrichten*, 8 January.

McAdams, A. James (1985), *East Germany and Détente. Building Authority after the Wall*, Cambridge University Press: Cambridge.

McAdams, A. James (1993), *Germany Divided. From the Wall to Reunification*, Princeton University Press: Princeton.

McCardle, Arthur W. and Boenau, A. Bruce (eds.) (1984), *East Germany: a new German Nation under Socialism?* University Press of America: Lanham and London.

McCauley, Martin (1984), *The GDR since 1945*, MacMillan: London.

McCauley, Martin and Carter, Stephen (eds.) (1986), *Leadership and Succession in the Soviet Union, Eastern Europe and China*, MacMillan: London.

McElvoy, Anne (1992), *The Saddled Cow. East Germany's Life and Legacy*, Faber: London and Boston.

McKay, Joanna (1994), 'The SED's Interpretation of Marxist-Leninist Theory regarding the Nation: the Problem of Language', in Dunleavy, Patrick, and Stanyer, Jeffrey (eds.), *Contemporary Political Studies 1994*, UK Political Studies Association: Belfast.

McNeill, Terry (1979), 'State and Nationality under Communism', in Hayward, J. S. and Berki, R. N. (eds.), *State and Society in Contemporary Europe*, Martin Robertson: Oxford.

Meier, Helmut (1973), 'Zur Entwicklung der sozialistischen Nation in der DDR. Rezension', *Einheit*, Vol. 28, pp. 1376-1379.

Meier, Helmut and Schmidt, Walter (1975), 'Die DDR - Verkörperung der besten Traditionen der deutschen Geschichte', *Einheit*, Vol. 30, pp. 463-471.

Meier, Helmut and Schmidt, Walter (1978), 'Tradition und sozialistisches Bewußtsein', *Einheit*, Vol. 33, pp. 1220-1227.

Merkl, Peter (1995) *The Federal Republic at 45. Union without Unity*, MacMillan: London and Basingstoke.

Meuschel, Sigrid (1988), 'Auf der Suche nach Madame L'Identité? Zur Konzept der Nation und Nationalgeschichte' in Glaeßner, Gert-Joachim (ed.), *Die DDR in der Ära Honecker*, Westdeutscher Verlag: Opladen.

Meuschel, Sigrid (1992), *Legitimation und Parteiherrschaft in der DDR. Zum Paradox von Stabilität und Revolution in der DDR*, Suhrkamp: Frankfurt.

Mitchell, I.R. (1983), 'The Changing Image of Prussia in the GDR', *German Life and Letters*, Vol. 37, pp. 57-69.

Mittenzwei, Ingrid (1979), *Friedrich II von Preußen. Eine Bibliographie*, Dietz Verlag: East Berlin.

Moreton, N. Edwina (1978), *East Germany and the Warsaw Alliance: the Politics of Détente*, Westview Press: Boulder, Colerado.

Motschmann, Klaus (1979), *Sozialismus und Nation. Wie Deutsch ist die DDR?* Wirtschaftsverlag Langen-Müller/Herbig: Munich.

Mushaben, Joyce (1994), *The Persistence of East German Identity*, MacMillan: London.

Nak-Chung, Paik (1996), 'Habermas of National Unification in Germany and Korea', *New Left Review*, No. 219, pp.14-21.

Naumann, Gerhard and Trümpler, Eckhard (1991), *Der Flop mit der DDR-Nation 1971*, Dietz Verlag: Berlin.

Navari, Cornelia (1981), 'The Origins of the Nation-State', in Tivey, Leonard (ed.), *The Nation-State. The Formation of Modern Politics*, Oxford: Martin Robertson.

Neues Deutschland, 16 November 1946, 26 March 1962, 5 February 1964, 1 January 1967, 21 January 1967, 19 December 1967, 20 January 1970, 15 March 1973, 7/8 February 1976, 26 August 1983, 10 April 1987, 7 September 1987, 11 January 1991.

Norden, Albert (1966), 'Arbeiterklasse und Nation', *Einheit*, Vol. 20, pp. 451-465.

Norden, Albert (1967), 'Anklage gegen Bonns revanchistische Politik', *Neues Deutschland*, 19 December, pp.3-4.

Nordon, Albert (1973), 'Zwei deutsche Nationalstaaten', *Deutschland Archiv*, Vol. 5, pp. 416-417.

Oelssner, Fred (1951), 'Die Ideologischen Hauptaufgaben in der DDR', *Einheit*, Vol. 6, pp. 1347-1352.

Oldenburg, Fred (1975), 'Blick zurück nach vorn. Zum 13. Plenum des Zentralkomitees', *Deutschland Archiv,* Vol. 8, pp. 2-4.
Osmond, Jonathan (ed.) (1992) *German Reunification: a Reference Guide,* Longman: London.
Plessner, Helmuth (1966), *Die Verspätete Nation,* Kohlhammer: Stuttgart.
Pletsch, Carl (1979), 'The "Socialist Nation of the GDR" or the Asymmetry in Nation and Ideology between the two Germanies', *Comparative Studies in Society and History,* Vol. 21, pp. 323-345.
Plock, Ernst (1993), *East German-West German Relations and the Fall of the GDR,* Westview Press: Boulder, Colerado.
Polak, Karl (1962), 'Über fehlerhaften Auffassungen in Fragen unseres Kampfes um Frieden und nationale Wiedergeburt', *Einheit,* Vol. 17, pp. 106-121.
Pollak, Wolfgang and Rutter, Dereck (eds.) (1986), *German Identity: 40 Years after Zero,* Liberal Verlag: Sankt Augustin.
Prittie, Terence (1961), 'East Germany: record of failure', *Problems of Communism,* Vol. 10, pp. 1-7.
Protokoll der Verhandlungen der 1. Parteikonferenz der SED (1949), Dietz Verlag: East Berlin.
Protokoll der Verhandlungen der 2. Parteikonferenz der SED (1950), Dietz Verlag: East Berlin.
Protokoll der Verhandlungen des 3. Parteitages der SED (1951), Dietz Verlag: East Berlin.
Protokoll der Verhandlungen des 7. Parteitages der SED (1967), Dietz Verlag: East Berlin.
Protokoll der Verhandlungen des 8. Parteitages der SED, 2. vols., (1971), Dietz Verlag: East Berlin.
Protokoll der Verhandlungen des 9. Parteitages der SED (1976), Dietz Verlag: East Berlin.
Protokoll der Verhandlungen des 10. Parteitages der SED (1981), Dietz Verlag: East Berlin.
Protokoll des Vereinigungsparteitages der SPD und KPD (1946), Dietz Verlag: East Berlin.
Przybylski, Peter (1992), *Tatort Politbüro,* 2 vols, Vol. 1: Die Akte Honecker, Vol. 2: Honecker, Mittag und Schalk-Golodkowski, Rowohlt: Berlin.
Read, Anthony and Fisher, David (1994), *Berlin. The Biography of a City,* Pimlico: London.
Reinhold, Otto (1989), 'Zur Gesellschaftskonzeption der SED', *Einheit,* Vol. 44, pp. 483-489.
Remnek, Richard B. (1975) *Soviet Scholars and Soviet Foreign Policy. A Case Study of Soviet Foreign Policy Towards India,* Carolina Academic Press: Durham, North Carolina.
Riege, Gerhard, and Kulke, Hans-Jürgen (1979), *Nationalität Deutsch, Staatsbürgerschaft DDR,* Dietz Verlag: East Berlin.

Röder, Karl-Heinz (1961), 'Arbeiterklasse und Nation', *Deutsche Zeitschrift für Philosophie*, Vol. 9, pp. 1157-1163.

Röpke, Wilhelm (1960), 'National Socialism and Intellectuals', in De Huszar, George B. (ed.), *The Intellectuals*, Free Press of Glencoe: Illinois.

Rothschild, Joseph (1979), 'Political Legitimacy in Contemporary Europe', in Denitch, Bogdan, *Legitimation of Regimes. International Frameworks for Analysis*, Sage: London and Beverly Hills.

Rubens, Franziska (1951), 'Die deutsche Nation ist nicht zu zerstören!' *Einheit*, Vol. 6, pp. 124-128.

Rudolph, H. (1983), 'Wie sieht das Selbstverständnis der DDR-Gesellschaft aus?' in Weidenfeld, Werner (ed.), *Die Identität der Deutschen*, Hanser Verlag: Munich and Vienna.

Sandford, John (1983), 'The GDR and the German Question: the Unofficial Debate in the Peace Movement', in Gerber, Margy (ed.), *Studies in GDR Culture and Society 7*, University Press of America: Lanham and London

Säuberlich, Dietmar (1985), 'Das Problem der Nation in der Strategie und Taktik der SED in der ersten Hälfte der 60er Jahre', *Thematische Information und Dokumentation*, No. 48, pp. 70-78.

Schabowski, Günther (1990), *Das Politbüro. Ende eines Mythos. Eine Befragung*, Rowohlt: Hamburg.

Scharf, C. Bradley (1990), 'Necessity and Vision in East German Identity', in Harms, K., Reuter, L.R. and Dürr, V. (eds.), *Coping with the Past: Germany and Austria after 1945*, University of Wisconsin Press: Wisconsin and London.

Scheuch, Erwin K. (1991), *Wie Deutsch sind die Deutschen? Eine Nation wandelt ihr Gesicht*, Bastei Lübbe Verlag: Bergisch Gladbach.

Scheuner, Ulrich (1982), 'The Problem of the Nation and the GDR's Relationship with the FRG', in Schulz, E., Jacobsen, H-A., Leptin, G. and Scheuner, U. (eds.), *GDR Foreign Policy*, M.E. Sharpe Inc.: New York and London.

Schiller, Klaus J. and Thiemann, Manfred (1979), *Geschichte der Sorben*, 4 vols., VEB Domowina Verlag: Bautzen.

Schmidt, Walter and Meier, Helmut (eds.) (1988), *Erbe und Tradition in der DDR. Die Diskussion der Historiker*, Akademie-Verlag: East Berlin.

Schmidt, Walter (1993), 'The Nation in German History', in Teich, Mikulás and Porter, Roy (eds.), *The National Question in Europe in Historical Context*, Cambridge University Press: Cambridge.

Schulz, Eberhard (1982), *Die Deutsche Nation in Europa. Internationale und Historische Dimensionen*, Europa Union Verlag: Bonn.

Schweigler, Gebhard Ludwig (1973), *Nationalbewußtsein in der BRD und in der DDR*, Bertelsmann Universitätsverlag: Düsseldorf.

Schweigler, Gebhard Ludwig (1975), *National Consciousness in Divided Germany*, Sage: London and Beverly Hills.

Shlapentokh, Vladimir (1990), *Soviet Intellectuals and Political Power. The Post Stalinist Era*, I.B. Tauris & Co.: London and New York.

Shoup, P. (1972), 'The National Question and the Political Systems of Eastern Europe', in Sinanian, S., Deak, I. and Ludz, P-C. (eds.), *Eastern Europe in the 1970s,* Praeger: New York and London.

Smith, Anthony D. (1991), *National Identity,* Penguin: London.

Smith, Duncan (1988), *Walls and Mirrors. Western Representations of Really Existing Socialism in the GDR,* University Press of America: Lanham and London.

Smith, Gordon (1981), A Future for the Nation-State?' in Tivey, Leonard (ed.), *The Nation-State. The Formation of Modern Politics,* Oxford: Martin Robertson.

Smith, Helmut Walser (1991), 'Socialism and Nationalism in the East German Revolution 1989-1990', *East European Politics and Societies,* Vol. 5, pp. 234-246.

Smith, Jean Edward (1967), *Germany beyond the Wall,* Little Brown: Boston.

Smith, Jean Edward (1967), 'The Red Prussianism of the GDR', *Political Science Quarterly,* Vol. 82, pp. 368-385.

Sommer, Theo (1964), 'Kommunisten oder Deutsche?' in Dönhoff, M., Leonhardt, R.W. and Sommer, T. (eds.), *Reise in ein Fernes Land,* Die Zeit Bücher: Hamburg.

Spittmann, Ilse (1966), 'Soviet Union and DDR,' *Survey,* Vol. 6, pp.165-76.

Spittmann, Ilse (1967), 'East Germany: the swinging pendulum', *Problems of Communism,* Vol. 16, pp. 14-20.

Spittmann, Ilse (1970), 'Deutscher Gipfel in Erfurt', *Deutschland Archiv,* Vol. 3, pp. 431-440.

Spittmann, Ilse (1971), 'Warum Ulbricht stürzte', *Deutschland Archiv,* Vol. 4, pp. 568-570.

Spittmann, Ilse (1972), 'Honecker und die Nationale Frage', *Deutschland Archiv,* Vol. 5, pp. 1-2.

Staadt, Jochen (1993), *Die geheime Westpolitik der SED 1960-1970. Von der gesamtdeutschen Orientierung zur sozialistischen Nation,* Akademie-Verlag: Berlin.

Stalin, Joseph (1960), 'The Old and New Intellegensia', in De Huszar, George B. (ed.), *The Intellectuals,* Free Press of Glencoe: Illinois.

Staritz, Dietrich (1985), *Geschichte der DDR 1945-1985,* Suhrkamp: Frankfurt.

Steiniger, Peter-Alfons (1966), 'Das Selbstbestimmungsrecht im allgemeinen Völkerrecht', *Einheit,* Vol. 21, pp. 1226-1227.

Stern, Carola (1965), *Ulbricht: A Political Biography,* translated by Abe Farbstein, Pall Mall Press: London.

Stone, Gerald (1972), *The Smallest Slavonic Nation. The Sorbs of Lusatia,* Athlone Press: London.

Studien- und Seminarhinweise für Teilnehmer und Propagandisten der Seminare zur Entstehung und Entwicklung der DDR unter Führung der SED (1989), Dietz Verlag: East Berlin.

Sturrels, John (1974), 'Nationalism in the GDR', *Canadian Review of Studies in Nationalism*, Vol. 10, pp. 23-37.

Thompson, Mark R. (1996) 'No Exit: "Nation-stateness" and Democratisation in the GDR', *Political Studies*, Vol. 44, No. 2, pp.267-286.

Trommler, F. (1991), 'The Creation of History and the Refusal of the Past in the GDR', in Harms, K., Reuter, L.R. and Dürr, V. (eds.), *Coping with the Past: Germany and Austria after 1945*, University of Wisconsin Press: London and Wisconsin.

Ulbricht, Walter (1952), 'Die gegenwärtige Lage und die neuen Aufgaben der SED', *Einheit*, Vol. 7, pp. 728-774.

Ulbricht, Walter (1967), *Die gesellschaftliche Entwicklung der DDR bis zur Vollendung des Sozialismus*, Dietz Verlag: East Berlin.

Ulbricht, Walter (1968), *On Questions of Socialist Construction in the GDR*, Zeit im Bild: Dresden.

Uschner, Manfred (1993), *Die Zweite Etage. Funktionsweise eines Machtapparates*, Dietz Verlag: Berlin.

Veen, Hans-Joachim, and Zelle, Carsten (1995), 'National Identity and Political Priorities in Eastern and Western Germany', *German Politics*, Vol. 4, No. 1, pp. 1-26.

Verheyen, Dirk (1993), *The German Question. A Cultural, Historical and Geopolitical Exploration*, Westview Press: Boulder, Colorado.

Vorholzer, Jörg (1962), *Willfähriger Untertan oder bewußter Staatsbürger?* Dietz Verlag: East Berlin.

Vucinich, Alexander (1956), *The Soviet Academy of Sciences*, Stanford University Press: Stanford.

Vucinich, Alexander (1984), *Empire of Knowledge. The Academy of Sciences of the USSR 1917-1970*, University of California Press: Berkeley and London.

Wallace, Ian (1987), *East Germany*, World Bibliographical Series. Vol. 77, Clio Press: Oxford.

Watson Alan, (1992), *The Germans. Who are they now?* Methuen: London.

Weber, Hermann (1980), *Kleine Geschichte der DDR*, Edition Deutschland Archiv: Cologne.

Weidenfeld, Werner, and Korte, Karl-Rudolph (1991), *Die Deutschen - Profil eine Nation*, Klett Verlag: Stuttgart.

Weidenfeld, Werner (ed.) (1993), *Deutschland - eine Nation, doppelte Geschichte*, Verlag Wissenschaft und Politik: Cologne.

Weinreich, Max (1946), *Hitler's Professors. The Part of Scholarship in Germany's Crimes against the Jewish People*, Yiddish Scientific Institute: New York.

Wettig, Gerhard (1975), *Community and Conflict in the Socialist Camp*, translated by Edwina Moreton and Hannes Adomeit, St Martin's Press: New York.

Wettig, Gerhard (1987), 'The Soviet View', in Edwina Moreton (ed.), *Germany between East and West*, Cambridge University Press: Cambridge.

Wetzel, Rudi (1953), 'Was ist Patriotismus?' *Einheit*, Vol. 8, pp. 312-317.

Williams, H., Bishop, C. and Wright, C. (1996), 'German (Re)Unification: Habermas and his Critics', *German Politics*, Vol. 5, No. 2, pp.214-239.

Wright, A. W. (1981), 'Socialism and Nationalism', in Tivey, Leonard (ed.), *The Nation-State. The Formation of Modern Politics*, Oxford: Martin Robertson.

Wolle, Stefan (1993), 'Im Labyrinth der Akten. Die archivalische Hinterlassenschaft des SED-Staats', in Weidenfeld, Werner (ed.), *Deutschland - eine Nation - doppelte Geschichte*, Verlag Wissenschaft und Politik: Cologne.

Die Zeit, 11 September 1987, 11 January 1991.

Zieger, Gottfried (1987), *Die Haltung von SED und DDR zur Einheit Deutschlands 1949-1987*, Verlag Wissenschaft und Politik: Cologne.

Zimmermann, Hartmut (ed.) (1985), *DDR-Handbuch*, 3rd ed., 2 vols., Verlag Wissenschaft und Politik: Cologne.

Unpublished Sources

Theses and Unpublished Papers:

AfG/IfGA (1980), 'Probleme der Entwicklung der sozialistischen deutschen Nation und der Aufeinandersetzung mit neuen Tendenzen des bürgerlichen Nationalismus in der Politik und Ideologie des Imperialismus in der BRD'.

AfG/IfGA (1988), 'Fragen der Entwicklung der sozialistischen Nation in der DDR und der Auseinandersetzung mit dem gegenwärtigen Nationalismus in der BRD'.

Braumann, Marianne (1985), 'Zum Zusammenhang von sozialistischen Nationalbewußtsein und sozialistischen Geschichtsbewußtsein in der DDR. Ergebnisse und Probleme geschichtsideologischer Arbeit nach dem 10. Parteitag der SED', Doctoral thesis, IfGA: East Berlin.

Cordell, Karl (1991), 'Nation-building Strategies in the GDR: An Assessment', Paper presented at the ECPR joint sessions, University of Essex.

Hofmann, Jürgen (1983), 'Studien zur Entwicklung der sozialistischen deutschen Nation und zur Nationspolitik der SED', Doctoral thesis, IfGA: East Berlin.

Koch, Klaus-Uwe (1971), 'Das Problem der Nation in der Strategie und Taktik der SED in der zweiten Hälfte der sechziger Jahre', Doctoral thesis, IfGA: East Berlin.

Rentsch, Peter (1982), 'Die Nation und das Nationalspezifische in der Programmatik und Strategie der SED', Doctoral thesis, IfGA: East Berlin.

Stephan, Gert-Rüdiger and Küchenmeister, Daniel (1993), 'Die nationale Frage in der Politik der SED am Ende der achtziger Jahre', Unpublished paper.

Trompelt, Wilfried (1985), 'Nationalstaatliche Konstituierungsprozesse in der Entwicklung der sozialistischen Nation in der DDR, 1945 bis Anfang der sechziger Jahre', Doctoral thesis, IfGA: East Berlin.

Archive material:

Stiftung Archiv der Parteien und Massenorganisationen der DDR im Bundesarchiv (SAPMO-BArch):

Politbüro: J IV 2/2A/1178, 1202, 1205, 1211, 1218, 1228, 1232, 1273, 1275,1281, 1283, 1287, 1296, 1302, 1315, 1346, 1379, 1384, 1399, 1402, 1403, 1405, 1407, 1416, 1425, 1428, 140, 1441, 1443, 1445, 1459, 1460, 1478, 1481, 1484, 1488, 1489, 1497, 1500, 1504, 1509, 1514, 1515, 1519, 1606, 1687, 3045, 3054.
Sekretariat: J IV 2/3A/1771, 1784, 1847, 2035, 2049, 4668.
Zentralkomitee: IV 2/1/46, 72, 122, 220, 347, 356, 357, 370, 402, 408, 409, 415, 416, 419, 427, 460, 471, 473, 495, 685, 692, 699.
Büro Hager: IV 2/2.024/1.
Büro Hager: IV A2/2.024/55.
Büro Hager: IV B2/2.024/11, 12.
Büro Norden: IV A2/2.028/14, 42, 122.
Büro Lamberz: IV 2/2.033/1, 4, 9, 10, 11, 24, 33.
Büro Krenz: IV 2/2.039/64.
Büro des Politbüros: IV A2/2.01/31.
Abteilung Agitation: IV A2/9.02/3, 31, 32, 44, 158.
Abteilung Propaganda: IV A2/9.03/3, 5, 32, 72.
Abteilung Wissenschaften: IV A2/9.04/13.
Abteilung Wissenschaften: IV B2/9.04/4, 11, 20, 21, 29, 43, 67, 90, 115.
Westabteilung: IV A2/10.02/14.
Agitationskommission: IV 2/2.106/6, 20.
Nachlaß Ulbricht: NL 182/798, 922, 926 1105, 1106, 1107, 1179, 1306, 1312, 1362.
Nachlaß Verner: NL 281/73, 85.
8. Parteitag: 1/VIII/17, 18, 123.

Institut für die Geschichte der Arbeiterbewegung (IfGA):

Altregistratur Agitation: 11527, 11533, 14350.
Internes Parteiarchiv: IPA NL 2/31, 32.

Bundesarchiv Abteilungen Potsdam (BArchP):

Staatssekretariat für Westdeutsche Fragen: D-2/2, 13, 16, 37, 59, 67, 68, 186.

Interviews

Hofmann, Dr Jürgen, Berlin, 5 February 1993, 1 March 1993, 11 May 1993.
Kosing, Prof. Alfred, Berlin, 11 February 1993, 3 March 1993, 7 July 1993.
Krenz, Egon, Berlin, 15 July 1993.
Meier, Prof. Helmut, Berlin, 15 March 1993, 28 May 1993.
Neumann, Alfred, Berlin, 7 April 1993, 4 May 1993.
Schmidt, Prof. Walter, Berlin, 3 June 1993.
Uschner, Dr Manfred, Berlin, 21 July 1993.